You CAN
Stop Stupid

You CAN Stop Stupid

Stopping Losses from Accidental and Malicious Actions

Ira Winkler
Dr. Tracy Celaya Brown

WILEY

You CAN Stop Stupid: Stopping Losses from Accidental and Malicious Actions

Copyright © 2021 by John Wiley & Sons, Inc., Indianapolis, Indiana

Published simultaneously in Canada

ISBN: 978-1-119-62198-0
ISBN: 978-1-119-62206-2 (ebk)
ISBN: 978-1-119-62204-8 (ebk)

Manufactured in the United States of America

For general information on our other products and services please contact our Customer Care Department within the United States at (877) 762-2974, outside the United States at (317) 572-3993 or fax (317) 572-4002.

Wiley publishes in a variety of print and electronic formats and by print-on-demand. Some material included with standard print versions of this book may not be included in e-books or in print-on-demand. If this book refers to media such as a CD or DVD that is not included in the version you purchased, you may download this material at booksupport.wiley.com. For more information about Wiley products, visit www.wiley.com.

Library of Congress Control Number: 2019956718

SKY10021973_102820

To my incredible wife, Adriana, who pushed me harder to write this book than I pushed myself. —Ira

To my extraordinary husband, Mel, and my wonderful family, I love and appreciate you more than words can ever express. —Tracy

About the Authors

Ira Winkler, CISSP, is president of Secure Mentem and author of *Advanced Persistent Security*. He is considered one of the world's most influential security professionals. Ira began his career at the National Security Agency (NSA), where he served in various roles as an intelligence and computer systems analyst. He has since served in other positions supporting the cybersecurity and risk management programs in organizations of all sizes. His specialty is the human aspects of technology and loss mitigation. He has received several lifetime achievement awards, including the CSO COMPASS Award, which dubbed him "The Awareness Crusader." Ira has written books and speaks around the world about cybersecurity, risk management, and the human aspects of security and technology. Ira can be reached through his website at www.irawinkler.com.

Dr. Tracy Celaya Brown, CISSP, is a sought-after IT and business consultant and the president of Go Consulting International. Clients consider her their "secret weapon" as she helps organizations define and implement their security strategy and develop a solid organizational culture of security. Committed to making the digital world more secure and influencing the next wave of IT and security professionals, she is also a facilitator, researcher, author, innovative leader, and an award-winning international speaker. Dr. Tracy Celaya Brown can be reached through her website at DrTre.com.

About the Technical Editors

Adam Shostack is a leading expert on threat modeling, and a consultant, entrepreneur, technologist, author, and game designer. He's a member of the BlackHat Review Board, and he helped create the CVE. He currently assists many organizations to improve their security via Shostack & Associates and advises startups, including as a Mach37 Star Mentor. While at Microsoft, he drove the Autorun fix into Windows Update, was the lead designer of the SDL Threat Modeling Tool v3, and created the *Elevation of Privilege* game. Adam is the author of *Threat Modeling: Designing for Security* and the co-author of *The New School of Information Security*.

Dr. Lance Hayden has 30 years of experience in the information security field, a career that includes roles in industry, government, and academia. He is the chief information security strategist for Vericast, as well as a professor at the University of Texas School of Information. Dr. Hayden's research and expertise includes understanding information security awareness and behavior, and he is the author of *People-Centric Security: Transforming Your Enterprise Security Culture*.

Acknowledgments

A book like this represents the experiences and lessons learned throughout our entire careers. As such, we owe a debt of gratitude to many people, some of whom we've lost touch with. So to all of you, the best we can do is send you good karma and hope we have somehow returned the favor. There are, however, a few people to whom we need to truly express our thanks.

First is Jim Minatel, who worked with us to determine the book we really wanted to write and allowed us to share our passion and experiences with you, the reader. We also owe an immense debt of gratitude to Kelly Talbot, our development editor, who kept us from sounding stupid and helped us get our points across. During the review process, we cringed every time we saw comments from Lance Hayden and Adam Shostack, our technical editors. The cringes were due to the fact that we knew that each of their comments were well thought out, would add immensely to the quality of the book, and would require us to do a lot of research and hours of more writing. They both have an incredible breadth and depth of experience in the field and truly know how to incorporate research into practice. If you find value in this book, it is as much a credit to them as it is to us. Dr. Nicklas Dahlstrom of Emirates also provided incredibly valuable guidance in forming our thoughts on the integration of safety science with mitigating user-initiated loss. We likewise owe a massive thanks to Adriana Winkler, who read everything to ensure that it made sense to laypersons as well as to the technical experts. We also want to give a special thanks to Rupin Kotecha of Digital Guru, who was the catalyst for putting us in contact with Jim Minatel to get this book started. Finally, we need to thank Britta Glade of RSA Conference, who was the instigator for our working together.

—Ira Winkler and Dr. Tracy Celaya Brown

Foreword

So, here it is, in your hands. A book with a message that took the field of cybersecurity only a couple of years—decades at most—to come around to. Its premise is something that human factors professionals wish they could get through to the people they work with every day: the medical device manufacturers, the cockpit designers, the "autonomous" vehicle developers, the construction site planners, the procedure writers—if they could just get this simple message. Spoiler alert, this is the message: If your people are doing stupid things, it's not because you have stupid people. It's because you have a stupid system.

And then to think that human factors is a field that's been around for almost 80 years. It was at the basis of the discoveries that led to this premise. Design a cockpit that puts two toggle switches next to each other—one for the landing gear, and the other for the flaps—and you are going to get belly landings. Which the new, bigger, badder Boeing B-17 bomber was getting a lot of during WWII. The solution was not punishing the errant pilots. It wasn't putting up posters exhorting them to try harder. It wasn't mounting an incident counter on the wall that announced how many days had gone by without a fellow B-17 pilot planting the aircraft on its belly. As long as the toggle switches were inviting pilots to mix them up, then pilots would mix them up.

In 1943, Alphonse Chapanis, a human factors pioneer, fashioned a little flap handle and a little wheel in a workshop and mounted them on the respective toggle switches of some of the B-17s. The ones that were thus equipped never belly-landed again. A gear lever that looks and feels like a wheel, and a flap handle that looks and feels like a flap, now constitute a design and certification requirement for airplane cockpits. If your people are doing stupid things, then you have a stupid system. So, go fix your system. As Ira and Tracy put it, "The simple fact is that a user can't initiate loss unless an organization creates an environment that puts them in a position to do so."

When you suffer a loss, it is, of course, attractive to gravitate to emotionally satisfying and low-cost interventions. Blame the person who messed things up. Hold them accountable. But Ira and Tracy have a different, and more sustainable, message for you. If you want to talk about accountability, then *you* are actually accountable for setting your people, your users, up for success. *You* are accountable for avoiding safety barriers that get unreasonably in the way of work, which leads to undesired side effects. *You* are accountable for showing nonjudgmental curiosity in how work actually gets done, rather than how you, or your designers, imagined it to be done. *You* are accountable for giving your people error-resistant and error-tolerant designs to work with. *You* are accountable for reducing the resource constraints and goal conflicts that set your system up for drifting into failure. *You* are accountable for valuing your people's native resilience and adaptive capacity over dogmatic, strict rule-following. And *you* are accountable for identifying and enhancing the capacities in your people that make things go well.

There is so much you can do to stop "stupid." But you need to see "stupid," not as the root cause of your problems. If you discover "stupid" somewhere, then that is just the beginning of your inquiry, of your curiosity, of your journey toward improvement. "Stupid" comes from somewhere. It is an effect, an outcome—not a cause. When you start looking behind that label "stupid," you will find lots of things that actually make sense: where people were looking at the time, which things they considered important to focus on, what knowledge they brought to bear, which interacting goals they were trying to achieve simultaneously, what resource constraints they were trying to make up for, what work they were trying to get done despite all the obstacles you may well have helped put in their way.

If you think your people were doing "stupid" things, then muster the courage to go behind that label and face up to what you find. Stop stupid by fixing your system. Because otherwise the label "stupid" might well stop with you, and stick.

Sidney Dekker

Professor, Griffith University (Australia)

and Delft University of Technology (Netherlands)

Contents at a Glance

Contents

Introduction

We believe that the title of a book is perhaps its most critical characteristic. We acknowledge that the title, *You Can Stop Stupid* is controversial. We had considered other possible titles, such as Stopping Human Attacks, but such a title does not convey the essence of this book. Although we do intend to stop attacks that target your users, the same methodology will stop attacks by malicious insiders, as well as accidents.

The underlying problem is not that users are the targets of attacks or that they accidentally or maliciously create damage, but that users have the ability to make decisions or take actions that inevitably lead to damage.

That is the fundamental issue this book addresses, and it makes a critical distinction: The problem lies not necessarily in the user, but also in the environment surrounding the people performing operational functions.

What Is Stupid?

Managers, security specialists, IT staff, and other professionals often complain that employees, customers, and users are stupid. But what is "stupid"? The definition of "stupid" is having or showing a great lack of intelligence or common sense.

First, let's examine the attribute of showing a great lack of intelligence. When your organization hires and reviews people, you generally assess whether they have the requisite intelligence to perform the required duties. If you did hire or retain an employee knowing that they lacked the necessary intelligence to do the job, who is actually stupid in this scenario: the employee or the employer?

Regarding a person who shows a great lack of common sense, there is a critical psychological principle regarding common sense: You cannot have common sense without common knowledge. Therefore, someone who is stupid for demonstrating a great lack of common sense is likely suffering from a lack of common knowledge. Who is responsible for ensuring that the person has such common knowledge? That responsibility belongs to the people who place or retain people in positions within the organization.

In general, don't accuse someone in your organization of being stupid. Instead, identify and adjust your own failings in bad employment or training practices, as well as the processes and technologies that enable the "stupidity."

Do You Create Stupidity?

When people talk about employee, customer, and other user stupidity, they are often thinking of the actions those users take that cause damage to your organization. In this book, we refer to that as *user-initiated loss (UIL)*. The simple fact is that a user can't initiate loss unless an organization creates an environment that puts them in a position to do so. While organizations do have to empower employees, customers, and other users to perform their tasks, in most environments, there is little thought paid to proactively reducing UIL.

It is expected that users will make mistakes, fall for tricks, or purposefully intend to cause damage. An organization needs to consider this in its specification of business practices and technological environments to reduce the potential for user-initiated loss.

Even if you reduce the likelihood for people to cause harm, you cannot eliminate all possibilities. There is no such thing as perfect security, so it is folly to rely completely on prevention. For that reason, wise organizations also embed controls to detect and reduce damage throughout their business processes.

How Smart Organizations Become Smart

Consider that large retail stores, such as Target, have a great deal to lose from a physical standpoint. Goods can be physically stolen. Cashiers can potentially steal money. These are just a couple of common forms of loss in retail environments.

To account for the theft of goods, extensive security controls are in place. Cameras monitor areas where goods are delivered, stored, and sold. Strict inventory control systems track everything. Store associates are rewarded for reporting potential shoplifters. Security guards, sometimes undercover, patrol the store. High-value goods are outfitted with sensors, and sensor readers are stationed at the exits.

From a cash perspective, cashiers receive and return their cash drawers in a room that is heavily monitored. They have to "count in" the cash and verify the cash under the watchful eyes of the surveillance team. The cash registers keep track of and report all transactions. Accounting teams also verify that all cash receipts are within a reasonable level of expected error. Also, as important, the use of credit cards reduces the opportunity for employees to mishandle or steal cash.

Despite all of these measures, there are still losses. Some loss is due to simple errors. A cashier might accidentally give out the wrong change. There might be a simple accounting error. Employees might figure out how to game the system and embezzle cash. Someone in the self-checkout line might accidentally not scan all items. Criminals may still be able to outright steal goods despite the best controls. Regardless, the controls proactively mitigate and detect large amounts of losses. There are likely further opportunities for mitigating loss, and new studies can always be consulted to determine varying degrees to which they might be practical.

An excellent example of an industry that intelligently mitigates risk is the scuba diving industry. Author Ira Winkler is certified as a Master Scuba Diving Trainer and first heard the expression "you can't stop stupid" during his scuba instructor training. The instructor was telling all the prospective instructors that there will always be some students who do not pay attention to safety rules. It is true that scuba diving provides for an almost infinite number of ways for students to do something potentially dangerous and even deadly.

Despite this, scuba diving is statistically safer than bowling. When you consider how that may be, you have to understand that most scuba instruction involves safety protocols. Reputable dive operators are affiliated with professional associations, such as the Professional Association of Diving Instructors (PADI). PADI examines how dive accidents have occurred and works with members to develop safety protocols that all members must follow.

For example, when Ira would certify new divers, all students had to take course work specifying safe diving practices. They also had to go through a health screening process and demonstrate basic swimming skills and comfort in the water. They then had to demonstrate the required diving skills in a pool.

When it comes to certifying people in open water, all equipment is inspected by the students and instructors prior to diving. The potential dive location is chosen based upon the calmness and clarity of the water and limited depth so that students don't accidentally go too deep. Before the dive, there is a complete dive briefing, so students know what to expect, as well as safety precautions and instructions about what to do if a diver runs into trouble. The instructors are familiar with the location and any potential hazards. The number of students is limited, and dive master assistants accompany the group as available to ensure safety. Additionally, instructors are required to ensure there is a well-equipped first aid kit, an emergency oxygen supply, and information about the nearest hospital and hyperbaric chamber.

To become an instructor, Ira went through hundreds of hours of training, especially including detailed training about how to handle likely and unlikely problems. This training includes extensive first aid training. From a risk mitigation strategy, instructors maintain personal liability insurance. Similarly, the sponsoring school maintains liability insurance while also paying for supplemental insurance to cover potential injuries to students. The dive facilities, be they pools, boats, quarries, or so on, also maintain liability insurance.

Essentially, PADI and other professional associations have proactively examined where potential injuries may occur and determined how to prevent them as best as possible. Although some accidents will inevitably occur, there is extensive preparation for those incidents, and the result is that diving is a comparatively safe activity.

Not All Industries Are as Smart

Retail loss prevention and dive instruction have clearly created comprehensive strategies for preventing and mitigating loss that accounts for human error and malfeasance. Unfortunately, many industries, and ironically even many practices within the same industries that are otherwise relatively secure, are not dealing with human error well. For example, Target, which generally has an outstanding loss prevention practice, failed when it came to a data breach where 110,000,000 credit records were stolen.

When an organization fails to account for humor error and malfeasance, and fails to put in sufficient layers of controls, the losses can be devastating. When organizations fail to implement an effective process of risk mitigation to account for user-initiated loss, there is a great deal of blame to go around, but organizations tend to point to the "stupid user" who made a single error.

No case is more notorious for this than the massive Equifax data breach. When Richard Smith, former CEO of Equifax, testified to Congress regarding the infamous data breach, he laid the blame for the data breach squarely on an administrator for not applying a critical patch for a vulnerability in a timely manner. Not immediately applying a patch is not uncommon for organizations the size of Equifax. However, a detailed investigation showed that there was a gross systemic failure of Equifax's security posture.

After all, not only did Equifax allow the criminal in, the criminal was able to explore the network undetected for six weeks, breach dozens of other systems, and download data for another six weeks. The attack was detected only after Equifax renewed a long-expired digital certificate that was required to run a security tool.

This type of scenario is common in computer-related incidents. Whether it is the failing of an individual user or someone on the IT team, a single action, or failure to act, can initiate a major loss. However, for there to be a major loss, there has to be a variety of failures to allow an attack to be successful.

Similar failures happen in all operational units of organizations. Any operational process that does not analyze where and how people can intentionally or unintentionally cause potential loss enables that loss.

The goal of this book is to help the reader identify and mitigate actions where users might initiate loss, and then detect the actions initiating loss and mitigate the potential damage from the harmful acts.

Just as the diving and loss prevention industries have figured out how to effectively mitigate risk arising from human failures, you can do the same within your environment. By adopting the proper sciences and strategies laid out in this book, you can effectively mitigate user-initiated loss.

Deserve More

When we consult with organizations, we find that one of the biggest impediments to adequately addressing user-initiated loss is not getting the required resources to do so. The underlying reason is that all too frequently, people responsible for loss reduction fail to demonstrate a return on investment. In short: You get the budget that you deserve, not the budget that you need. You need to deserve more.

If people believe scuba diving is dangerous, the scuba industry will collapse. If accounting systems fail, public companies can suffer dire consequences. These industries recognize these dangers, and they take steps to demonstrate their value and viability. However, many other professions do not adequately address risk and prove their worth.

The common strategy of dealing with user-initiated loss is to focus on awareness and letting people know how not to initiate a loss. Clearly, this fails all too frequently. Therefore, money put into preventing the loss appears wasted. There is no clear sense of deserving more resources.

It is our goal that you will be able to apply our strategies and show you are deserving of the resources you need to properly mitigate the potential losses that you face.

Reader Support for This Book

We appreciate your input and questions about this book. You can contact us at www.YouCanStopStupid.com.

How to Contact the Publisher

If you believe you've found a mistake in this book, please bring it to our attention. At John Wiley & Sons, we understand how important it is to provide our customers with accurate content, but an error may occur even with our best efforts.

To submit your possible errata, please email it to our Customer Service Team at wileysupport@wiley.com with the subject line "Possible Book Errata Submission."

How to Contact the Authors

Ira Winkler can be reached through his website at www.irawinkler .com. Dr. Tracy Celaya Brown can be reached through her website at DrTre.com. Additional material will be made available at the book's website, www.youcanstopstupid.com.

Stopping Stupid Is Your Job

While professionals bemoan how users make their job difficult, the problem is that this difficulty should be considered part of the job. No matter how well-meaning or intelligent a user may be, they will inevitably make mistakes. Alternatively, the users might have malicious intent and intend to commit acts that cause loss. Considering the act "stupid" assists a malicious party in getting away with their intent.

Fundamentally, you don't care about an individual action by a user; you care that the action may result in damage. This is where professionals need to focus. Yes, you want to have awareness so users are less likely to initiate damage. However, you have to assume that users will inevitably make a potentially harmful action, and your job is to mitigate that action in a cost-effective way.

Part I lays the groundwork for being able to address the potential damage that users can initiate. The big problem that we perceive regarding the whole concept of securing the user—as some people refer to it, creating the human firewall—is that people think that the solution to stopping losses related to users is awareness. To stop the problem, you have to understand that awareness is just one tactic among many, and the underlying solution is that you need a comprehensive strategy to prevent users from needing to be aware, to create a culture where people behave appropriately through awareness or other methods, and to detect and mitigate loss before it gets out of hand.

Any individual tactic will be ineffective at stopping the problem of user-initiated loss (UIL). As you read the chapters in Part I, you should come away with the holistic nature of the problem and begin to perceive the holistic solutions required to address the problem.

1

Failure: The Most Common Option

As security professionals, we simultaneously hear platitudes about how users are our best resource, as well as our weakest link. The people contending that users are the best resource state that aware users will not only *not* fall prey to the attacks, they will also respond to the attacks and stop them in their tracks. They might have an example or two as well. Those contending that the users are the weakest link will point to the plethora of devastating attacks where users failed, despite their organizations' best efforts. The reality is that regardless of the varying strengths that some users bring to the table in specific circumstances, users generally are still the weakest link.

Study after study of major data breaches and computer incidents show that users (which can include anyone with access to information or computer assets) are the primary attack vector or perpetrator in an overwhelming percentage of attacks. Starting with the lowest estimate, in 2016, a Computer Technology Industry Association (CompTIA) study found that 52 percent of all attacks begin by targeting users (www.comptia.org/about-us/newsroom/press-releases/2016/07/21/comptia-launches-training-to-stem-biggest-cause-of-data-breaches). In 2018, Kroll compiled the incidents reported to the UK Information Commissioner's Office and determined that human error accounted for 88 percent of all data breaches (www.infosecurity-magazine.com/news/ico-breach-reports-jump-75-human/). Verizon's *2018 Data Breach Investigations Report* (DBIR) reported that 28 percent of incidents were perpetrated by malicious insiders (www.documentwereld.nl/files/2018/Verizon-DBIR_2018-Main_report.pdf). Although the remaining 72 percent of incidents were not specifically classified as resulting from an insider mistake or action, their nature indicates that the majority of the attacks perpetrated by outsiders resulted from user actions or mistakes.

Another interesting finding of the 2018 DBIR is that any given phishing message will be clicked on by 4 percent of people. Initially, 4 percent might sound extremely low, but an attack needs to fool only one person to be successful. Four percent means that if an organization or department has 25 people, one person will click on it. In an organization of 1,000 people, 40 people will fall for the attack.

> **NOTE** The field of statistics is a complex one, and real-world probabilities vary compared to percentages provided in studies and reports. Regardless of whether the percentages are slightly better or worse in a given scenario, this user problem obviously needs to be addressed.

Even if there are clear security awareness success stories and a 96 percent success rate with phishing awareness, the resulting failures clearly indicate that the user would normally be considered the weakest link. That doesn't even include the 28 percent of attacks intentionally perpetrated by insiders.

It is critical to note that these are not only failures in security, but failures in overall business operations. Massive loss of data, profit, or operational functionality is not just a security problem. Consider, for example, that the WannaCry virus crippled hospitals throughout the UK. Yes, a virus is traditionally considered a security-related issue, but it impacted the entire operational infrastructure.

Besides traditional security issues, such as viruses, human actions periodically result in loss of varying types and degrees. Improperly maintained equipment will fail. Data entry errors cause a domino effect of troubles for organizational operations. Software programming problems along with poor design and incomplete training caused the devastating crashes of two Boeing 737 Max airplanes in 2019 (as is discussed in more detail in Chapter 3, "What Is User-Initiated Loss?"). These are not traditional security problems, but they result in major damage to business operations.

History Is Not on the Users' Side

No user is immune from failure, regardless of whether they are individual citizens, corporations, or government agencies. Many anecdotes of user failings exist, and some are quite notable.

The Target hack attracted worldwide attention when 110,000,000 consumers had their personal information compromised and abused. In this case, the attack began when a Target vendor fell for a phishing attack, and then the attacker used the stolen credentials to gain access to the Target vendor network. The attacker was then allowed to surf the network and inevitably accomplish their thefts.

While the infamous Sony hack resulted in disaster for the company, causing immense embarrassment to executives and employees, it also caused more than $150,000,000 in damages. In this case, North Korea obtained its initial foothold on Sony's network with a phishing message sent to the Sony system administrators.

From a political perspective, the Democratic National Committee and related organizations that were key in Hillary Clinton's presidential campaign were hacked in 2016 when a Russian intelligence GRU operative sent a phishing message to John Podesta, then chair of Hillary Clinton's campaign. The resulting leak of the email was embarrassing and was strategically released through Wikileaks.

In the Office of Personnel Management (OPM) hack, 20,000,000 U.S. government personnel had their sensitive information stolen. It is assumed that Chinese hackers broke into systems where the OPM stored the results of background checks and downloaded all of the data. The data contained not just the standard name, address, Social Security number, and so on, but information about their health, finances, mental illnesses, among other highly personal information, as well as information about their relatives. This information was obtained through a sequence of events that began by sending a phishing message to a government contractor.

From a physical perspective, the Hubble Space Telescope was essentially built out of focus, because a testing device was incorrectly assembled with a single lens misaligned by 1.3 mm. The reality is that many contributing errors led to not only the construction of a flawed device but the failure to detect the flaws before it was launched.

In an even more extreme example, the Chernobyl nuclear reactor had a catastrophic failure. It caused the direct deaths of 54 people, another approximately 20,000 other people contracted cancer from radiation leaks, and almost 250,000 people were displaced. All of this resulted from supposed human error, where technicians violated protocols to allow the reactor to run at low power.

These are just a handful of well-known examples where users have been the point of entry for attacks. The DBIR also highlights W-2 fraud as a major type of crime involving data breaches. Thousands of businesses fall prey to this crime, which involves criminals pretending to be the CEO or a similar person and sending emails to human resources (HR) departments, requesting that an HR worker send out copies of all employee W-2 statements to a supposedly new accounting firm. The criminals then use those forms to file fraudulent tax refunds and/or perform other forms of identity theft. Again, these attacks are successful because some person makes a mistake.

> **NOTE**   If you are unfamiliar with U.S. tax matters, W-2 statements are the year-end tax reports that companies send to employees.

Other human failures can include carelessness, ignorance, lost equipment, leaving doors unlocked, leaving sensitive information insecure, and so on. There are countless ways that users have failed. Consequently, sometimes technology and security professionals speciously condemn users as being irreparably "stupid." Of course, if technology and security professionals know all of the examples described in this section and don't adequately try to prevent their recurrence, are they any smarter? The following sections will examine the current approach to this problem and then how we can begin to improve on it.

Today's Common Approach

There are a variety of ways to deal with expected human failings. The three most prevalent ways are awareness, technology, and governance.

Operational and Security Awareness

As the costs of those failings have risen into the billions of dollars and more failings are expected, the security profession has taken notice. The general response has been to implement security awareness programs. This makes sense. If users are going to make mistakes, they should be trained not to make mistakes.

Just about all security standards require that users receive some form of awareness training. These standards are supposed to provide some assurance for third parties that the organizations certified, such as credit card processors and public companies, provide reasonable security protections. Auditors then go in and verify that the organizations have provided the required levels of security awareness.

Unfortunately, audit standards are generally vague. There is usually a requirement that all employees and contractors have to take some form of annual training. This traditionally means that users watch some type of computer-based training (CBT) that is composed of either monthly 3- to 5-minute sessions or a single annual 30- to 45-minute session. CBT learning management systems (LMSs) usually provide the ability to test for comprehension. Reports are then generated to show the auditors to prove the required training has been completed.

As phishing attacks have grown in prominence, auditors started to require that phishing simulations be performed. Organizations also unilaterally decided that they want phishing simulations to better train their users. Phishing simulations do appear to decrease phishing susceptibility over time. These simulations vary greatly in quality and effectiveness. As previously stated, this optimistically results in a 4 percent failure rate.

In general operational settings, training is provided, but there are few standards or requirements for such training. There may or may not be a safety briefing. There are sometimes compliance requirements for how people are to do their jobs, such as in the case of handling personally identifiable information (PII) in certain environments covered by regulations or requirements, such as the Healthcare Insurance and Portability and Accountability Act (HIPAA) and the Payment Card Industry Data Security Standard (PCI DSS). The PCI DSS even requires that programmers receive training in secure programming techniques. NIST 800-50, "Building an Information Technology Security Awareness and Training Program," even attempts a more rigorous structure in the context of the Federal Information Security Management Act (FISMA).

Unfortunately, awareness training, security-related or otherwise, is poorly defined and broadly fails at creating the required behaviors.

Technology

Independent of awareness efforts, IT or security technology professionals implement their own plans to try to reduce the likelihood of humans falling for attacks or otherwise causing damage. For the most part, these are preventative in nature. For example, a user cannot click on a phishing message if the message never gets to the user. For that reason, organizations acquire software that filters incoming email for potential attacks.

There are also different technologies that can stop attacks from being completed. For example, data leak prevention (DLP) software reviews outgoing data for potentially sensitive information. An example would be if a file attached to an email contains Social Security numbers or other PII, DLP software should catch the email before it goes outside the organization.

The purchase of these technologies is generally random to the organization. While awareness and phishing simulation programs are generally accepted as a best practice, there are no universally accepted best practices for many specific technologies, with a few notable exceptions such as for anti-malware software, which is a staple of security programs.

Cloud providers like Google and Microsoft are becoming increasingly proficient at building effective anti-phishing capabilities into their platforms like Gmail and Office 365. As a result, many organizations are considering whether purchasing third-party solutions is even necessary. Either way, every software solution has its limitations, and no single tool (or collection of tools) is a panacea.

Governance

Although we discuss governance in more detail in Chapter 13, "Governance," for an initial introduction it is sufficient to know that governance is supposed to be guidance or specification of how organizational processes are to be performed. The work of governance professionals involves the specification of policies, procedures, and guidelines, which are embodied in documents.

These documents typically reflect best practices in accordance with established laws, regulations, professional associations, and industry standards. In theory, governance-related documents are expected to be living documents and used for enforcement of security practices, but it is all too common that governance documents only see the light of day during a yearly ritual of auditors reviewing them for completeness in the annual audit.

In an ideal world, governance documents should cover how people are to do their jobs in a way that does not make them susceptible to attacks and in a way that their work processes do not result in losses. This includes how specific actions are to be taken and how specific decisions are to be made in performing job functions.

That ideal world represents the embodiment of a system. A good example of this is McDonald's. Generally, McDonald's expects to hire minimally qualified people to deliver a consistent product anywhere in the world. This involves specifying a process and using technology to consistently implement that process. Although people may be involved in performing a function, such as cooking and food preparation, technology is now driving those processes. A person might put the hamburgers on a grill, but the grill is automated to cook the hamburgers for a specific time at a given temperature. The same is true for french fries. Even the amount of ketchup that goes on a hamburger is controlled by a device. Robots control the drink preparation. McDonald's is now distributing kiosks to potentially eliminate cashiers. Although a fast-food restaurant might not seem to be technology-related, the entire restaurant has become a system, driven by governance that is implemented almost completely through technology.

We Propose a Strategy, Not Tactics

We described in the book's introduction how the scuba and loss prevention industries look at the concept of mitigating loss as a comprehensive strategy. When organizations fail to do this, they attempt to implement random tactics that are not cohesive and supporting of each other. For example, if you think the fact that users create loss is an awareness failing and that the solution is better awareness, you are focusing on a single countermeasure. This approach will fail.

A comprehensive strategy is required to mitigate damage resulting from user actions. This book provides such a strategy. This strategy is something that should be applied to all business functions, at all levels of the organization. Wherever there can be a loss resulting from user actions or inactions, you need to proactively determine whether that loss is worth mitigating and then how to mitigate it.

NOTE Implementing the strategy across the entire business at all levels doesn't mean that every user needs to actively know and apply the depth and the breadth of the entire strategy. (The fry cook doesn't need to know how the accounting department works, and vice versa.) The team that implements the strategy coordinates its efforts in a way that informs, directs, and empowers every user to accomplish the strategy in whichever ways are most relevant for their role.

In an ideal world, you will always look at any user-involved process and determine what damage the user can initiate and how the opportunity to cause damage may be removed, as best as possible. If the opportunity for damage cannot be completely removed, you will then look to specify for the user how to make the right decisions and take the appropriate actions to manage the possibility of damage. You then must consider that some user will inevitably act in a way that leads to damage, so you consider how to detect the damaging actions and mitigate the potential for resulting loss as quickly as possible.

Minimally, when you come across a situation where a user creates damage, you should no longer think, "Just another stupid user." You should immediately consider why the user was in a position to create damage and why the organization wasn't more effective in preventing it.

2

Users Are Part of the System

Users inevitably make mistakes. That is a given. At the same time, within an environment that supports good user behavior, users behave reasonably well. The same weakest link who creates security problems and damages systems can also be an effective countermeasure that proactively detects, reports, and stops attacks.

While the previous statements are paradoxically true, the reality is that users are inconsistent. They are not computers that you can expect to consistently perform the same function from one occurrence to the next. More important, all users are not alike. There is a continuum across which you can expect a range of user behaviors.

Understanding Users' Role in the System

It is a business fact that users are part of the system. Some users might be data entry workers, accountants, factory workers, help desk responders, team members performing functions in a complex process, or other types of employees. Other users might be outside the organization, such as customers on the Internet or vendors performing data entry. Whatever the case, any person who accesses the system must be considered a part of the system.

Clearly, you have varying degrees of authority and responsibility for each type of user, but users remain autonomous, and you never have complete authority over them. Therefore, to consider users to be anything other than a part of the system will overlook their capacity to introduce errors and cause security breaches and thus lead to failure. The security and technology teams must consider the users to be one more part of the system that needs to be facilitated and secured. However, without absolute authority, from a business perspective, you must never consider users to be a resource that can be consistently relied upon.

It is especially critical to note that the technology and security teams rarely have any control over the hiring of users. Depending upon the environment, the end users might not be employees, but potentially customers and vendors over whom there is relatively little control. The technology and security teams have to account for every possible end user of any ability.

Given the limited control that technology and security teams have over users, it is not uncommon for some of these professionals to think of users as the weakest link in the system. However, doing so is one of the biggest copouts in security, if not technology management as a whole.

Users are not a "necessary evil." They are not an annoyance to be endured when they have questions. Looking down upon users ignores the fact that they are a critical part of the system that security and technology teams are responsible for. In some cases, they might be the reason that these teams have a job in the first place.

It is your job to ensure that you proactively address any expected areas of loss in the system, including users. Users can only be your weakest link if you fail to mitigate expected user-related issues such as user error and malfeasance.

Perhaps one of the more notable examples is that of the B-17 bomber troubles. Clearly, a pilot is a critical part of flying the airplane. They are not just a "user" in the most limited sense of the term. When the B-17 underwent the first test flights in 1935, it was the most complex airplane at that time. The pilots chosen as the test pilots were among the top pilots in the country. Yet, these top test pilots crashed the plane. The reason was that they failed to disengage a locking mechanism on the flight controls.

It was determined that the pilots were overwhelmed by the complexity and made a simple mistake. As the pilots were a critical part of the system, removing them was not an option. They were highly experienced and trained professionals, so the problem was not that they were poorly trained. The government could have sent the pilots for additional training, but retraining top pilots in the basics of how to fly the plane was not going to be an efficient approach. Instead, they recognized that the problem was that the complexity of the airplane was overwhelming.

The solution was the implementation of a checklist to detail every basic step a pilot had to take to ensure the proper functioning of the airplane. Similar problems have since been solved for astronauts and surgeons, among countless other critical "pieces of the system."

Users Aren't Perfect

Users can be both a blessing and a curse. For the most part, if the rest of the system is designed appropriately, users will behave accordingly. At the same time, you must understand and anticipate that despite your best efforts, users sometimes do the wrong thing.

For example, in one case that is unfortunately not isolated, author Ira Winkler ran a phishing simulation against a large company. Employees were sent a message that contained a link to a résumé. The sender claimed that one of the company's owners suggested they contact the recipient for help in referring them to potential jobs. If the employees clicked on the fake résumé, they received a message explaining that the email was fake and how they should have recognized it as such. In at least one case, the user replied, still believing it was a real message, saying there was a problem with the attached résumé. This sort of phishing training exercise can improve some user behaviors, but it is certainly far from making users a foolproof part of the system.

Anticipating how people will behave helps you design better systems to capitalize on predictable behaviors, leading to better security. Even though people make mistakes, good systems should anticipate that and not break when they do.

"Users" Refers to Anyone in Any Function

When we use the term *users* throughout the book, it might seem that we are implying end users or low-level workers. The reality is that we mean anyone with any function. This can be managers, software developers, system administrators, accountants, security team members, and so on.

Anyone who has a job function or access that can result in damage is technically a user. Administrators can accidentally delete data and cause system outages. Security guards can leave doors open. Managers can leave sensitive documents in public places. Auditors can make accounting errors. Everyone is a user at some level.

Our use of the term *users* can also include outside contractors, customers, suppliers, cloud service providers, or anyone else who interacts with your organization. If they can take an action that can potentially cause harm to your organization, they must be considered in your risk model.

Cloud services and remote workers create additional concerns, where you potentially lose control over your information and users. For example, if a user goes into Starbucks and uses the free WiFi to connect to your network, that user creates a whole new class of users, increasing the risk profile. Cloud services change the profile of your users, given that access control methods change to allow for someone to theoretically log in from anywhere in the world. The risk can be mitigated, but you have to plan for it.

Perhaps some of the more overlooked groups of users are the people who are responsible for mitigating risk. They tend to look at the errors caused by others and believe that they themselves would have never caused the errors. This causes two types of problems.

The first is that if they don't conceive that an error can occur, they cannot proactively mitigate it. We have been on software test teams and found problems with potential uses of the software and told the developers. The developers have often responded that "nobody would ever do that" and fought us on implementing the fixes.

The second issue is that the risk mitigation teams, like information security, IT, physical security, operations, and so on, don't perceive themselves as being the source of errors. They do not believe they will make mistakes. They can have tremendous privileges and access, which provides the capabilities for their errors to create more damage than any normal user would.

Malice Is an Option

Although the natural assumption is that user-initiated loss happens through ignorance or carelessness, a great deal of damage is caused by malicious users. The 2018 DBIR found that 28 percent of incidents result from malicious insiders who have clear intent to either steal something of value or create other forms of damage. That is a staggering number.

More critical is that malicious insiders typically know the best ways to access whatever it is they are trying to steal or destroy. Additionally, if they are intelligent in their planning and execution, they might be able to identify and bypass your protection, detection, and reaction capabilities.

When malice is involved, awareness efforts can sometimes even work against an organization. Awareness efforts typically educate people about how malicious actors accomplish their goals. This provides your malicious employees with information about how they too can commit those types of crimes. It also gives them ideas about how and where you allocate defensive resources and what countermeasures they need to bypass. Clever malicious insiders use this information to improve their own attacks.

As a percentage of overall users, the number who will launch malicious attacks, let alone succeed at them, is fortunately small. Even so, the reality is that malicious users exist, so you must account for them. There have been various studies that have shown that a small percentage of users create the most damage. This is intuitively obvious. Such users will always exist. The best you can do is acknowledge this reality and prepare for them.

What You Should Expect from Users

Users need to perform their jobs properly in a fundamentally safe and secure manner. You need to ensure that security is embedded in job functions and that people know how to perform those functions properly. This should be well defined, and just like any other job function, you should set the expectation for those users to follow those definitions. We would love to say that you should also expect users to be fundamentally aware of security concerns beyond what is specifically defined, but that will not likely happen on a consistent basis.

Therefore, businesses should factor the users' limited awareness into their risk management calculations and plans. You should provide awareness training and opportunities to further reduce risk. Although we don't want organizations to rely too strongly on awareness, it is a critical component of any security program to reduce risk.

Although user ignorance can be partially improved with training, carelessness is another matter. Assuming you have properly instructed users in how they should perform their functions, if some users still consistently violate policies and cause damage, you may need to take disciplinary action against them.

Beyond ignorance and carelessness, you also must account for malicious actions. We discussed this in the previous section, and we will explore options to address it as we discuss security measures throughout the book.

It is important to follow our recommended strategies to ensure that your systems reduce the opportunities for users to make errors or cause malicious damage and then mitigates any remaining potential harm. Then regardless of whether the harmful actions are due to malice, ignorance, or carelessness, your environment should be far more powerfully positioned to minimize or even stop the resulting damage.

3 What Is User-Initiated Loss?

U sers are expected to, and do, make mistakes, and some attempt to maliciously cause damage. However, those actions do not have to result in damage. There is a tendency to place all of the blame for mistakes on users. Instead, a better approach is to recognize the relationship between users and loss and work to improve the system in which they exist.

For this reason, we will use the term *user-initiated loss* (UIL), which we define as loss, in some form, that results from user action or inaction. As Chapter 2, "Users Are Part of the System," discussed, users are not just employees but anyone who interacts with and can have an effect on your system. These actions can be a mistake, or they can be a deliberate, malicious act. Obviously, sometimes the system is attacked by an external entity, so the attack itself is not user-initiated. But when the user initiates an action that enables the attack to succeed, the user's action has initiated the actual loss.

It is important to also note that not all mistakes or malicious acts result in loss, and not all loss happens when the action takes place.

First, we must consider that some actions might not be sufficient to result in loss, or the loss may be prevented. For example, if a person clicks to open a ransomware program in a phishing message, if the user does not have admin privileges on their system, the ransomware should not be able to encrypt the system.

Then we must consider that should there be loss, the loss may or may not happen immediately. Consider that the data entry error may take years to create a problem, if at all, like the iconic error with the Hubble Space Telescope referred to in Chapter 2, where the error wasn't realized until the telescope was already in orbit and ultimately required $150,000,000 in repairs. This error was years in the making.

The Target, Sony, OPM, and Equifax hacks all happened over a period of time. They each resulted in some form of user action or inaction as the initial attack vector. However, none of them had to result in massive damage from the single user failing. Yes, an Equifax employee was slow in patching a new vulnerability, but the massive data breach did not have to occur if there weren't the systematic technical failings within the Equifax infrastructure, especially given that the thefts took months to complete.

These examples begin to imply some potential solutions for UIL. However, before we begin exploring solutions, we intend to set a foundation of understanding the types of losses that may be initiated through user actions. With this foundation, we can then discuss how to avoid putting users in a position where they might initiate loss, instruct them how to take better actions, and then prevent their actions from resulting in loss. We will also explore how to take the opportunity away from malicious actors, as well as how to detect and mitigate the malicious acts.

Because there are an infinite number of user actions and inactions that can result in loss, it is helpful to categorize those actions. This allows you to identify which categories of user error and malice to consider in your environment and what specific scenarios to plan to mitigate. This chapter will examine some common categories where UIL occurs. We'll begin by considering processes, culture, physical losses, crime, user error, and inadequate training. Then we'll move on to technology implementation. Future chapters will explore ways of mitigating UIL.

Processes

Although this might seem to have no direct relationship to the users, how your organization specifies work processes is one of the biggest causes of UIL. Every decision you make about your work processes determines the extent to which you are giving the user the opportunity to initiate loss.

Clearly, the user has to perform a business function. If you can theoretically remove people from processes, you can reduce all UIL associated with those processes. For example, in fast-food restaurants, cashiers have the ability to initiate loss in multiple categories. A cashier can record the order incorrectly. This causes food waste and poor customer satisfaction, which can reduce profit and impede future sales. A cashier can also make mistakes in the handling of cash. They might miscount change, steal money, or be tricked by con artists. These are just a few of the problems. Restaurant chains understand this and implement controls within the process to reduce these losses. McDonald's, however, is going even further to control the process by implementing kiosks where customers place their orders directly into a computer system. This removes all potential loss associated directly with the cashiers.

Obviously, there are a variety of potential losses that are created by removing a human cashier from the process (such as loss of business from customers who find interacting with a kiosk too complicated), but those are ideally accounted for within the revised process. The point is that the process itself can put the user in the position to create UIL, or it can remove the opportunity for the user to initiate loss.

A process can be overly complicated and put well-intentioned users in a position where it is inevitable that they will make mistakes. For example, when you have users implement repetitive tasks in a rapid manner, errors generally happen. Such is the case with social media content reviewers. Facebook, for example, through outside contractors, pays content moderators low wages and has them review up to 1,000 reported posts a day. (See "Underpaid and Overburdened: The Life of a Facebook Monitor," *The Guardian*, www.theguardian.com/news/2017/may/25/facebook–moderator–underpaid–overburdened–extreme–content.) This can mean that legitimate content is deleted, while harmful content remains. The situation is ripe for UIL and also for causing significant harm to the content moderators, who have stress both from the working conditions and from reviewing some of the most troubling content on the Internet.

A process may also be poorly defined and give users access to more functionality and information than they require to perform their jobs. For example, companies used to attach credit card numbers to an entire sales record, and the credit card numbers were available to anyone in the entire fulfillment process, which included people in warehouses. Payment Card Industry Data Security Standard (PCI DSS) requires that only people who need access to the credit card numbers can actually access the information. Removing access to the information from all but those with a specific requirement to access it reduces the potential for those people to initiate a loss, maliciously or accidentally.

Processes can also lack checks and balances that ensure that when a loss is initiated, it is mitigated. For example, well-designed financial processes regularly have audits to ensure transactions are validated. A financial process that does not have sufficient audits is ripe for abuse by insiders and crime from outsiders. For example, we worked with a nonprofit organization and found that they paid thousands of dollars to criminals who sent the organization invoices that looked real. However, when we asked what the invoices were specifically for, it turns out that nobody knew. They modified the process to ensure that future invoices required internal approval by a stakeholder familiar with the charges. Clearly, establishing proper checks and balances is equally important for anyone who has access to data and information services as well.

All processes need to be examined to ensure that users are provided with minimum ability to create loss. Additionally, all organizations should have a process in place to prevent, detect, and mitigate the loss should a user initiate it.

Culture

Establishing a great process is awesome. However, as stated in the famous Peter Drucker quote, "Culture eats strategy for breakfast."

Consider all of the security rules that exist in an organization. Then consider how many are usually followed. There are generally security rules that are universally followed and those that are universally ignored.

As consultants, we are frequently issued badges when we arrive at a client's facility. We diligently don the badges, at least until we walk around and determine that we are the only people actually wearing a badge. While we intend to adhere to security policies, we also have a need to fit in with and relate to the people inside the organization. Badge wearing is a symptom of a culture where security policies inspire people to ignore them.

Conversely, if many people in an office lock their file cabinets at the end of the day or whenever they leave their desk, most of their colleagues will generally do the same. Culture is essentially peer pressure about how to behave at work. No matter what the defined parameters of official behavior are within the organization, people learn their actual behavior through mirroring the behavior of their peers.

Culture is very powerful, enabling vast amounts of UIL and facilitating losses in other categories. If your culture doesn't adequately support and promote your processes, training, and technology implementation, then crime, physical losses, and user errors all increase as a consequence. Let's consider some examples where culture can be shown to have a direct relationship to UIL.

When the Challenger space shuttle exploded, the explanation given to the public was that O-rings, cold weather, and a variety of other factors were the combined cause. However, internal investigations also revealed that there was a culture that was driven to take potentially excessive risk to stay on schedule. (See "Missed Warnings: The Fatal Flaws Which Doomed Challenger," *Space Safety Magazine*, www.spacesafetymagazine .com/space-disasters/challenger-disaster/missed-warnings-fatal-flaws-doomed-challenger/.) Despite many warnings about safety concerns relevant to the Challenger launch, NASA executives chose to downplay the warnings and continued with the launch. Even if the Challenger explosion was due to a mechanical failure, it was clearly a UIL because someone made the conscious decision to ignore warnings and proceed despite the risks.

While it shouldn't take a crippling of the entire space program to initiate culture fixes, NASA subsequently issued engineers challenge cards that they could place on the table in the middle of discussions and demand that their concerns be heard.

In perhaps one of the most iconic cases of culture-based UIL, in 2017, the U.S. Navy destroyer *USS Fitzgerald* crashed into a large freighter, resulting in severe damage and 7 deaths. Another destroyer, the *USS John S. McCain*, crashed into another large ship 9 weeks later, resulting in massive damage and 10 deaths. Investigations determined that there were major failures in leadership and communications on the individual vessels. (See "Worse Than You Thought: Inside the Secret Fitzgerald Probe the Navy Doesn't Want You to Read," *Navy Times*, www.navytimes.com/news/your-navy/2019/01/14/worse-than-you-thought-inside-the-secret-fitzgerald-probe-the-navy-doesnt-want-you-to-read/.) Essentially, the investigators determined that there was a culture on the ship that created those failures. Further studies found that the problems resulting in these collisions were due to a culture that created systematic failings throughout the 7th Fleet, creating poorly trained sailors, failing equipment, and other failures. (See "Years of Warning, Then Death and Disaster," *ProPublica*, features.propublica.org/navy-accidents/us-navy-crashes-japan-cause-mccain/.)

In the cybersecurity world, there are many massive failings due to cultural causes. The Equifax hack demonstrated systematic failures that went beyond a straight failing of technologies. (See "Data Protection: Actions Taken by Equifax and Federal Agencies in Response to the 2017 Breach," U.S. Government Accountability Office, www.warren.senate.gov/imo/media/doc/2018.09.06%20GAO%20Equifax%20report.pdf.) The technological failures would not have occurred without a management infrastructure that allowed them to take place. Some people claimed the Equifax CISO was made a scapegoat and fired, but it is clear that there were management failings.

There is a wide spectrum to the forms that culture-based UIL can take, from small behaviors to widespread negligence. Strong cultures tend to be consistently strong, although they may have some isolated shortcomings to address. Likewise, when you have a weak culture with regard to control of loss, you will find the culture to be consistently weak. Even so, culture is not static. It evolves and changes. If you let culture change organically on its own, you will more likely increase loss. If you take an active role in understanding and influencing culture by determining the desired user behaviors, taking steps to architect those behaviors, establishing open channels of communication for feedback, initiating and improving training, and so on, you can improve your culture and reduce UIL.

Chapter 9, "Security Culture Defined," explores culture further.

Physical Losses

Physical losses are generally straightforward to categorize. If a user leaves a computer behind on an airplane, it is technically a physical loss. An automobile accident can be considered a physical loss. If a user is somehow responsible for creating a fire, or at least ignoring conditions that would lead to a fire, the resulting damages can be considered a physical UIL.

While there may be some overlap with culture, the *USS Fitzgerald* is arguably a physical UIL, at least with regard to the resulting damage. We categorize losses in order to determine how the potential loss might be mitigated in any applicable category. Even if the U.S. Navy culture was perfect, it is possible that the freighter could have still steered toward the *USS Fitzgerald*. No matter what the cause of the accident was, deaths resulted from the actual collision, and it would be legitimate to ask if the construction of the ship could be improved to stand up to future collisions.

We can dissect the 9/11 terrorist attacks to determine many categories of UIL, but there was clearly a successful countermeasure that saved lives. Specifically, prior to the attacks, the Pentagon was renovated to include blast resistant walls and glass. (See "September 11, 2001," U.S. Department of Defense Pentagon Tours Office, `pentagontours` `.osd.mil/Tours/september11.jsp`.) Those renovations were credited with saving lives when an airplane flew directly into the side of the building. Although there were still deaths, the trauma was greatly contained.

The Pentagon renovations were specifically designed to prevent hostile attacks, but they also prepared for other forms of physical damage. Similarly, other building construction often takes into account fire and earthquake protection.

People often think of planning for physical loss in terms of their own immediate organization, but it extends beyond that. If a cloud computer center isn't adequately air-conditioned, the servers can be damaged, affecting an organization's data. To prevent that type of loss, the organization needs to consider not only their own immediate physical assets but those of users in partner organizations as well.

Huge, dramatic losses get a lot of attention, but seemingly small losses accumulate quickly and can be even more damaging. This is what we refer to as "death by 1,000 cuts." With death by 1,000 cuts, small, inconsequential losses can add up to significant losses. International grocery chains operate on a tiny profit margin. Their meat, produce, deli, and dairy products are highly perishable and have a limited shelf life. Those are physical assets, and any increase in their loss can drastically damage the company's profit. To safeguard that product against loss, many factors need to be considered such as proper training of employees on stock rotation and inventory control, regular maintenance of refrigeration units, and partnering with vendors that will provide the freshest, most reliable product possible.

If an organization has a fleet of delivery trucks, those trucks age. If you don't regularly change the oil, you replace expensive engine parts more quickly. If you don't occasionally balance and rotate the tires, they wear unevenly, and you buy expensive truck tires more often. When equipment wears out and needs to be replaced, that is still a physical loss, and it can be planned for and minimized.

Also consider that people exist physically and thus, are themselves physical resources. If an organization has a high turnover rate, they enter into a constant cycle of acquiring and training new employees. Even if employee retention isn't a problem, it is important to maintain the condition of your people just as you do any other physical resource. For example, one study found that 98 percent of medical residents made a medical error in large part because of the lack of sleep incurred by their required and strenuous schedules (see journalofethics .ama-assn.org/article/after-apology-coping-and-recovery-after-errors/2011-09). Organizations that use trucks or airplanes perform oil changes, tire inflation, and other routine maintenance on their vehicles to keep them working efficiently as physical components in the system. Similarly, regularly addressing the processes, culture, and training maintains an organization's physical users to maximize their efficiency and effectiveness, thereby reducing loss.

To properly mitigate a physical loss, you need to consider what physically exists and how to best safeguard it. Often, this needs to be done in conjunction with addressing other categories that contribute to loss as well, such as training, processes, culture, and so on.

Crime

Criminal acts are unfortunately a part of business operations that need to be accounted for. There are many types of crime that affect an organization. Some crimes are the theft of equipment. Others involve embezzlement of money. Still others include a robbery of an employee traveling for work or a robbery intended to steal company assets. Whatever the type of crime, it should be something to account for in your risk reduction programs.

Some users can be malicious and have clear intent to cause loss, while others are normal users who simply want to perform their ordinary functions. Regardless, both are frequently a conduit for crime. The studies cited in Chapter 1, "Failure: The Most Common Option," indicate that in the majority of significant computer-related losses, users were the primary attack vector. This impacts the tactics you need to use to mitigate the threats.

From a more comprehensive perspective, crime impacts a variety of operations. Disrupted supply chains, depending on their nature and scope, can cause operations to cease. Theft of funds can cripple an organization's cash flow, which can cause an organization to go bankrupt. Data theft involving intellectual property cause organizations to go out of business, particularly when it enables competitors to make the same products at significantly cheaper prices. Data theft involving personally identifiable information (PII) can cause significant fines and embarrassment for an organization.

In general, all of these crimes involve another category of UIL as well. It can be physical, computer usage, user error, and so on. UIL in the criminal category has specific consideration in how you potentially stop the attack from reaching the user and how to mitigate the loss resulting from the crime.

For example, if you know criminals may attempt to steal equipment from traveling employees, you can perform awareness campaigns to ensure that users know how to best protect the equipment during travel. If you assume that at least one user will inevitably fail to protect the equipment, you know to encrypt devices and enable remote data deletion capabilities, also known as *wiping*. You may also provide the employee with travel equipment that stores only the data needed during the trip. Acknowledging that crime is a possibility allows you to prepare countermeasures that might not otherwise be considered.

All organizations have exposure to varying levels of criminal activity. If you consider how to mitigate UIL from any perspective, you can solve most of the problems, as users still have to initiate the loss. Then you can focus on addressing the finer points.

A couple of types of crime that warrant additional scrutiny are user malice, which is generally an internal attack, and social engineering, which is commonly an external attack. The following sections will examine these types of crime more closely.

User Malice

Malice is the intent to cause loss to an organization. User malice can take many forms. Sometimes it simply involves theft for personal gain. This theft can be money, physical equipment, data, other valuables, and so on.

Other times people are motivated to cause loss out of revenge for a variety of perceived wrongs. Many organizations are notorious for poor working conditions or their general mistreatment of employees, and it is inevitable that some employees may act out. In these instances, the people might commit theft, destroy property or data, or sabotage the organization's processes or reputation to reduce sales, productivity, or efficiency.

According to Dr. Martha Stout in her book, *The Sociopath Next Door* (Harmony, 2006), sociopaths make up approximately 4 percent of the population. The FBI estimates that an additional 1 percent of the population will become psychopaths (see www.leb .fbi.gov/articles/featured-articles/psychopathy-an-important-forensic-concept-for-the-21st-century). Combined, this means that 5 percent of the population might do harm if given the opportunity. This can take the form of the previously discussed personal gain or revenge. However, some of these people sometimes just create damage for their personal entertainment.

Frequently, malicious users may work with outsiders. Malicious users can solicit the support from the outsiders to assist with their acts. Alternatively, they can facilitate the crimes of outsiders who approach them. There are a variety of reasons for both scenarios. Whatever the scenario, it is important that you acknowledge it as a possibility.

> **NOTE**   Not all user malice comes from greed or hostility. Some users are coerced or manipulated by outside parties. Others find themselves in a desperate financial situation and perform actions that they normally wouldn't. It is important to recognize that it isn't only disgruntled users who can become malicious users.

Malice has caused loss across every industry, so it is important to recognize that UIL may not always be the result of some type of unintentional action. There is frequently a focus on awareness to stop unintentional UIL, but any security or loss mitigation program that does not also consider and mitigate actions due to intentional UIL will fail. Even though an aware user might be one of your best defenses, an aware user can also be your worst enemy if their intent is to use their awareness against you.

Social Engineering

Social engineering is the broad category of attacks typically associated with the computer security field. However, social engineering can take a variety of forms and can be used to facilitate other crimes beyond just computer-based ones. Social engineering can be defined as manipulating an individual to take an action they would not normally take. In the computer field, it is essentially any nontechnical attack to gain access to a computer.

People perceive social engineering as tricking someone into providing them with information or access. In many common scenarios, that is an accurate working definition. This can be achieved through telephone calls, emails, in-person interactions, online chat systems, and so on.

Other forms of social engineering include people essentially sneaking into locations. Dumpster diving, where you literally go through the trash to find useful information, can be considered a form of social engineering. Some people don construction hard hats and reflective vests or utility worker uniforms and walk into a facility. Other people check doors and gates to see if they are locked. Still others try to follow people into facilities through tailgating.

While these tactics can be used to obtain computer access, clearly they can be used for a variety of other types of crimes. A company once tasked us to perform a social engineering simulation to see how outsiders can gain access to a building, because there had been a tragic workplace shooting, where a man had snuck into the building and shot his ex-wife. These things unfortunately can happen.

From a computer attack perspective, social engineering frequently takes the form of phishing, where someone sends a message attempting to get a user to download malware or to disclose login credentials or other useful information.

Sometimes criminals, frustrated with failing to technically hack an organization, will resort to pretext telephone calls attempting to get users to disclose usernames and passwords. Pretext phone calls are also used for a variety of other nefarious purposes to support crimes, such as trying to defraud people for money with fake Microsoft support, claiming the people owe taxes and immediate payment is required, and false claims of needing medical insurance information from the elderly.

Another form of social engineering involves criminals creating USB drives loaded with malware. They place the USB drives in the vicinity of the target and hope that someone from the targeted organization will plug one of them into a computer inside the company. Clearly, this is a hit or miss type of social engineering, but if successful, it can be a very fruitful attack.

The takeaway from our discussion of social engineering is that while insiders may not intend to be malicious, they can be exploited by a malicious outsiders who can obtain insider-level access, both physically and technically. This has to be a critical consideration for any UIL mitigation strategy.

User Error

User error is a commonality within most of the other categories in this chapter. Some errors are more consequential than others. Some errors cause loss of life, which is sometimes the case in medical procedures and diagnoses. Other errors cause large losses of money. Many errors cause inconvenience. Some errors have no consequence at all.

In the other categories within this chapter, we assume error to be induced in part by other factors, such as confusing interfaces. In this section, we focus primarily on error due to carelessness or accidents. Users are human beings, and the fact is that they sometimes just make mistakes.

Many people who are overworked, underpaid, or otherwise not treated well are less motivated to avoid making errors. Other people may be distracted for a variety of reasons such as personal issues, medical conditions, lack of sleep, drug use, or similar issues. Sometimes, even good people can feel apathetic, overwhelmed, or pressured. All of this is to be expected. While you hope carelessness is not the norm, its gravity is more dire in some situations than others. Ideally, culture should help to assist in creating more attentiveness in situations where people have to perform at higher levels. Even in less critical situations, you can try to prevent carelessness as much as possible.

We classify accidents as being different than carelessness because even the best people in the best situations will make an error. For example, many users have experienced accidentally deleting a message instead of forwarding it because they mistakenly clicked on the wrong button on an interface, particularly when they encounter an unexpected lag in cursor speed.

Sometimes there can be multiple supposedly legitimate actions to take, and a person makes an error in determining which action is correct. Everyone has made a legitimate mistake while driving. It is assumed that in accounting, even the most attentive accountant makes a mistake.

Whether it occurs through a legitimate accident or carelessness, you must assume that users will make an error. You need to proactively plan for such errors and have audit procedures, warning systems, redundancies, and so on, to ensure that potential errors are mitigated before a loss can be initiated.

> **NOTE** One of the most common examples of preventing accidental errors is providing a confirmation message that has to be acknowledged prior to the permanent deletion of an email message.

Inadequate Training

One fundamental aspect of awareness training is that people believe a properly trained user will not make mistakes. The reality is that even with the best training, a user will make fewer mistakes, not no mistakes.

Many people take for granted that common sense will help prevent a lot of mistakes. That might be an overly optimistic assumption. Either way, there can be no common sense without common knowledge. It is critical to ensure that all users are grounded in common knowledge. Training attempts to establish and strengthen this common knowledge.

However, training frequently falls short. Some training provides an adequate amount of knowledge but is short on practical experience. Knowledge without application is short lived. A random piece of information will rapidly dissipate from memory and, without reinforcement, will be quickly forgotten. We explore this further when we discuss the concept of the forgetting curve in Chapter 5, "The Problem with Awareness Efforts."

Proper training should ensure that users understand what their responsibilities are and how to perform them. Ideally, training also impresses the need for users to be attentive in the performance of their duties. This requires accuracy and completeness in training, as well as motivation.

Some training is grossly inadequate, inaccurate, and irrelevant. In 2019, two Boeing 737 MAX airplanes crashed. There were multiple causes of these incidents, including technology implementation and user error (as will be discussed further in the upcoming "Technology Implementation" section). However, training requirements were also insufficient and led to pilots not knowing how to handle the malfunctioning equipment. While that is an extreme example, failed training plagues all organizations to varying levels.

Everyone has experience with inadequate training and can relate to the fact that such training results in loss. Fortunately, training can be strengthened to make it more effective. Chapter 15, "Creating Effective Awareness Programs," addresses the improvement of training.

Technology Implementation

As we talk about UIL, it is important to consider contributing factors to those losses. Everyone has experience with difficult-to-use systems that inevitably contribute to loss of some type. Some systems cause typographical errors that cause people to transfer the wrong amount of money. Some navigational systems cause drivers to go to the wrong destination or to drive the wrong way on a one-way street.

Some user interfaces contribute to users making security-related mistakes. For example, one of the most common security-related loss results from autocomplete in the Recipients field of an email. People frequently choose the wrong recipient from common names. In one case, after one of our employees left our organization to work for a client and solicited bids from a variety of vendors, we received a proposal from a competitor. The competitor apparently used an old email to send the proposal to our former employee. In another case, we had a client issue an email with a request for proposals to various organizations, including us and our competitors. One competitor mistakenly clicked Reply All, and all potential bidders received a copy of their proposal.

These are minor issues compared to some more serious losses. For example, as mentioned earlier, in 2019 two Boeing 737 MAX airplanes crashed. In both cases, Boeing initially attributed the crashes to pilot error, but it appeared that malfunctions of a mechanical device, an angle of attack sensor (AOA), caused the computer system to force the plane to descend rapidly. There are two AOAs on each plane, and computer systems in similar Boeing 737 models would let the pilot know that there was a discrepancy between the readings of the two AOAs. In the 737 MAX airplanes, the warning for the discrepancy was removed and made an optional feature, and pilots were not properly warned about the differing functionality. (See "Boeing Waited Until After Lion Air Crash to Tell Southwest Safety Alert Was Turned Off on 737 Max," CNBC, www.cnbc.com/2019/04/28/boeing-didnt-tell-southwest-that-safety-feature-on-737-max-was-turned-off-wsj.html.) Clearly, even if there was some pilot error involved, it was only enabled due to the technological implementation of the system.

There are many aspects of technological implementation that contribute to UIL. The following sections examine design and maintenance, user enablement, shadow IT, and user interfaces.

Design and Maintenance

There are a wide variety of decisions made in the implementation of technology. These design decisions drive the interactions and capabilities provided to the end users. Although it is easy to blame end users when they commit an act that inevitably leads to damage, if the design of the system leads them to commit the harmful action, it is hard to attribute the blame solely to the end user. Such is the case in attempting to blame the Lion Air and Ethiopian Airlines pilots of the doomed Boeing 737 MAX airplanes.

In the implementation of technology, there are many common design issues that essentially automate loss. Programming errors can cause the crash of major computer systems. If this happens to a financial institution, transactions can be blocked for hours. If it happens to an airline's schedule systems, planes can be grounded until the problem is resolved.

People maintaining systems fail to properly maintain and update them for a variety of reasons. Trucks that are not properly maintained will break down. Computers that are not properly maintained may crash or be more easily hacked. Such was the case with the Equifax hack. As we described earlier, one administrator failed to update one system, which allowed the criminals into their infrastructure. Other failings, including a simple maintenance function of renewing a digital certificate, which is essentially paying a fee, caused the data breach to go undetected. No end user initiated a loss in this case, but other people initiated the loss through their actions, and as we explained in Chapter 2, anyone who interacts with the system should be considered to be a user who can initiate loss.

Another category of loss that many professionals fail to consider is the disposal of equipment. Just about all technology seems to have local storage. Before an organization discards computers, they generally know to remove the storage drives. Many people know that they should delete everything on their cellphones. However, many organizations and individuals fail to consider that the same diligence should apply to printers, copy machines, and other devices that had access to the organization's network or data.

If a loss results from the decisions, actions, or inactions of a person, it is a loss that you have to consider in your risk reduction plans, and that includes loss that relates to design and maintenance.

User Enablement

While you can expect end users to make mistakes or be malicious, you do not have to enable the mistakes or malice. Unfortunately, some technology teams are doing exactly that. It is a given that users have to be able to perform their required business functions. However, you can design a user's access and function to limit the amount of loss they can initiate.

As we discussed earlier, McDonald's eliminates the possibility for cashiers to steal or miscount money by removing the cashier from the process. Similarly, ransomware is a constant problem for organizations, but that problem can be greatly reduced by not providing users with administrator privileges on their computer systems. Without administrator privileges, new software, even malicious software, cannot be installed on a computer.

There are limits to any measures that you employ to reduce user enablement. Some malware can bypass administrator privileges. While the elimination of cashiers eliminates risk of cashier theft, it also increases the risk posed by the people maintaining the kiosks, including those who count the cash collected by the kiosks. Even so, there is a significant reduction in the overall risk.

Just as users rarely need administrator privileges on their computers, they are frequently provided with much more technological access and capability than they require to do their jobs. In one extreme example, Chelsea Manning was a U.S. Army intelligence analyst in an obscure facility in Iraq. Manning was allowed to download massive amounts of data from SIPRNet, which is a communications network used by the U.S. Department of Defense and U.S. Department of State for data classified up to the SECRET level. Manning had access to data well beyond what her job function required. Some might argue that Manning's excessive access was part of an effort to ensure intelligence analysts had access to needed information and that compartmentalization of data was a contributing factor in the 9/11 failures. However, in the case of Manning, such access was not implemented with the appropriate security controls (see abcnews.go.com/US/top-brass-held-responsible-bradley-mannings-wikileaks-breach/story?id=12276038). After all, the United States has been dealing with insider threats since Benedict Arnold. Examples like Manning's excessive information access are not unique to the military, and they're often even worse in commercial organizations.

In college, author Ira Winkler worked for his college's admissions office and was responsible for recording admission statuses in the college's mainframe computer. He realized that he also had menu options that provided access to the school registrar's system, which maintained grades. Although he never abused the access, you can assume that other people were not as ethical. You can also assume that many people in other university offices with access to legitimate functions also had excessive access privileges. As you can see, such information access is a combination of both technology and process.

In short, any time a user is provided with the ability to access information or perform tasks more than is required for their work, there is a risk to potentially be contained. Sometimes, expanded information access and enhanced capabilities can help empower people to do their jobs more effectively. Empowering users to succeed while reducing loss is always about finding the right balance. For example, there is no reason for employees to have access to other people's PII, unless their job specifically requires such access.

Shadow IT

Shadow IT is a term for computing equipment, software, and access that is unknown to the IT department. It is typically acquired and introduced outside of the organization's normal process. It may or may not be purchased through the use of organizational funds.

One example is people's choices of laptops. Some people prefer to use Macs, as opposed to corporate PC-compatible systems, and they purchase a Mac directly and use it as their primary system. The problem is that the Mac systems are generally unknown to the IT department and will not be maintained per organizational standards. For example, if the Mac is lost, there will not be an ability to remotely erase company data on the system.

Shadow IT also includes software. Users add software to their personal and corporate devices that has not been vetted by the organization. Frequently, the organization has made a conscious choice not to use the software because of a variety of issues, including adherence to regulations, security requirements, and proper maintenance and patching. In one of the most notorious cases, Jared Kushner, advisor to President Trump, installed and used WhatsApp to communicate with foreign leaders. (See "Jared Kushner's Use of WhatsApp Raises Concerns Among Cybersecurity Experts," CNN, www.cnn.com/2019/03/23/politics/kushner-whatsapp-concerns/index.html.) WhatsApp violates the law in that it does not adhere to record-keeping requirements.

Additionally, while communications may be encrypted, there are a variety of security concerns. Shadow IT systems may not be patched properly or have updated anti-malware software, which puts the whole organization at risk. If the employee leaves the organization, nobody knows to collect the system or at least delete the organizational data on the system.

In one case we are familiar with, which is not uncommon for organizations, an employee was unhappy with the available Internet access bandwidth, as well as the fact that his access was both filtered and monitored, so he had a new Internet connection installed in a corporate office. This created a rogue connection that bypassed the organization's security posture and created a backdoor for outside criminals.

Another case of Shadow IT is the use of online storage systems, such as Box, Dropbox, and Google Drive. Users frequently use third-party services to perform their jobs and bypass obstacles. Some services might not have strong security. Either way, the organization loses control of its information once it's placed on the servers and they are not otherwise aware of it.

Shadow IT includes aspects of both user enablement and design and maintenance. Because the infrastructure has to allow for rogue devices, no matter the source, it is a network maintenance issue. Because organizations are directing that IT departments allow users to bring their own personal devices to work, it is a form of user enablement. One typical example of this is that organizations want employees to use their own cell phones to save costs because the organization doesn't have to purchase cell phones for the employees. They create an infrastructure to allow employee cell phones to connect to the network and to also access and store organizational information.

You do not need to categorize Shadow IT. You just need to understand it for the risk that it is and incorporate it into your strategy to mitigate UIL.

Confusing Interfaces

It is safe to say that everyone has looked at some document, computer screen, electronic or mechanical device, or a general situation and found it confusing. This is the case where even the experienced pilots in the Boeing 737 MAX airplanes could not figure out that the computer had the wrong readings and was forcing the airplanes down.

Fortunately, there are few interfaces involving such drastic consequences. Even so, a great deal of loss can be attributed to well-meaning users who fail to properly interact with some system. This is often not the user's fault. It is an area where design, maintenance, and user enablement overlap.

There is a discipline within the fields of psychology and mechanical engineering of ergonomics that is sometimes referred to *human factors*. Within the computer field, a similar discipline is referred to as *human-computer interaction* (HCI). While these fields intend to optimize human interaction with systems, the net result is to also reduce loss, which sometimes even includes reducing the loss of life. We recommend that you look into the relevant fields for additional guidance.

As you can see, how you configure work and computers to interact with users can have a substantial impact on loss. You need to understand that if you see otherwise intelligent and capable people initiating losses that it may very well be caused by how they are required to interact with your systems.

UIL Is Pervasive

To prevent and mitigate UIL, you have to acknowledge it for what it is: pervasive and natural to your organization. Some categories of loss lend themselves to preventing the potential attacks from reaching users. Some attacks are clearly intentional, and the only way to prevent them is to remove the capability of the user to cause the loss.

Sometimes awareness alone can mitigate a particular loss, but in all likelihood the loss will only be mitigated through a layered approach of countermeasures. This unfortunately goes against much of the current hype that users are your first and last line of protection and that awareness is a silver bullet that will stop user-related losses. Again, awareness is a tactic, and solving UIL requires a comprehensive strategy.

Foundational Concepts

Ideally, you now have an understanding that the nature of the problem is not necessarily that users make mistakes but that user actions can initiate loss in some form. This empowers you to know that users do not control the destiny of the organization. Instead, your job is to prevent users from making potentially harmful actions and then mitigate the resulting loss.

However, before we detail a holistic strategy, we need to set the foundation for that strategy. We have to ensure there is common knowledge, if for no other reason than to practice what we preach. While many of the disciplines covered in Part II appear unrelated, they all play a part in ensuring a comprehensive strategy.

4 Risk Management

People often mistakenly assume that "mitigating loss" means preventing all potential loss. That is impossible. There will always be some form of loss in operations. Perhaps one of the best definitions of risk is this one from ISO 27000:

Risk is the effect of uncertainty on objective.

Similarly, we want to be careful about what we mean when we discuss "optimizing risk." People generally believe that minimizing risk implies you should spend whatever it takes to avoid as much risk as possible. Trying to prevent all risk and loss might cost more to achieve than the actual loss you hope to mitigate.

What you are actually trying to do is manage the loss. The concept of balancing potential loss with the cost of mitigating it is called *risk management.*

As this book specifically addresses user-initiated loss (UIL), including malice and other potential forms of loss, you need to not just understand the concept of risk management as a whole, but also consider it in the context of mitigating the risk that is inherent in users.

This means you need to open your mind to potentially changing workflows and reducing some capabilities of users within your organization. While there may be some pushback against doing this, the reality is that while you are removing the ability of users to initiate loss, you are also simplifying the process and making it more efficient at the same time. In Chapter 1, we discussed the timers for cooking at McDonald's. Removing the discretion of the cooks delivers a more consistent product while reducing the potential stress for "eyeballing" properly cooked food and the inevitable reprimands when food is undercooked or overcooked.

In a traditional white-collar environment, there is usually concern about reducing the capabilities of an employee. However, the capabilities being removed are often those that are unneeded or unused. For example, many organizations provide employees with PCs and knowingly or unknowingly provide those employees with administrator access to their PCs. Having administrator access can enable the employee to potentially make more use of the PC, for example by giving them the ability to load new software, perform preventative maintenance, and so on. However, not all users will perform preventative maintenance how and when they should, and the software they load can create security vulnerabilities due to its source, its configuration, and so on. As a result, having users with admin access also opens the door to more ransomware attacks. In theory, the organization should have a process in place for acquiring software and performing maintenance (generally managed by a technology, security, or management department). Consequently, there are fewer benefits to users having administrator privileges, and those are outweighed by the potential loss.

These are the types of decisions that you have to make during the process of "stopping stupid." You need to weigh the benefits of giving users specific capabilities against the potential loss those capabilities might cause. This requires a consideration of risk. The better you understand risk, the better you can make such determinations.

Death by 1,000 Cuts

People normally assume that "risk" means the likelihood that something catastrophic is going to happen. In a manufacturing setting, it could mean that an error causes a major recall. From a safety perspective, it could mean that death or a major injury could happen to an employee or a client. From an IT perspective, it could mean that something causes a major network outage and takes down the organization. There is a fallacy that addressing risk merely means that you should try to prevent a disaster from occurring.

A smart risk reduction program looks at the breadth and depth of risks, large and small. The reality is that small risks, in aggregate, add up to major losses. This is the metaphorical death by 1,000 cuts, where a single cut is inconsequential, but with enough cuts, the loss of blood is deadly.

Risk can also include security concerns. The infamous WannaCry worm of 2017 was a worldwide ransomware attack that clearly had the impact to cripple enterprises. While regular malware does not usually have the devastating impact of WannaCry, in aggregate, all of the individual incidents combined add up to an impact that could potentially be as significant, if not worse than, WannaCry.

The concept of total quality management (TQM), discussed in Chapter 12, addresses the fact that small losses throughout a process add up to major losses. For example, if you have a manufacturing process that has 10 steps, and the defect rate is around 1% in each step, in total, your manufacturing process has a defect rate of roughly 10%. That is significant.

It is the same with all disciplines involving security and risk. A single incident involving a small loss may not be recorded. In organizations with strong safety programs, every injury reported, from a small cut to death, is recorded and tracked. However, in most organizations, few incidents are recorded and tracked. As we talk about risk management and security programs deserving more attention and resources, a significant way to begin to improve results is to record and track as many incidents as possible.

The Risk Equation

To address UIL, you need to understand where it comes from. You also need to know where and how to mitigate the loss, and even whether you want to do so in the first place. That might sound counterintuitive. Clearly, you want to mitigate loss as effectively as possible, but only when it makes sense to do so. It is possible that sometimes mitigating a particular loss is more expensive than to actually letting it happen.

To make these determinations, you need to understand how to approach them rationally. Unfortunately, there are many ways people react irrationally when it comes to loss. It is easy to get overwhelmed by anxiety and uncertainty when thinking about loss. It is also easy to be lulled into a false sense of security and ignore loss altogether, because a major loss seems so unlikely, while a minor loss seems unnecessary to worry about.

A similar problem is when organizations resign themselves to loss as a seemingly inevitable cost of doing business. This fallacy is where the sentiment of the user as the weakest link comes from. There is always something that can be done, but organizations, or more specifically, the people within the organization responsible for addressing the problem, don't know where to start or perceive it as useless to try.

To approach risk more rationally, it helps to think of it in terms of value, threats, vulnerabilities, and countermeasures and how they relate to each other. Figure 4.1 represents these concepts as a high-level equation.

$$Risk = \left(\frac{(Threat * Vulnerability)}{Countermeasure} \right) * Value$$

Figure 4.1 The risk equation

Looking at Figure 4.1, *value* is what is at stake. *Threats* are entities that will do you harm if given the opportunity. *Vulnerability* is a weakness that can result in harm if exploited. *Countermeasures* are efforts to mitigate a potential loss.

With specific regard to UIL, we want to differentiate between a threat and a vulnerability. For the purposes of dealing with UIL, you need to understand that a user is actually also a threat. As a threat, users cannot actually initiate loss unless there are vulnerabilities that allow them to do so. And even then, the threat can't successfully exploit those vulnerabilities unless there are insufficient countermeasures to prevent them from doing so.

In other words, yes, a user may have a moment of carelessness or malicious intent. However, the resulting action cannot result in loss unless there is both an environment that allows that user's action to initiate loss and insufficient countermeasures to mitigate that loss. When you understand and embrace the concept of risk from this perspective, you can begin to see UIL is clearly an addressable problem.

In the sections that follow, we will examine each of the elements of the risk equation, beginning with value.

NOTE   The risk equation discussed in this chapter is a high-level representation to help deal with risk on a conceptual level. It isn't a mathematical formula intended to be directly used with quantifiable figures. Although some disciplines, such as actuarial science, attempt to quantify risk for business purposes, that isn't our focus. We do, however, discuss practical metrics throughout the book, particularly in Chapter 10.

Value

Value is perhaps the most important element of risk. It is essentially what you have to lose. More important, it is both separately identifiable elements and their totality that you have to lose. Too many organizations and decision-makers misperceive the value that is at risk. Either they have a myopic view as to what value is exposed to loss or they underestimate the potential for overall value to be lost.

Consider, for example, the infamous Sony hack, where North Korea attacked Sony in retaliation for the movie *The Interview*, which depicted the killing of North Korea's leader, Kim Jung Un. Prior to the attack, the Sony CIO was quoted as saying that he wasn't going to spend $10,000,000 to prevent a $1,000,000 loss. While the logic was sound, the underlying assumption of potential loss was incredibly wrong. Sony didn't lose $1,000,000 in the incident. The combined loss from the interrupted release of the movie, the incident response, the compromise of PII of Sony employees, and the embarrassment resulting from leaked emails, operational interruption, and so on, cost Sony in excess of $150,000,000.

Unfortunately, there are numerous losses of this scope. While your organization will ideally not suffer such a loss, even small losses can become significant, as we discussed earlier in the "Death by 1,000 Cuts" section. At the least, you want to have a realistic consideration of the value that you are protecting.

There are many types of value. Monetary, opportunity, and reputation are some of the most significant forms. It is also important to consider the value that your organization has to potential attackers, which clearly impacts the level of effort that they will go through to target you. The following sections will explore these types of value.

Monetary Value

Monetary value is the clear financial amount that your organization possesses or can lose. To a large extent, this is pretty straightforward. Organizations typically have financial metrics for predicted income, estimated costs for outages, estimates for injuries, estimates for supply chain interruptions, and so on.

Airlines are an easy-to-recognize example of what happens when there are computer outages that interrupt operations. In 2017, a power outage at the Hartsfield-Jackson International Airport in Atlanta caused the cancellation of 1,173 flights. This caused disruption to the lives and business of hundreds of thousands, if not millions, of people given the cancelled flights and the other people impacted. While a good portion of the loss was intangible, Delta Airlines estimated a hard loss of up to $50,000,000.

All organizations with reasonable financial practices have clear estimates of the financial costs of incidents. If you are responsible for mitigating UIL, it would benefit you to talk to your risk or accounting departments to see whether they have any metrics regarding the value of operations, interruptions, and so on. When it comes to technology, computer incidents, unfortunately, have not been generally well defined regarding the resulting loss. However, you can, gather costs from third parties that track such information and extrapolate it for your own purposes. The good news is that there have been significant incidents documented in the technology field to provide you with a good start.

You should try to use any metrics available to you in calculating the financial impact of UIL. You can use this data in justifying the efforts and resources you require to mitigate UIL. The resources include cash and people to prevent the initiation of loss, as well as to mitigate the loss, should it be initiated. You also need to justify the organizational impact you may create in changing processes and otherwise impacting the organization. While the other categories of loss discussed can assist in making your case, demonstrating the potential loss in monetary value is the easiest way to justify the resources you require.

Opportunity Value

Opportunity value is the potential benefit lost or gained as a result of a harmful action. Opportunity value can include the growth or loss of your customer base, business opportunities, profits, and so on. It can also include strategic positioning of your organization and its business-to-business relationships, the timing of taking a company public, and the strength of your corporate culture.

Unless there are already detailed plans with financial projections, it is sometimes hard to assign a specific monetary value to an opportunity value loss. For example, when contracts are lost internally unless they were large contracts that were calculated into financial projections, it is unlikely that those losses are tracked. If those losses could be quantified financially, they would likely be considered a loss of monetary value as well as opportunity value. There generally is a monetary value that relates to opportunity value, and it can't always be tracked.

We have worked incidents where former employees stole proposals and other corporate information to use for the benefit of their new employers. In some cases, a contract was lost. It is hard to attribute the lost contract to the specific theft, as these situations can be complex and many factors apply. Besides the lost profit from not having the contract, it reduces the likelihood of future work with the client. It might also reduce the money available for future marketing efforts, which can impact future income from other sources.

Some opportunity values can be identified and even quantified, particularly if they align with your organization's goals. For example, if your organization wants to raise its profile in the public's general awareness, being positively reported on in major media has opportunity value. Tracking the number of hits on social media can reveal some level of engagement with people as well.

Opportunity value comes in many forms, and it is usually difficult to calculate. However, it is something to consider in the justification of your efforts. And in the situations when you actually can attach metrics to the opportunity value, you can turn it into something more recognizably quantifiable. Any outage or disruption reveals opportunities for improvement in operations.

Reputation Value

For many organizations, reputation value is critical. For example, Uber relies on passengers' trust that they will get to their destinations safely. Whenever a negative incident with a ride is reported, it impacts the organization's image, customer satisfaction, and future profits. Clearly, claims of sexual assaults committed by Uber drivers is a major concern that can impact the willingness of people to use Uber in the future. Uber has been in the unenviable position of being sued by passengers who got into cars and were assaulted by drivers. Some of those lawsuits deal with legitimate Uber drivers, but some even deal with impostors who are not even affiliated with Uber.

Whenever an organization's name is disparaged in some way, it can result in lost revenue, diminished customer base, damaged relationships with other organizations, or other costs. Cambridge Analytica purchased access to Facebook users' data. Cambridge Analytica's use of that data resulted in a sequence of events that generated negative media coverage, increased the potential regulation of the service, decreased usage by some individuals, and raised the potential for fines. While billions of dollars in fines is a clear monetary loss, the reality is that Facebook's brand suffered further punishment in the loss of trust, respect, and confidence of consumers, investors, regulators, governments, and other businesses.

There are many academic studies that indicate that there is a decrease in stock value after a data breach, for example. The effect is clear in the short to mid-term. While the impact likely dissipates over time, it does put an organization in a weaker position should there be compounding circumstances.

Clearly, brand reputation has distinct value to the organization. You need to be able to identify how user actions can potentially compromise the brand's value so that you can get the support you require to protect the brand.

Value to Potential Attackers

The road to business hell seems to frequently begin with, "Nobody would bother attacking me." We once heard this from the CEO of a credit union that had assets of "only" $20,000,000,000. His thought was that criminals would go after bigger banks. While this is clearly an extreme case, every organization has some people who believe they don't work with anything of value that people would target.

Many people don't realize that a seemingly inconsequential computer or website can be used as part of a botnet to serve malware to others. The location of the computer is irrelevant to the criminals. Excess equipment may seem outdated, but such units frequently contain hard drives that still contain sensitive information. Printers, for example, might have a copy of every document that they ever printed.

Clearly, successes are critical to protect. However, even failure can provide valuable data to potential attackers. In research and development environments, knowing the details of your failures can show your competitors where they should not waste time and effort in their own endeavors. In a sales environment, even rejected proposals can give a competitor an idea of your pricing structure and methodologies.

As you begin to create your business case, it pays to consider how your threats look at the value of your organization. It helps to understand what is actually at risk. It might also help you more completely determine what is truly valuable to your organization. Every so often, it pays to refresh your perspective regarding what you have to protect.

Threats

A *threat* is a person or entity that will do you harm if provided with the opportunity. While the common assumption is that threats are malicious people or groups, they are just one type of threat. There is a wide variety of threats that any given organization has to address.

As opposed to listing all possible threats, we focus on categorizing them. Threats can be malicious or malignant. A malicious threat is one that intends to do you harm. A malignant threat is one that causes harm by its mere existence.

Malignant threats can further be broken down into "who" threats and "what" threats. There are many examples of malignant "who" threats. Users accidentally delete or enter the wrong data. Administrators make mistakes. Travelers lose their laptops or USB drives. Workers are careless on factory lines. There is no malicious intent on the part of any of these people, but ultimately these users are still malignant threats.

Besides the "who" malignant threats, there are also "what" malignant threats. Computers crash. Machinery breaks. Power outages occur. Natural disasters, such as hurricanes, earthquakes, floods, and tsunamis, cause incredible damage. Consider the deaths and damage caused by Hurricane Katrina, for example. A large hurricane causes tens of billions of dollars of damage. That does not include its impact to businesses within the area that lose revenue and suffer other losses. And of course, how users react to such "what" threats is also a "who" factor, which has the potential to compound the malignant threat.

Beyond malignant threats, we also need to consider malicious threats. There are two types of malicious threats: outsider threats and insider threats.

Outsider malicious threats are generally people with criminal intent. These people target your users with the intent to exploit them. Either they intend to get your users to commit actions on their behalf or they essentially assume the identity and access of your users. For example, an outsider might attempt to trick employees into sending them sensitive information. Alternatively, outsiders might steal credentials through phishing attacks and then use those credentials, appearing to be your own user, to steal information.

We can further breakdown malicious outsider threats by the scope of their ability and resources. Nation-states have nearly unlimited resources and ability. When North Korea targeted Sony, they poured an incredible amount of resources into finding a way into Sony's corporate network. They eventually compromised administrator credentials and, once in, had a large enough team to quickly scour the Sony network to both steal information and create massive damage.

On the lower end of malicious outsider threats, you have opportunists who take what is easily available. From an IT perspective, low-skilled hackers target people randomly with tools available on the Internet. If they are successful in gaining a foothold, they take whatever they find available.

Beyond the malicious outsider threats, we have malicious insider threats. These can be employees within an organization, users, business partners, customers, or any other type of user who deals with your organization. Some of these users steal equipment, software, or materials for personal use. Other malicious insiders sabotage the organizations' products, services, or reputation. Others actively try to undermine the morale or productivity of other users.

People often focus on malicious outsiders when they think of threats. But from the perspective of reducing UIL, one of the primary threats is the user. That might sound counterintuitive, but consider the following points. The DBIR reports that 28% of incidents are the result of malicious insiders. Add to that the number of malicious outsider threats that are attempting to exploit the user in some way, and the user as a malignant "who" threat that unwittingly (or uncaringly) enables those attackers. Then add to that the number of other ways that users function as a malignant "who" threat and accidentally or unknowingly initiate loss. Obviously, it is important to address malicious outsider threats. However, it is equally important to address users, as they have the potential, intentional or otherwise, to be involved in your organization experiencing vast amounts of loss.

Vulnerabilities

Without a vulnerability to exploit, threats would be irrelevant. The reality, though, is that vulnerabilities are plentiful in just about any business environment. If you do any business at all, there will be vulnerabilities.

When we give presentations, we sometimes ask the audience, "Can anyone describe how to achieve perfect computer security?" The most common answer is, "Unplug the computer." Our response is,

"Congratulations! You just committed a denial-of-service attack against your own computer."

There can never be a complete absence of vulnerability. You need to provide users with the ability to perform their job functions, and that will inevitably create vulnerabilities. Increasing the depth and breadth of functions provides an ability to provide more value, but doing so also provides the opportunity to create more loss. It all boils down to finding the right balance.

Different categories of vulnerabilities are more prominent than others in various organizations, and it is important to be aware of each of them and consider their relevance to your users. The following sections address some basic types of vulnerabilities to consider as you look to mitigate UIL. These include physical, operational, personnel, and technical vulnerabilities.

Physical Vulnerabilities

Physical vulnerabilities are tangible in some way. Such vulnerabilities allow for access to an organization or its resources.

Most organizations have buildings, and many have outside properties where materials are stored. These facilities generally have perimeters that are protected by walls and fences. While people assume perimeters keep outsiders out, the reality is that the perimeters usually possess many vulnerabilities.

Such vulnerabilities may include doors and gates that are not closed and locked, unmonitored entrances, materials left on the property but outside of the protective perimeter, information visually exposed due to open windows, materials exposed to the weather, poor monitoring of visitors, and so on. All of these physical vulnerabilities present opportunities for your resources to be damaged by the environment or by outsiders.

Sometimes organizations take their physical perimeter for granted, and they unknowingly circumvent it. One example of this is leaving materials on the property but actually outside of the protective perimeter. Another example is having users work remotely. If users can access the facility without having to cross the physical perimeter, that is effectively a physical vulnerability.

Often, organizations put some level of faith into perimeter security and then leave resources vulnerable inside their facilities. In reality, internal physical vulnerabilities are as important as external vulnerabilities.

If a malicious outsider makes it past your perimeter security, they can pass as an insider. And it is a rare organization that has absolutely no malicious insiders.

What vulnerabilities might a malicious threat see inside your perimeter? Things that come to mind include equipment to steal, computers left logged in and unattended, papers left on printers in public areas, unattended desks, file cabinets unlocked, sensitive information left on whiteboards, telecommunication equipment rooms left unlocked, USB drives untracked, and countless other things. You don't have to be a world-renowned penetration tester to see how your organization leaves resources vulnerable to anyone with malicious intent.

At the same time, you also need to recognize what leaves you vulnerable to accidental compromises or damages. For example, do people leave coffee cups on printers? Is fragile equipment transported in an unsafe manner? Is information stored on USB drives that are easy to lose? Accidental damage to resources sometimes creates greater loss than malicious actions.

Vulnerabilities are not just relevant to equipment, materials, and data. You must also be concerned about physical vulnerabilities of your environment that put people at risk. Unattended doors allow for intrusions where outsiders can enter and do harm to your people. Obstacles and sharp edges can cause injuries. Moving vehicles can hit people. While there are some freak injuries, with an open mind, you can identify a great deal of vulnerabilities that can result in injury. These factors relate to safety science, which we discuss in Chapter 7.

Operational Vulnerabilities

Operational vulnerabilities are vulnerabilities in business processes that can cause loss. Within every business operation, there are some steps that allow for human error or facilitate malicious activity. For example, the collection of information itself is a potential vulnerability, but collecting excessive information is an additional, unnecessary vulnerability.

There will always be a vulnerability in any business process. You need to identify the vulnerabilities to potentially proactively account and prepare for their potential exploitation. You also need to watch for operational vulnerabilities that do not need to exist.

Websites are an example of this. You need to provide information. However, that information does not have to be excessive. Social media is an extension of this concept. Individuals want to share their lives, yet at the same time, they share so much that they expose themselves unnecessarily to criminal activity. For example, online banking account reset security questions include questions such as the name of your pet or your birthday, which are frequently available on social media.

Physical inventory is also affected by operational processes. When you are dealing with physical inventory, sometimes there are good accounting practices to ensure that every piece is properly tracked from the manufacturing to final sale to a customer and all steps in between. More often, there are less effective processes in place, and loss occurs over time.

Operational processes should be defined by organizational governance through policies, procedures, and guidelines. Governance should specify every process in your organization and should tell people how to specifically perform their job responsibilities and how to make decisions. Chapter 13 discusses governance further, but at this point it suffices to say that most governance is poorly defined and increases operational vulnerabilities.

Personnel Vulnerabilities

Personnel vulnerabilities are vulnerabilities in the hiring, management, and termination of personnel involved with the organization. Obviously, you want to hire law abiding and ethical employees. However, hiring processes frequently are flawed. Poor background checks can let people slip through the cracks. Even when there are processes in place, they are sometimes ignored.

Such was the case with Edward Snowden. Snowden resigned from the CIA in anticipation of being fired due to a variety of troubles. However, he was able to obtain a job as an NSA contractor, because USIS, the company responsible for performing his background check, did not interview Snowden's CIA co-workers, who would have disclosed his questionable activities.

Personnel vulnerabilities extend beyond hiring and into the day-to-day management of employees. Some organizations fail to review employees on a regular basis and fail to take action when warranted. Chelsea Manning reportedly had violent confrontations with her parents before enlisting in the U.S. Army, which included threatening her stepmother with a knife. Before Manning stole classified information, she was involved in several incidents, including assaulting a supervisor and sending an email to superiors that literally stated she was emotionally troubled. There should have been adequate enforcement of policies in place so that these incidents would have resulted in rescinding access to classified information long before she stole it.

Most environments do not typically see behaviors and circumstances as egregious as those of Manning and Snowden. However, there is a great deal of mismanagement of employees who give signs of concern. While you do not want to overreact to less than ideal circumstances and behaviors, you do not want to let them go unexamined. It is important to have policies and procedures in place to govern personnel vulnerabilities, and these should be driven by the balance of your risk equation.

Similarly, there needs to be a process when people leave an organization, regardless of whether they are fired or leave voluntarily. When people depart, they frequently take information with them. They can cause other damages. There need to be specific processes implemented for employee separation.

You also need to have criteria for anyone else with access to your organization. Contractors, vendors, temporary employees, and any other individual who has any involvement with sensitive processes or data, or might be able to create loss, represents the same potential vulnerability as your employees.

Much as with operational vulnerabilities, poor governance and its implementation are significant vulnerabilities with regard to the management of personnel.

Technical Vulnerabilities

Technical vulnerabilities can be software, hardware, or firmware based. They can also be vulnerabilities in equipment that cause injuries. Generally, with technical vulnerabilities, people assume they can bypass the users. However, we need to expand the discussion of technical vulnerabilities to include how technology is configured or maintained.

For example, poor passwords can be considered a technical vulnerability as they can be technically exploited by someone who guesses the passwords. This results in an external malicious attack directly against the computer, as the result of a technical vulnerability that was enabled by a user, who in turn was enabled to do so by their IT department, which happened to be governed by the existing policies of the organization. So, as you can see, the technical vulnerability is not just something that is inherent in the software or hardware independent of any user interaction. Users are involved at many levels.

As we are primarily interested in UIL, it is also important to recognize that technical vulnerabilities include the user interface design. While this can refer to computer interfaces, it can also refer to any interface on any piece of equipment. Such technology can cause users to initiate a loss. Interfaces can be confusing and almost force errors. For example, the DBIR highlights that a significant percentage of data breaches are caused by the email address autocomplete function filling in the wrong email address, after which sensitive data ends up being sent to the wrong person.

Generally, you can consider a technical vulnerability as anything in the organization's environment that can be exploited or can cause an error or damage. This is an important distinction to embrace as too many people are intimidated by the underlying technology (such as esoteric programming languages), but it is the surface technology (such as user interfaces) that they regularly interact with that can be the most damaging.

THE TWO WAYS TO HACK A COMPUTER

People are in awe of computer hackers, believing that they are some form of modern-day magicians who can manipulate computers at will. The reality is that these hackers in general know a few extra tricks that the average person does not. Fundamentally, there are two ways to hack a computer: take advantage of problems built into the software (or hardware) or take advantage of the way that users or administrators set up and maintain the computer.

Regarding problems built into a computer, everyone can accept that all programs have bugs. Some bugs cause the computer to crash. Other bugs create bad output. Some bugs cause elevated privileges or information leakage. These are all examples of security vulnerabilities.

Regarding how users and administrators set up and maintain a computer, consider how bad passwords can be guessed by another party. Administrators can configure computers to provide users with unnecessary privileges. They can leave the computer open to people from outside of the organization. They can fail to enact encryption on files. There are countless ways that such user actions can make a device vulnerable.

Again, all technology fails either by its design or through its use. Other than researching the track record of known vulnerabilities in software and hardware before you acquire it and knowing what patches can be applied to existing problems, there is little that you can do to affect technology design. That makes it all the more important to do what you can to help protect your users from hackers.

Countermeasures

When you look at the risk equation in Figure 4.1, you can see that countermeasures can be used to mitigate threats and vulnerabilities. However, you must consider that mitigating threats is frequently not possible or realistic. For example, you are not going to prevent hurricanes. Hurricanes will always exist. You are not going to prevent a nation-state from existing, unless you are likewise a nation-state and willing to invest significant resources. The average organization is not going to prevent outside criminals from making attacks. Even if you work with law enforcement, your abilities to stop a threat from existing are negligible.

You should plan to implement countermeasures to mitigate what is within your control. So while you might not be able to prevent a hurricane, you can choose to locate resources outside of hurricane zones. You can create backup systems and files. You can have backup power sources in case of power outages.

Also consider that when you mitigate a vulnerability, you mitigate the opportunity for a threat to exploit that vulnerability. For example, if a user has a bad password, the password can be exploited by any threat, from nation-states to nosy co-workers. However, if you implement multifactor authentication, it helps prevent nation-states and other attackers from exploiting the bad password.

For these reasons, you want to prioritize countermeasures that mitigate vulnerabilities that are most likely to be exploited and result in loss. This is a critical theme in Part III of this book.

Protection, Detection, and Reaction

It is also important to recognize that countermeasures not only apply to protection but apply to detection and reaction as well. When people think of countermeasures, they typically perceive them to provide protection, in other words, stopping a loss from occurring in the first place and keeping the bad guys out. The reality is that countermeasures can provide protection, detection, or reaction. There is no such thing as perfect protection. Because protection will inevitably fail, it is just as critical to invest in detection and reaction capabilities.

Different studies indicate that up to 80% of investment in countermeasures is in protection. This unfortunately results in massive success for perpetrators who are able to get through the initial protection measures. In many cases, it is sometimes more feasible to focus on detection of malicious activity and not put effort into prevention, as it is too costly. For example, if you are trying to secure a public network, any people with malicious intent are already allowed on the network. Likewise, even well-meaning users might violate policies. For that reason, it might be more effective to look for potentially harmful activities and, where appropriate, reduce the users' capabilities.

Accept, Avoid, Mitigate, Transfer

When you consider countermeasures, you must consider that the goal of countermeasures is not always to stop an attack. There is a widely accepted risk management paradigm known as accept, avoid, mitigate, and transfer.

Accepting risk implies that you acknowledge the risk exists but consciously choose not to take further action on the risk. This is appropriate, for example, when a risk involves an inconsequential loss or has a low probability of occurring.

Avoiding risk implies that as opposed to directly addressing the risk, you find a way to make it a moot issue. For example, a company might decide that it is not worth doing business within a specific region.

Mitigating risk means that you implement specific countermeasures to address a risk.

Transferring risk implies that you will not mitigate the risk directly, but you acknowledge it occurs and choose to transfer liability. This is the primary purpose of insurance, where you choose to be financially compensated, if a loss is realized, as opposed to proactively stopping the loss.

As you examine a potential risk, you need to consider how you want to manage that risk. There are many factors that are unique to your organization, and you must determine which method of addressing risk is best for your circumstances.

TIME'S ROLE IN COUNTERMEASURES

It is critical to understand the importance of time in a security program. When author Ira Winkler worked at the NSA, he learned that any encryption algorithm will inevitably by cracked. Given sufficient time and resources, an attacker can eventually crack an algorithm. However, you can endeavor to use encryption that is strong enough to prevent the code from being cracked for as long as the data is valuable.

For example, a commander in battle has to give tactical commands to troops in the field. Knowledge of the individual commands becomes worthless at the end of the battle in most cases. In this case, very low-grade encryption can be used. However, if you consider a military communications satellite that may be in orbit for a decade, you need to employ encryption that will not likely be cracked for much more than a decade. You cannot just upgrade the encryption hardware. The encryption does not just have to be strong enough to withstand current attacks but to withstand anticipated improvements in technology and the changing attacks that will occur over that time period.

Similarly, when you consider a physical safe that contains valuables, the security can potentially be compromised. A safe is intended to be heavy so that it isn't easy to physically remove. The removal of the safe will take time, and the expectation is that by the time the safe can be removed, police or other responders will arrive to stop the theft. Likewise, if someone intends to crack the safe, the time it takes to crack the safe should be long enough for responders to arrive.

Types of Countermeasures

As with vulnerabilities, we address four basic types of countermeasures: physical, operational, personnel, and technical. It is important to note that you do not need to mitigate a vulnerability with a countermeasure of the same type. Also, you may choose to mitigate a vulnerability with countermeasures from multiple categories.

For example, the case of Edward Snowden demonstrates personnel vulnerabilities. Several types of countermeasures could have helped in this case. Better personnel countermeasures could have identified and addressed the problem. However, technical countermeasures, such as multifactor authentication and better network security controls, as well as operational controls, such as Snowden's co-workers having better awareness about not giving out their passwords to others, would have combined to stop Snowden's theft.

You should likewise look for diverse sets of countermeasures to mitigate vulnerabilities. Know that no single type of countermeasure is perfect. However, when combined effectively, they should ideally stop UIL from actually being realized. The following sections further examine physical, operational, personnel, and technical countermeasures.

Physical Countermeasures

Physical countermeasures are those that implement some tangible security control to prevent a loss through physical means. Some common physical countermeasures are access controls, such as gates, locks, filing cabinets, and so on. They include physically securing unattended materials or workstations when you are away from the area. They also include getting someone to take custody of valuable materials.

Guards and surveillance cameras are physical countermeasures. Surveillance is a form of detection, while guards provide a combination of protection, detection, and reaction, depending upon their assignment and deployment. It is also important to consider that known detection is also an indirect form of protection. For example, when criminals know that a house or office has an alarm system, which is a form of detection, they might choose to avoid the facility and choose a different target.

When considering physical countermeasures for UIL, keep in mind that countermeasures may be put in place to prevent error. For example, covers on power switches prevent accidental pressing of the off buttons. Guards inspecting outgoing materials can detect when users accidentally take things out of the facility. It may also prevent a malicious act. Again, it is key to understand that physical countermeasures can simultaneously mitigate malicious and malignant threats.

Operational Countermeasures

Operational countermeasures are procedures designed to perform work properly and mitigate loss. For example, procedures on how to safely handle sensitive materials or perform work safely are operational countermeasures. Likewise, audit procedures to detect and mitigate loss and deviations from expectations are operational countermeasures.

Ideally, operational countermeasures that deal with security are embedded in business processes so that security concerns are integral to the organization. Security awareness programs are operational countermeasures, especially when they inform people on how to perform their functions properly. There are also practices that can be put in place to authenticate and verify the identity of individuals and their need to have access to information, facilities, or other resources. This extends to website interactions and requesting critical services to include reset of passwords and access to sensitive information.

Operational countermeasures also include legal agreements and enforcement. For example, nondisclosure agreements are a common form of protection that should be used whenever exchanging sensitive information with potential business partners.

Insurance is also a critical operational countermeasure. It is inevitable that there will be a loss, and insurance provides for a way to potentially mitigate losses.

Personnel Countermeasures

Personnel countermeasures are those that deal with the hiring, managing, and firing of people. We say specifically say "people" and not "employees" because this applies to everyone, including customers, business partners, and any and all users. Anyone with access to your facilities and information needs to be considered a potential threat and should be subject to these countermeasures.

Applying requirements to people who are giving you money and you technically serve is a sensitive matter, but you have to at least limit their access to only the functions required. You may also need to audit those customers and potentially pursue penalties against them. Such is the case where Cambridge Analytica violated Facebook's policies to use Facebook users' information by misrepresenting to users the scope and use of the information collected.

When you hire or otherwise bring someone into your organization, countermeasures include background checks and a consistent process to have people sign the appropriate agreements and to make them aware of their responsibilities. Regarding background checks, this should ideally include criminal and financial checks, as well as confirmation of stated employment and educational histories. When possible, this would also include talking to past employers to ensure there were no concerns. This again is where Snowden's background check failed.

Countermeasures for personnel can vary depending on the nature of your organization. In high security environments, this may include periodic updates of background and criminal records checks. There should be tracking of incidents to ensure that there are not patterns of concerning behaviors. There should also be periodic training and reinforcement of employee responsibilities. In major financial organizations, it is common practice to force employees to take a two-week vacation. During that vacation, there are teams in place to go through all business functions, financial transactions, records, and so on, to ensure there are no concerning behavior or actions.

During separation, there should be established processes for people's departure. This should include review of information access, equipment in their possession, and any other concerns. When possible, there should be a review of activities to see whether the person in question took any information with them. There should also be a reinforcement of any obligations to include protection of sensitive information.

It is critical to involve the IT department to ensure that the individual's access is proactively limited, as feasible, and that their accounts are deactivated as soon as possible. We have investigated incidents where a salesperson still had access to his former company's proposal system. The salesperson would download proposals from his former company and then create a proposal from his new company that was more competitive. This is unfortunately not an uncommon circumstance.

Enforcement also must be consistent. You can't punish one employee for mishandling information and not punish another employee for the same infraction. Inconsistent enforcement exposes your organization to claims of bias, confuses your users about which policies they're truly expected to follow, and emboldens people who are inclined to commit violations.

Technical Countermeasures

Technical countermeasures are technological in nature. Technical countermeasures have a broad scope that extends beyond computers and information. For example, to stop car thefts, which are physical in nature, there is technology that can deactivate the engine remotely. Given the Internet of Things (IoT), almost any piece of equipment, no matter how basic, can now implement technical countermeasures.

Technical countermeasures mitigate some form of UIL by providing protection, detection, and/or reaction capability. Protection involves the user not having the ability to initiate loss, either because an attack is filtered or because the user does not have the ability to initiate the loss in the first place.

Detection can involve two aspects of the UIL problem. Technology can detect that malicious parties are attempting to interact with users or that a user has done something that can initiate a loss. So, for example, you can detect phishing messages are being sent to users. Another example is that you may detect that a user is attempting to go to a malicious website.

Obviously, the circumstances of reaction are similar. If you detect attacks targeting users, there are a variety of technologies that can react to and mitigate the attacks before they get to the users. Also, if you detect a user action that might initiate loss, you can then mitigate that action in progress. Following up with examples described in the previous paragraph, detected phishing messages can be deleted before reaching the user. The messages can also be analyzed, and any websites or Internet systems involved can be proactively blocked and reported. If you detect a user going to a malicious website, you can lock the user's account, block the website, or investigate the user to see whether the action is malicious or perhaps is being made by a person who has compromised the user's account.

Technical countermeasures can be the failsafe for a security and risk mitigation program. Users will fail. Procedures will fail. However, if you have the right technology in place, you can detect and react to the other failures. Obviously, technological countermeasures can also fail. However, if you implement the methodology in Part IV properly, technical countermeasures can be your first and last line of defense.

Risk Optimization

When people think of risk, there is frequently an unstated assumption that risk should be minimized. This assumption is wrong. Risk is about balancing loss with the cost to mitigate the loss. This balance should be optimized, not minimized.

Minimizing loss implies that you do absolutely everything possible to stop a loss. That is far from practical. Consider what you might do to minimize your chance of being robbed or accidentally injured on the street. You can buy an armored car that is heavily weighted and has a reinforced metal frame. You can hire a driver so that you can stay in the back in a padded area. You can travel surrounded by armed body-guards and escort vehicles.

Taking these measures would minimize a great deal of risk, but they would not guarantee your safety and would likely cost more than you stand to lose from an injury or robbery. In fact, for the average person they would be prohibitively expensive. On the other hand, if you were carrying a great deal of money in a high-risk area, some of these pre-cautions might be more practical. The important point is that the cost of your countermeasures is balanced with your potential loss.

NOTE   Risk optimization is clearly a complicated concept that we cannot do justice to within a reasonable length. For those people who want to look further into this topic and want to be more effective in a risk mitigation position, we recommend the work of Lawrence Gor-don and Martin Loeb. Their book, *Managing Cybersecurity Resources: A Cost-Benefit Analysis* (McGraw-Hill Education, 2005), is a helpful work on the subject.

Figure 4.2 depicts the relationship of the cost of countermeasures compared to potential loss. The vertical axis represents cost. The curve that begins on the top left represents the potential loss associated with your vulnerabilities. The curve that begins at the bottom left repre-sents the cost of your countermeasures. Figure 4.2 assumes that you are implementing the countermeasures that are appropriate to your organization's needs.

As you can see, when countermeasures are 0, your potential loss is at its maximum. As you begin to implement countermeasures, your vulnerabilities begin to be mitigated and your potential loss decreases.

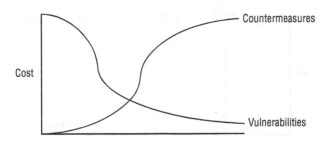

Figure 4.2 Cost of countermeasures compared to vulnerabilities

Your potential loss should decrease rapidly, as there is usually a strong payback with the initial and practical countermeasures.

At some point, however, the cost of your countermeasures exceeds your potential loss. This is when you know that you are spending too much on countermeasures. The users running your security program can actually drain finances disproportionately to benefits, which effectively creates another form of loss.

Keep in mind that there can also be intangible forms of loss other than monetary, such as loss of life, reputational costs, and so on, and these might justify spending more than would otherwise be justified. Even then, you want to try to place a potential monetary value on such intangible loss and not put excessive investment into countermeasures.

Generally, you want the cost of your countermeasures to be significantly less than the potential loss. If you invest in countermeasures to the point where they exceed the potential loss, you are also likely wasting a great deal of money. In Figure 4.2, the area under the vulnerabilities line represents potential loss, not actual loss. It is rare that all potential loss becomes fully realized into actual loss.

For these reasons, you want to determine a good point where you have mitigated most of the potential loss and a minimal amount of potential loss might be acceptable. You will never be completely free from risk or loss, but you can consciously prepare for optimizing the loss. Figure 4.3 represents this concept by introducing the risk optimization point to the vulnerabilities/countermeasures balance.

As you can see in Figure 4.3, the risk optimization point is located where vulnerabilities have greatly decreased while the relative costs of their countermeasures have only modestly increased. The implication is that a reasonable investment in your security program's countermeasures dramatically mitigates potential loss. Clearly, the location of

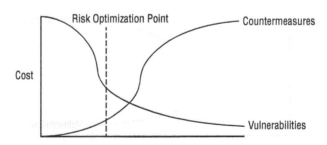

Figure 4.3 The risk optimization point

the risk-optimization point relative to the vulnerabilities/countermeasures balance will vary depending on your organization's specific needs. You want to determine the level of potential loss that you are willing to accept and then determine the costs of the countermeasures that will reduce your potential loss to that level.

That might sound obvious, but that is not the way security programs are typically budgeted. Security programs generally get some percentage of the IT budget and then have to determine how to spend that money. Obviously, this number is frequently inadequate, which results in major losses.

Understanding that last sentence is essential. There is typically no relationship between the potential loss a security program is trying to prevent and the budget the organization is willing to allocate. That is a critical issue that will lead to the failure of the security program.

Consider the example of how the city of Baltimore was the victim of a ransomware attack in 2019, due to malware based on EternalBlue. EternalBlue had been identified as one of the tools exploited by the Shadow Brokers breach of the NSA. EternalBlue was patched in 2017, and should not have been an issue for anyone in 2019. After the successful attack on Baltimore, it and other cities around the United States improved their security budgets to address such attacks. However, the patch was widely known and had already been around for two years. Their budgets should have already accounted for patching, but they apparently had not previously invested sufficient funds to provide for a basic countermeasure.

When you understand your organization's vulnerabilities/countermeasures balance and its risk-optimization point, you develop greater insight into how you might better mitigate UIL.

Risk and User-Initiated Loss

When you consider how UIL impacts risk, you realize that organizations generally do not fund UIL mitigation efforts well in many industries. Generally, it is a combination of failing to appreciate the holistic nature of countering the problem, a resignation to the fact that users can never be perfect, and not allocating the proper resources. The failure to allocate resources includes funding, staff, and expertise.

In the accounting and safety fields, for example, there is a clear understanding of risk. They understand that user actions can result in serious financial losses, and they treat the problems holistically and with the appropriate resources. They determine where loss occurs, and they track the financial metrics to determine the success of the program.

In other fields such as cybersecurity, there is rarely effective tracking of losses and a holistic approach in applying countermeasures to them. While the problems are bemoaned, there is not a clear understanding of the value lost due to UIL.

To address UIL, you must be able to demonstrate in clear financial terms the value at risk. Chapter 10 covers metrics, which should help you make the argument about the value that users put at risk. However, that will still not do any significant good, if you do not look beyond the awareness as the primary countermeasure to the problem. Chapter 5 will look at the limitations of awareness, and going forward, the book will examine the more holistic approach to all aspects of addressing UIL.

NOTE Risk management, as a whole, is complicated and rarely performed effectively. While we hope that we provide a working knowledge to apply the concepts in the book, risk management is a core component of all loss mitigation efforts. We recommend you also look to other resources, such as *The Failure of Risk Management: Why It's Broken and How to Fix It* (Wiley, 2009), for further information.

5

The Problems with Awareness Efforts

A s we highlight throughout the previous chapters, organizations frequently believe that as users initiate a loss, the solution is to educate users better through awareness efforts. The logic is that if users know the right actions to take, they will not make mistakes and, therefore not initiate loss. This only speciously addresses the issue.

The unfortunate fact is that most awareness efforts have serious and fundamental shortcomings that can undermine their possible returns. Many organizations know of these shortcomings and unfortunately, consider awareness programs to be a waste of effort. This creates a self-fulfilling prophecy given that the organizations have low expectations for awareness programs' return on investment and, therefore allocate resources accordingly.

Awareness Programs Can Be Extremely Valuable

People often have the impression that awareness efforts are a waste of resources. Nothing could be further from the truth. Along with governance and technology, awareness is one of the three pillars of mitigating user-initiated loss (UIL), and it can have a critical return on investment. We need to dispel the misperceptions that arise about awareness programs and UIL, both as a whole and involving their usage and implementation.

Beyond misperceptions, we also need to address the actual shortfalls of awareness programs. Most of those shortfalls relate to poor implementation of awareness efforts. A large portion of the shortfalls involve the fact that awareness, by itself, is not a complete solution to UIL. As with all loss countermeasures, there is no such thing as perfection. There will be failures in even the best awareness programs.

At the same time, awareness is relevant only at the point where a user can make a decision to act (or fail to act) in the prescribed way. So even in the best situations, awareness must be proceeded by processes and technologies that focus on preventing users from being in the position where they can initiate loss, and followed by technology and processes to mitigate loss after it has been initiated.

Chapter 15 discusses how to create a successful awareness program, which is an essential aspect to our methodology. The remainder of this chapter identifies concerns in both the perception and implementation of awareness programs.

Check-the-Box Mentality

One of the biggest problems with awareness efforts is a check-the-box mentality. Frequently, organizations only have awareness programs because they are required by various compliance standards. Generally, the standards imply that there has to be some form of awareness training. They feel that the practical implication is that they therefore only need to do what is minimally required to achieve compliance, basically checking this box off their list of duties to perform.

This check-the-box mentality is pervasive across many organizations and departments, and it even extends to cybersecurity awareness. Consider the ramifications of approaching cyberspace security this way, especially given the scope of the problem. You are going to have poor results from such awareness efforts, and the scope and range of the resulting UIL can be extreme.

A range of prominent standards attempt to address cybersecurity requirements, some more directly than others. For example, the Health Insurance Portability and Accountability Act (HIPAA) identifies the need for security, and the U.S. Department of Health and Human Services (HHS) offers some guidance on HIPAA-specific security awareness programs (www.hhs.gov/about/agencies/asa/ocio/cybersecurity/security-awareness-training/index.html). PCI DSS does the same for credit card transactions (www.pcisecuritystandards.org/documents/PCI_DSS_V1.0_Best_Practices_for_Implementing_Security_Awareness_Program.pdf). NIST SP 800-50, *Building an Information Technology Security Awareness and Training Program*, goes into some depth on security awareness programs from a government perspective, which could be construed as applicable to HIPAA as well (csrc.nist.gov/publications/detail/sp/800–50/final). Even so, many such sources discuss the form and content fairly broadly in an attempt to make them applicable to many organizations. Situation-specific implementation is often a matter of interpretation, and organizations are often inclined to meet these responsibilities as expediently as possible in terms of time, money, and resources. Consequently, this feeds into organizations sliding into the check-the-box mentality.

Organizations generally purchase off-the-shelf content from a vendor with the hope that it will require little time and effort on the users' part. Vendors try to convince customers that their content is funny or otherwise memorable and thus will effectively remain in the users' minds and improve awareness. However, the reality is that the content will soon be forgotten without constant reinforcement or hands-on implementation. This relates to a concept known as the *forgetting curve*, which describes how quickly people forget information over time that is not reinforced or otherwise put into practice.

The forgetting curve is a theory developed by German psychologist Hermann Ebbinghaus. It compares the strength of memory to the amount of time, often measured in days that it takes for a person to forget something they have newly learned. Most people forget more than half of their newly acquired information within a few days.

In short, if people don't use information that they've learned, they will quickly forget it. If you consider the half-life of information at a few days, you can generally assume that within one month, little, if any, information will be remembered. So, when you consider a typical awareness approach of showing a three-minute video, once a month, on varying subjects, it is unlikely that at the end of the year people will remember the intended principles. This is especially true given how few principles can be presented within a three-minute video.

Combatting the forgetting curve requires having students apply the information regularly. While some vendors and practitioners tout funny and entertaining videos as a way of making their materials more memorable, at best they slow the forgetting curve by a few days. People need to apply the information to retain the information.

There are some organizations that believe that they should have an awareness program, because it is a good practice regardless of compliance standards. However, if they only implement annual computer-based training (CBT), short monthly training sessions, or other basic aware-ness programs without any form of reinforcement, it is still, essentially, a check-the-box program.

For many organizations, the check-the-box mentality is a self-fulfilling prophecy as they will always result in minimal, if any, long-term improvements in behavior. Such awareness programs are, therefore wasting organizational resources, but that is primarily due to the approach of the organization, which has limited the potential effectiveness of the awareness program.

Training vs. Awareness

The way people think of the terms *training* and *awareness* is a major cause of perceived failures of such programs. Many people use the terms interchangeably, while others make a major distinction between them.

The National Institute of Standards and Technology (NIST) Special Pub-lication 800-50, *Building an Information Technology Security Awareness and Training Program*, defines training as providing people with a fixed body of knowledge and skills. This means it is a specific competency. In other words, you know how to do something. NIST 800-50 specifically states that awareness is not training. The purpose of awareness is for a person to recognize potential security concerns and act accordingly. In other words, while training may teach you how to create a good password, awareness is demonstrated by people implementing that training.

Although NIST 800-50 is intended for IT-related issues, the defini-tions are appropriate for any environment where user actions have to be both defined and encouraged. However, it is important to know that not everyone will use the terms *awareness* and *training* this way. The most important thing is to recognize the very profound distinction between a program that simply provides a description of how to do something, as opposed to a program that is designed to have an impact on improving actual behaviors.

The Compliance Budget

The compliance budget is a critical concept that not enough people seem to understand and employ. The compliance budget is not a financial budget, but the concept that users essentially budget their security efforts against competing resources; most frequently, time.

For example, security professionals realize the critical importance of performing backups of critical files, and they fully intend to run them. However, they are also busy professionals, and those backups take time and effort. Despite knowing the potential harm of postponing backups, security professionals frequently delay performing them, because they are immersed in myriad other responsibilities.

Similarly, consider how the average user inside an organization has a variety of responsibilities. They need to perform their basic job functions, respond to emails, attend meetings, meet deadlines, manage various reports, and interact with colleagues and clients. They likely also have a variety of stretch goals for their performance. Now, add training that is intended to reduce UIL to their responsibilities.

Although the typical user does not want to initiate loss, there is a limit to what they will voluntarily do to prevent UIL, if it is not a requirement and embedded with other functions. For example, many organizations have "clean desk" policies, which require users to not leave sensitive materials exposed in their work areas and to ensure that all sensitive materials are locked in storage before they leave for the day. However, it is common for users to rush out at the end of the workday. Unless there is some form of enforcement, the users, as a whole, have likely expended their compliance budget and will not adhere to the clean desk policy when they leave at the end of the day.

In dealing with their compliance budget, a user considers every potential action as having costs and benefits, both to themselves and to the organization. If users understand that good practices can reduce losses to the organization, they are more inclined to follow those practices, at least in proportion to how much they appreciate their organization. If they believe there is a cost to the organization, such as a security requirement slowing down organizational processes, they are less likely to follow guidance. Likewise, if the user believes there is a benefit to them to follow through on a requested action, they are more inclined to do it. Similarly, if they believe it is personally burdensome, they are less likely to do it.

Obviously, you need to include motivation in any outreach and awareness efforts. This can include the benefits to both the user and the organization. It is important to note that these need to be clear benefits. Although humor and education have their uses in some circumstances, they are not a substitute for true motivation. Motivation specifically involves a clear message that taking the desired action is beneficial.

At the same time, if there is a penalty (or "sanction" as it is referred to when discussing compliance budgets) for not adhering to a policy and the sanction is enforced, the user will likely put effort into adhering to the policy. For example, many organizations have very stringent travel reimbursement policies. The paperwork can be extremely onerous and time-consuming, and the sanction would be for the employee not to be financially reimbursed. Despite the burden this entails, employees collect every receipt and follow the procedures carefully so that they are properly reimbursed for the money they are owed.

Similarly, filling out timecards in some organizations can be a major burden, where employees have to account for every block of time. Despite the burden, they will do it, as the sanction would be that they are not paid.

Beyond such examples, you need to understand that although users may be very well-intentioned, there is a limit to what you can expect them to do on a daily basis. Not only is there a limit, complicating the issue is that the compliance budget may vary from day to day. For example, if an employee has a tight work deadline, they are less likely to put efforts into mitigating loss. However, if it is a slow workday, they would likely put more effort into loss mitigation.

The compliance budget is one of the reasons why you cannot entrust too much faith in the proverbial "human firewall." The human firewall varies from day to day, depending upon different circumstances that are completely outside of your control. At a high level, you have to understand that if your users have already expended their discretionary compliance budget, you cannot expect them to focus on your awareness efforts.

While the compliance budget applies aptly for our purposes, should you run into organizational roadblocks promoting this concept, you can also research and reference Dr. Eliyahu Goldratt's Theory of Constraints (ToC). Thousands of corporations around the world implement the ToC. ToC is also taught at hundreds of colleges.

Shoulds vs. Musts

When you look at awareness efforts, many of those efforts appear to convey awareness guidance as a "should." You should take great care in handling sensitive information. You should not share your password. You should follow safety precautions. You should treat the company information safely. You should have a nondisclosure agreement signed, before sharing information with outside parties. And the list goes on.

When you portray loss reduction countermeasures as a "should," you cannot expect people to adhere to what amounts to a recommendation. Consider the compliance budget. If you portray loss reduction countermeasures as something people should do simply because it is the right thing to do, the users will balance the loss mitigation among other priorities. However, when that same loss mitigation is portrayed as a "must" that is part of a person's job requirement, it gets done or there will be penalties. The compliance budget is changed when a potential action is actually required as part of the user's job.

Unfortunately, awareness materials are all too often portrayed as a "should." When we talk with users who are presented with awareness materials that way, we generally find that they take the tone of the awareness materials and believe they might implement the guidance after all other responsibilities are fulfilled. And it is a rare moment when any team member feels that they have fulfilled all of their duties and have free time on their hands.

We also find that in many cases, there is a trend to provide humorous content, which can likewise work against an awareness program. Humor can get someone's attention and engage them; it is true. However, when something is treated as comical, users frequently believe it is not a serious matter to the organization. For example, nobody trivializes sexual harassment in the workplace or portrays it in a comical manner. Nobody treats improper financial handling and accounting procedures as comical. By comparison, when computer security awareness is treated in a comical way, it implies that it may not be important to the organization or should not be taken as seriously as other concerns.

While there can never be a guarantee that a "must" will always be implemented by everyone as defined, "musts" are significantly more likely to be implemented than "shoulds." Unfortunately, though, many awareness efforts targeting UIL are portrayed as "shoulds."

SOMMELIER VS. GRANDMA

In trying to get across a variety of points regarding the tone of awareness programs and how to address them, we developed the concept of "Sommelier vs. Grandma."

If you buy a cheap bottle of wine at a grocery store, it might cost $10. When you sip the wine, it will ideally taste reasonably acceptable and likely last on your palate for perhaps three seconds. If you instead go to an expensive restaurant and want a bottle of wine, the house sommelier will come to your table and ask you about your meal and your preferences. The sommelier will then recommend a bottle that might likely cost $200. The wine will ideally taste better than the grocery store wine. However, does the flavor last for 60 seconds on your palate, given that it is 20 times more expensive? No, it might last for perhaps 6–7 seconds on your palate. So investing more money in the fancy restaurant does not translate to an equivalent return on investment (at least as far as your palate is concerned).

In many ways, the sommelier scenario is similar to using entertaining videos for training and awareness. Some vendors tell people that their videos are better, because they are "funny" or have some other attribute. The reality is that funny (or whatever else) does not equate to being more effective for a period of time worth the extra cost. It might have a minor effect on the forgetting curve, but not an extremely significant one.

In contrast to the sommelier, we have Grandma. While everyone has their own version of Grandma, generally people know that when they visit Grandma's house, there is an expected set of behaviors. You know that you have to hug and kiss her. You know what chores are expected of everyone. You know where you are supposed to sit. If a child does not know the rules of Grandma's house, everyone will tell them. You don't need funny videos or posters to tell you where to sit or how to behave at Grandma's house.

In short, at Grandma's house, there is a known culture that is enforced by the people within that culture over time. There is a set of "musts." The culture is the awareness. There is constant application of the important concepts. Chapter 9 discusses culture further, but for now understand that using humor or spending money doesn't generally translate into increased effectiveness. Establishing a loss prevention culture tends to be far more effective.

When It's Okay to Blame the User

Author Ira Winkler was on a keynote CISO panel, discussing security culture at an event in Europe. During the panel, Ira stated that users should potentially be punished for harmful actions. One of the other panelists interrupted Ira and said, "You can't blame the user!" Ira asked, "Why not?" The reply was, "Well, you can't." Of course, the conversation continued.

Unfortunately, there is what amounts to a widespread mantra of "You can't blame the user." However, if a user has the proper resources and knows what the expectations are and does not follow them, it is definitely okay to blame that user. If you don't enforce your policies, then for all practical purposes, you don't actually have real policies. So the first step is to provide the users with the proper resources to perform their functions effectively and then ensure users be properly trained and aware of the loss mitigation expectations. Then, it is also critical to adjust the compliance budget in favor of having users take the desired actions. If users believe that there is no penalty for failing to follow the appropriate policies, procedures, or guidelines, they are less likely to follow them.

In many industries, the entire organization can also suffer penalties for incurring a loss. If your organization is in such an industry, you need to ensure that your users take the appropriate actions. For example, in the medical profession, if an office worker mishandles patient information, and it is exposed, the entire office can be fined. If the worker was knowingly callous about mishandling the information, of course they should suffer penalties.

Keep in mind that it is appropriate to blame the users only when you have clearly identified the expected user actions in a way that they can understand and retain. Additionally, you should not implement conflicting requirements. For example, if you tell users in a medical practice how to properly handle information, but fail to provide the resources to do so properly, you cannot reasonably blame the users.

In a "just culture," users are clear about the expectations of them and have all the required resources to fulfill those expectations. In short, if there is such a just culture, users should be blamed as appropriate, and loss prevention professionals should not abdicate the importance of corporate processes.

Similarly, if you fail to consistently enforce policies, you cannot blame the users. In these cases, if you punish one user for losing information and you do not punish another user for a similar infraction, you send mixed messages and also open up your organization to legal claims of bias.

Before implementing sanctions, you must also consider the severity of the infractions and the possibility of issuing warnings. Some organizations fire employees for failing phishing simulations on multiple occasions. Employees who constantly fail phishing simulations are relatively rare, and they do represent a significantly increased threat to the organization. As with other matters of training and discipline, before you fire such a person, you should give them sufficient education and warning.

Before you are too quick to blame the user, don't forget that behind every "stupid" user is frequently an even more "stupid" loss reduction professional. After all, the professional (with the support of the organization's management team) is often responsible for establishing, managing, and following up on awareness efforts and loss mitigation programs. You must consider how much culpability you have if your users are initiating loss.

Awareness Programs Do Not Always Translate into Practice

The compliance budget considers whether users will consciously choose to behave in the way they are expected to at any given point in time. This presumes that everyone has been adequately made aware of exactly what they should do, why they should do it, and what the consequences are.

The reality, though, is that the user is frequently not making a conscious and aware choice. In such instances, this is more likely due to the awareness program itself, as opposed to the compliance budget. Just because there is an awareness program in place does not mean the awareness program itself is satisfactory. To be effective, the awareness materials need to be properly planned, completed, and well prepared.

There are many aspects to consider when deciding whether an awareness program is functioning well. For example, the importance and repercussions of following (and not following) the guidance needs to be sufficiently and effectively conveyed. Also, many user personality types exist, and each personality type requires a different form of communication to receive the desired message. There might not be sufficient motivation within the awareness message to have users follow through with the desired behaviors. As we mentioned at the beginning of the chapter, if your organization's management has a check-the-box mentality, there generally isn't the necessary support and follow-through to ensure the success of the program.

These are just a few considerations. It is important to examine your awareness program from many angles to identify and rectify its potential flaws.

Structural Failings of Awareness Programs

Generally, awareness programs are fundamentally flawed. We find that we can quickly tell whether an awareness program will be a success. There are several things we look at, including whether the person running the program is sufficiently qualified, the use of metrics, managerial support, whether a check-the-box mentality exists, and the use of off-the-shelf products.

The person running an awareness program is likely a serious professional who is trying hard, but they might not truly know what actually would work best for their circumstances. These people take small steps, and rightfully so, to test the proverbial waters to see what works. While such a program will not waste too many resources, success will be hit or miss.

Frequently, the person has not received proper training, nor do they have experience running awareness programs. There is limited training for awareness professionals. Even if a person is experienced, that does not mean they were successful in their previous efforts or that they know how to approach their current situation for maximum effectiveness. So, if you can't rely on training and experience to determine how qualified a person is to run the awareness program, what can you rely on?

There are several things we do to judge how qualified a person is and how successful their efforts have been. We ask them to explain the metrics they used and demonstrate why and how these particular metrics mattered and succeeded. They should also be able to tell us about how they attained management support for their programs. Additionally, we should learn about all of the different modalities of awareness that were implemented, along with how messages were reinforced, again, supported by metrics.

We ask an awareness manager those questions to determine their qualifications, because those are also generally the elements of a successful awareness program. We discuss metrics further in Chapter 10. For now, understand that most programs do not collect the appropriate metrics and, therefore have no reliable basis for determining their success or failure.

If a qualified professional is not running the awareness program, there is a greatly diminished chance of success. Sometimes, upper management doesn't know what to expect of the person running the program. Other times, the person doesn't know how to achieve satisfactory results and how to get the support of management. However, a lack of management support can be a problem, even if the awareness program is being run by a qualified professional.

An awareness program without executive support is destined for failure. Even if an awareness professional is outstanding at what they do, their best efforts will fail without having the support. For example, they will not get the required resources to have a satisfactory program. They will not get access to critical people within the organization. They will not have the support of the chain of command to ensure that awareness materials are distributed appropriately. Also, there will not be the appropriate level of sanctions required to ensure that employees prioritize loss reduction related to behaviors in their compliance budget.

Unfortunately, the majority of organizations are also content to implement a simple check-the-box awareness program. Those programs frequently choose one topic per month to focus on. They then distribute CBT, a newsletter, and perhaps a poster on the given topic. There is no other reinforcement. The information is general in nature and usually attempts to cover a highly complex topic in less than three minutes.

To more clearly see the problem of the check-the-box mentality, consider the example of using it to address social engineering. Social engineering is a broad term that involves tricking a well-meaning person to take an action against the best interests of themselves or their organization. Consider that there is an infinite set of scenarios for how a malicious party can use social engineering against your organization. Then consider how you are attempting to educate your users about this infinite set of scenarios in three minutes. To address social engineering in that small of a space, you have to make guidance so broad that it is almost useless. The following month, it is onto the next random subject.

Unfortunately, even awareness programs that don't have a check-the-box mentality frequently are not much different. There are definitely exceptions, where a qualified person manages the awareness effort.

However, those exceptions are not very common. It is far more common for organizations to license off-the-shelf awareness videos or other materials acquired from vendors and rely too strongly on just those materials in the state in which they were provided.

Some of these off-the-shelf videos are good and represent a useful addition to an awareness program. Regardless, you should consider that these videos provide guidance that becomes your default security policy. For example, if a video specifies how to create a good password and says that a good password has 8 characters, then your de facto password policy is that passwords have 8 characters, even if your organization's formally written policy specifies 10 characters. If you try to compensate for this by stressing to the users that they should disregard the 8 characters requirement from the video and adhere to the 10 characters requirement from the written policy, you are sending a mixed message. You end up teaching your users that you will provide them with multiple, conflicting guidelines, and you are likely to do the same in other instances as well. You've just trained them that you will be an unreliable partner in giving them proper guidance, undermining their respect, affecting the compliance budget, and ultimately reducing the success of your program.

Even if the off-the-shelf materials generally match your organization's policies, they are not designed for the specific work functions within your organization that can create or mitigate loss. Without loss mitigation guidance that is specific to work-related tasks, you will have incidents that will reflect the generic approach of using untailored off-the-shelf tools.

Further Considerations

As we have discussed, there are many common reasons why awareness programs fail. Depending on your organization and situation, there are likely other reasons beyond the ones that we have discussed. We've identified the problems with employing a check-the-box mentality or using off-the-shelf solutions without tailoring them to your needs. Similarly, you shouldn't only consider the common reasons we have discussed here. You need to actively assess your organization and your program, preferably using metrics, and determine where you can improve things. In this sense, awareness extends to you, too.

Likewise, it is critical to note that even great awareness programs will experience failure at some point, as no countermeasure is ever perfect. You must be prepared for that eventuality, as well.

We address how to address many awareness issues in Chapter 15. However, remember that even with the best awareness programs, you must also create a culture that promotes healthy user awareness while also proactively mitigating the inevitable UIL.

Along with governance and technology, awareness is one of the three fundamental pillars of mitigating UIL. Awareness is critical in mitigating loss. While awareness can never be perfect, awareness programs can dramatically reduce workplace injuries, successful phishing attacks, and myriad other forms of UIL. As we discuss in Chapter 10, metrics are a powerful tool you can use to measure the improvements that your program has. Considering that awareness programs generally receive significantly less funding than other countermeasures, such metrics can demonstrate that for a relatively small investment, your awareness program can be one of the most valuable investments that you make in loss mitigation.

6

Protection, Detection, and Reaction

There are many potential paradigms for loss mitigation strategies. We prefer to simply break loss mitigation down to three phases: Protection, Detection, and Reaction. This generally tracks to the NIST Cybersecurity Framework, which includes two additional phases: Identify and Recover. The NIST Cybersecurity Framework is a well-accepted paradigm for implementing a comprehensive cybersecurity program. At a high level, the framework is appropriate for any form of security or risk mitigation program.

We cover Protection, Detection, and Reaction throughout this chapter, and these names imply their purpose. For our purposes, we are going to include the Identify phase in Protection and the Recover phase in Reaction. Identify involves gathering information to understand what is within an organization so you know what there is to protect.

Recover, per the NIST framework, involves restoring proper business function. While you can choose to separate recovery from the reaction itself, Recover is integral to Reaction, and in many cases the actions overlap.

A three-phase paradigm is easier to understand for our purposes and maps well into the concept of Boom that we discuss in Part IV of this book.

Throughout the book, we emphasize the importance of this paradigm in the developing of a proactive strategy to mitigate loss. It encompasses the desire to protect what you have, the realization that there will be failure in your protection efforts, and the need to detect those failures and be able to respond. Just because protection fails, it does not mean that a loss has to occur, if you plan appropriately.

Conceptual Overview

Fundamentally, Protection, Detection, and Reaction are categorizations of countermeasures. Protection, Detection, and Reaction are typically delineated based upon when a countermeasure is put into action.

Clearly, anything that stops an attack from happening is protection. Security guards who check the belongings of people entering a facility to try to find weapons are a form of protection. However, security guards also perform rounds and can detect whether someone is behaving suspiciously, which makes them a form of detection. Security guards can also be called upon to respond to an ongoing incident and are, therefore, a countermeasure involved in reaction.

From a technology perspective, any tools that you put in place to stop an incident from happening can be considered a form of protection. However, some tools that you put in place proactively to prevent an incident are useful only after a loss is initiated. For example, many organizations implement data leak prevention (DLP) software that stops sensitive data from going out via email. It can legitimately be considered a form of protection as it stops the data from leaving the organization. It can also be considered a form of detection, as it is likely against policies for sensitive data to be sent outside the organization. DLP can also be considered a reaction, as it intercepts the data as it is sent outside the organization.

For the purposes of addressing UIL, we separate that into three phases in Part IV: Left of Boom, Boom, and Right of Boom. While the concept is discussed more thoroughly in Part IV, for now, suffice it to say that Boom is the point where a user is in the position that they might take some sort of action that can initiate a loss. In each phase, you can potentially implement protection, detection, and reaction. For example, consider the detection of a phishing message. When technology detects the phishing message before it gets to the user, that is detection in the Left of Boom phase. When the user detects the fact that the phishing message is a phishing message, that is detection during Boom. Finally, if the user clicks on the message and technology detects that the message intends to perform a malicious action, that is detection during Right of Boom.

When determining an overall UIL mitigation strategy, any potential countermeasure can be considered for any phase of protection, detection, and reaction when it is relevant, and even if used in another phase. The important aspect is that you consider protection, detection, and reaction at each phase of stopping UIL.

Protection

For our purposes, we define Protection as those efforts implemented to prevent users from initiating a loss. Anything that stops the initiation is a protection tool.

Even though this explains, at a high level, what protection is, it is not trivial to create a protection strategy. When addressing UIL, a protection strategy should be comprehensive, including elements of technology, governance, and awareness. Unfortunately, many loss mitigation efforts typically address protection efforts with independent tactics.

For example, when organizations address the phishing problem, the email team will ideally buy tools that filter out potential spam and phishing messages. Another team working on governance might address acceptable email use properties and what type of information can be sent out via email. Users should not send out PII-related information, for example. Independently, people might be assigned to an awareness program, and they might choose to implement phishing awareness programs that use off-the-shelf phishing awareness videos, and maybe implement phishing simulations.

However, as the saying goes, when everyone is in charge, no one is in charge. In the previous example, everyone is attempting to address phishing loss within their own small and limited sphere of influence. The result is essentially a set of independent tactics with no over-arching strategy.

As implied by the NIST model, to perform prevention properly, you need to first identify the assets that are potentially susceptible to loss. These could include the relevant computers, information, physical assets, money, etc. In other words, what *Value* do you possess and need to protect? It is beneficial to consider some of the previous losses your organization suffered, as they are a likely indicator of where your future loss can arise. Clearly, you want to consider what there is to lose beyond that, as well as additional assets that are coming to your organization.

It is also important to consider the threat you believe you face. This helps you identify what might be targeted and where you might want to prioritize your resources. As we discussed in Chapter 4, when you look to identify what is at risk and needs protection, consider Value and Threat.

Besides identifying what needs to be protected, a protection strategy should include governance. Governance defines both the high-level strategy and low-level procedures to be implemented by users.

Technologies that automate the strategy can then be chosen, and awareness can then be used to instruct users on how they are expected to behave. It is, however, the governance and the coordinated implementation of other countermeasures that determine whether you have an independent set of tactics or a coordinated protection strategy.

Detection

Detection in the context of UIL is that set of countermeasures implemented to detect when an attack targets a user, when a user is faced with a potential attack, and also when a user takes an action that has the potential to initiate a loss. These countermeasures also detect a loss in progress or even after the fact.

If there is an attack targeting your users, in the ideal world you detect the attack before it reaches them. Assuming the user falls prey to an attack or maliciously commits a harmful act, it is preferred to detect the potential loss as early as possible. Ideally, you immediately detect when a user makes an action that could initiate a loss. For example, you might immediately detect when a user opens up a phishing message. In the worst-case scenario, you don't determine that a loss occurred until long after the loss can be recovered. For example, an audit might show that money was illicitly transferred to an overseas bank account at a bank that won't cooperate and return the money.

In the case of the phishing message, there is the potential to prevent the loss completely. However, in the money transfer case, although the loss is irrecoverable, it is still beneficial to know that a loss occurred so it can be analyzed and future losses can be prevented. When you know about previous losses, you can then determine how to develop a strategy to better prevent, detect, and respond to future losses of a similar nature.

Chapter 4 refers to countermeasures at a high level. Those countermeasures generally represent specific tactics, and not a strategy. It is, however, useful to create a detection strategy as to where and when you intend to purposefully implement detection. This strategy should implement a combination of technology, process, and awareness.

Starting with awareness, the important aspect to consider is that you are looking to people to detect unusual actions. Co-workers are the most likely to detect unusual and unsafe behaviors among their peers. For example, when you work for an organization that uses access badges, co-workers can detect and remind their peers to put the badge away when they are outside the organization. In another example of a more heinous case, it was a failure of detection that allowed Edward Snowden to continue his data thefts, as Snowden solicited co-workers' passwords from them. If any of them would have reported this solicitation, Snowden would have been caught before fleeing the country.

Another part of the detection strategy is processes. Processes should be designed to integrate detection. For example, financial processes typically integrate auditing to detect any form of variation. Audits are agnostic regarding whether any variation is from malfeasance or error. Regardless of the reason for the discrepancies, the detection kicks off a reaction process to stop the actions. Ideally, the reason for the discrepancies should be determined, which should impact the reaction. However, detection itself is not dependent upon the reason for the initiation of the loss on the part of the user.

In addition to awareness and processes, the detection strategy should also address technology. Technology automates detection of the potential initiation of losses. However, like other countermeasures, technology is implemented as a tactic. Unfortunately, there is a great deal of misunderstanding of technology's limitations.

For example, in the IT environment, there are a variety of behavioral analytics tools that intend to identify potential misuse and abuse of computer systems. Some tools are network-based tools that look for abuses by analyzing the traffic between computers. Other tools are host based. In other words, they sit on a computer and analyze how a user accesses computer files, how critical processes are modified, and how the computer itself behaves.

For example, network-based analytics tools might identify when a user attempts to scour the network for information, while host-based tools will identify when a user copies information to a USB drive from their computer. Clearly, you would need both network-based and host-based behavioral analytics tools, as they each look for different types of activities. However, some people mistakenly believe that as long as they buy one type of behavioral analytics tool, they have implemented comprehensive behavioral analytics. There are a variety of implementation issues on top of that. However, the point is that when people choose to implement one tool over another, they are implementing a tactic and not designing a comprehensive detection strategy.

There are different technologies that detect a variety of user actions that can initiate loss. Part IV identifies how to choose the appropriate technologies as part of a comprehensive strategy that integrates them with process and awareness.

Detection should be implemented before the initiation of loss, after the fact, and at all points in between. The purpose of detection is to know that the system has failed and that a reaction should be considered. The last three words in the preceding sentence are critical. Just because you detect a possible harmful action, it doesn't mean that a reaction is warranted. For example, in a real case scenario, we investigated a string of large bank thefts, and in the process of investigating the specific thefts, we discovered other attempted compromises. We analyzed those attempts and determined that they were unsuccessful and very amateurish. No harm was inflicted, and there was little potential for future harm. Those particular attacks were not worth expending further resources.

Regardless of whether you decide to implement a reaction and regardless of whether you detect the problem before, during, or after an incident, detection is critical. As Chapter 7 discusses, any incident is a sign that there is a problem with the process, and that must be studied and, if warranted, corrected.

Reaction

The primary goal of reaction is to mitigate a potential loss in progress. However, if an attack is detected after it succeeds, reaction involves repairing the damage and potentially putting improvements in place. As with all the other steps in the protection, detection, and reaction chain, the reaction can be before an attack reaches the user, while a user is encountering an attack, or after the user makes a potentially harmful action.

Reaction can include any and all countermeasures involving process, technology, and awareness, and it is for the response team to determine the appropriate mix of such countermeasures.

Reaction is not as simple as just stopping an attack in progress. You have to determine the scope of the potential incident. You ideally need to have an incident response plan in place, as there are many issues that people typically do not consider when thrust into a crisis mode.

For example, whom do you alert to potential loss? Is public relations a consideration? Is there the willingness to prosecute a potential criminal? If so, do you have the necessary evidence collection processes in place? Do you actually own the resources that are being compromised, or do they belong to a third party, such as a cloud vendor? Do you know whom to interact with at the third parties? Do you have the equipment and people available to respond appropriately? Do you need to legally disclose the incident, because of the type of data or resources that may be compromised? The list can go on for pages, and that is the subject for other books.

Another aspect of reaction is to use the incident as a learning experience so that you can improve your protection to proactively mitigate future incidents. This requires a more thoughtful approach to how you analyze the incidents. All too often, there is a knee-jerk response where rash decisions are poorly chosen. For example, in the aftermath of the 9/11 attacks, all transportation systems were shut down. This included all airplane and train operations in the United States. While there was obviously a need to reassure the public of their safety, tremendous inconvenience was unnecessarily made for tens of millions of people.

Many people make bad risk-based decisions, especially when they have an irrational fear. Regarding terrorism, in 2003, a man heard dire news stories about how terrorists might use biological and chemical weapons. In response, he wrapped his entire house in plastic wrap. (See www.freerepublic.com/focus/news/842764/posts.) The reality is that the man was then exponentially more likely to die from carbon monoxide poisoning than any terroristic attack. In more rational but still poorly considered risk-based decision-making, many people choose to drive long distances, instead of fly, because of irrational fears of flying. (See www.researchgate.net/publication/46528808_Driving_Fatalities_After_911_A_Hidden_Cost_of_Terrorism.)

Even after the transportation systems resumed operations, useless security protocols were put in place, such as banning butter knives and tweezers from carry-on bags. These were not security countermeasures that addressed any viable, plausible threat.

An overreaction, or a reaction that does not take into account the reality of the situation, will result in both wasted efforts and an unhealthy skepticism of legitimate security efforts.

In a more traditional environment, such as a workplace, you need to factor in the compliance budget. If unproductive countermeasures are put in place that make work more difficult, they will be ignored, which will further result in a greater willingness to ignore other prescribed countermeasures.

Mitigating a Loss in Progress

When you want to stop a loss in progress, you ideally have an established incident response plan. More specifically, each department should have its own response plan identified. For example, what works for an IT department will be insufficient for physical incidents. Financial losses are a different type of incident, and a different plan should be in place for handling them. Incidents in manufacturing facilities that result in outages or injuries require their own specific plans as well. Supply chain incidents, too, require a different form of response. Even so, because many incidents can have a ripple effect across multiple departments, it is best for each of these plans to be coordinated with other departments.

In the ideal world, detection will indicate the type of loss that is in progress, and mitigating it will be straightforward. However, you need to understand that all may not be as it appears. It is often difficult to identify the attackers and their motives.

For example, if you are dealing with a phishing incident, the phishing message could be due to an amateur throwing a wide net and hoping for any random response. Likewise, the same message might be used by a nation-state that, if unsuccessful, will try other methods until they are successful.

Financial losses can be due to a simple error, or they can be the first sign of long-term, sophisticated financial fraud.

In an extreme example, Cliff Stoll, a computer administrator, became a legend because he discovered a seemingly minor accounting error in the computer usage accounts. In his attempts to clarify the discrepancy, he found an East German intelligence operation. His story was described in detail in the book *The Cuckoo's Egg*.

When mitigating a loss in progress, you need to proceed cautiously and in a way that does not create more damage than it stops. Taking down the entire transportation system after 9/11 created significant loss for no other reason than confusion on the part of people in charge.

The Risk Management field defines that there are several types of responses: accept, avoid, mitigate, and transfer. Accepting a risk means that you might detect a loss but consciously choose to ignore it. For example, this was the case in the incident involving an amateurish attempt to break into a bank's computers. It would have cost too much money to fully investigate an attacker who had little chance of causing the organization harm. Avoiding as a response implies that you take specific actions to not put yourself in a position where you are faced with a loss. In other words, you might change your business processes. For example, companies might choose not to put a business function on the Internet. Mitigating risk implies that you commit to a true response. Transferring risk means that you put other measures in place to deal with the loss associated with the potential risk. Buying insurance is such an example of risk transference.

In short, a reaction is much more complicated than just stopping an attack.

Mitigating Future Incidents

Once you are certain that an incident either has been mitigated or is otherwise over, you want to take steps to ensure that it doesn't happen again. Past incidents are perhaps the best indicators of future incidents. As Chapter 7 discusses, the errors you will find are not necessarily an indication of the deficiency of the user, but the deficiency of your system.

As our focus is on UIL, you need to understand why and how the user was allowed to initiate a loss. What environment put the user in a position where they could cause damage? What was the user thinking when they initiated the loss? Was the user provided appropriate guidance before initiating the loss? Why did the system allow the loss to be initiated and realized?

An equally important set of questions involves detection. How was the incident detected? Could the incident have been detected sooner? How could the incident have been detected as the incident advanced?

Again, we are looking for vulnerabilities of the system itself. Any way that you can improve the protection, detection, and reaction of the system against UIL is invaluable. While you do not want to rely on an incident to gather that knowledge, when an incident presents itself, you want to make the best of the situation.

Putting It All Together

Clearly this chapter does not provide a step-by-step description of how to implement protection, detection, and reaction. Not only is that a book in itself, it is a book in each operational field. If you are in the IT field, we recommend Ira Winkler's book, *Advanced Persistent Security* (Syngress, 2017).

However, for our purposes and specifically our focus on UIL, it is important to ensure that we stay focused. Every time a user makes an error and possibly initiates a loss, it is a sign of the weakness of the system itself. Yes, it is a given that users will initiate a loss, even if they are completely aware of what the correct actions are supposed to be. Still, every part of the system will fail at some point.

A failure by any individual part of the system is a failure of the system as a whole. You, therefore, need a comprehensive approach to protecting your organization from UIL, which includes all phases of protection, detection, and reaction.

7

Lessons from Safety Science

It is baffling to us that few people working in risk reduction positions, be they in security, financial, business process, etc., are familiar with the field of safety science. In the IT security field, many people cite psychology, mental models, and the like, to grasp for some scientific basis for what they are doing. But those sciences have yet to prove that they can consistently reduce user-initiated loss within an organization.

At the same time, there have been two fields that routinely look to reduce losses resulting from user error and that seem to have regular success. These are accounting and safety science.

Let's be clear, neither of these sciences is perfect and there will always be losses associated with users. However, they look hard at the sources of any errors and determine whether it can be cost-effective to reduce any given loss. In doing so, they realize that user error causes the organization a hard financial loss, and there is tremendous incentive to reduce such losses.

We should mention that the field of total quality management also looked into how to make processes more efficient by reducing errors, and there was enormous success in accomplishing loss reduction. However, the concept is not as popular as it was in the past. We do, however, cover total quality management in detail in Chapter 12, as it is critical in breaking down workflow in a way designed to reduce loss.

The accounting field is primarily designed to capture the financial aspects of processes and to accurately capture information related to those processes. This is not necessarily about human behavior, but the accurate collection of information. In large part, behaviors should not matter to accounting, as it is agnostic of such concerns and only cares about the accurate tracking of resources. While the accounting function is designed to accurately track resources, good procedures build in the detection of deviations, which might be the result of error and/or malfeasance. Good accounting systems also proactively reduce the opportunity for error and malfeasance. As useful as accounting is, safety science provides even better opportunities for addressing UIL, and that is where we will focus our energy in this chapter.

While there is clearly an altruistic nature to safety science, the primary purpose of the field is to reduce business losses due to human error, injury, and death. In an organization, there are tangible financial losses resulting from injuries and errors. For example, if there is an injury on a factory line, the entire factory line can be shut down to investigate the cause of the injury and to ensure the injured worker is treated in a safe environment. The injured worker can also be out of work for an extended period of time, and unexpected absences can cause a variety of operational issues and expenses. Insurance rates can increase. There can be lawsuits resulting from the injury. Total losses can be millions of dollars.

As Chapter 4 highlights, the value that can be lost includes much more than hard financial loses, and you can assume that if there are injuries in a factory, there is risk of intangible losses, such as increased regulations, reputational cost, loss in worker morale, etc. These combined losses can be extreme, which is why most fields consider safety science to be an infinitely more strategic approach than merely relying on awareness training alone.

The IT security and other operational fields seem to believe that if a user makes a mistake, the problem is that the user needs better awareness training. However, we believe that the problem is that the user was able to initiate actions that could result in loss. This should not be a novel concept, but it apparently is.

Safety science has been successfully applied in many fields for decades. For that reason, we provide this chapter as a primer on safety science, as opposed to the other sciences that awareness and other experts apply, which are essentially specious in their utility. To develop this primer, we scoured the work of Dr. Sidney Dekker, who is one of the true visionaries in the field of safety science. We also spoke in detail with Dr. Nicklas Dahlstrom, a colleague of Dr. Dekker's, and the Human Factors Manager of Emirates Airline, regarding the implications of safety science in security. For further details, we strongly encourage readers to review Dr. Dekker's books and especially *The Field Guide to Understanding Human Error* (Routledge, 2014).

As with all sciences, safety science is constantly evolving. In this chapter, we will first look at its past, discovering that despite its many strengths, it has also experienced limitations, some of which even linger to this day. Then we will look at the ongoing, emerging trends that are carrying safety science forward and making it a powerful means for reducing UIL.

The Limitations of Old-School Safety Science

With any field of science, there is an evolution in processes and what is considered state of the art at any given time. For example, we are trying to evolve how people think of UIL as more than an awareness issue. This evolution is especially true in safety science and how it relates to UIL.

There have been very different beliefs in how people perceive user error. Many misperceptions of user error result from societal ignorance at the time. For example, through the 19th century and even into the 20th century, there were many sexist beliefs about the supposed limitations of women in the workplace. Assuming that half your potential workforce is more prone to error based on an unfounded bias does not reduce UIL. It merely reduces your talent pool. These beliefs not only harmed the operational efficiency of organizations as a whole, but also skewed the validity of studies in the workplace. Fortunately, we continue to make progress in evolving beyond our gender, racial, class, and other biases, although we still have quite a distance to go.

Safety science has traditionally involved singling out user behaviors and actions to analyze the incidents in question. At any point in time, people analyzing incidents that involved some form of perceived user error focused specifically on the users being the source of the mistakes. Paraphrasing Dr. Dekker, safety investigators looked at canaries in a coal mine and blamed them for constantly dying.

If they looked at why the users made mistakes as part of a process to examine all the possible root causes, it would be one issue. However, the problem was that the users, by default, were considered to be the root cause of the error or incident. Unfortunately, some of these old-fashioned approaches to safety science still linger today.

It is common for hospitals to investigate the deaths or injuries incurred by patients while under the hospital's care. Typically, there is a forum where the doctors have to face tough questions regarding the choices that they made that led to the patient's injury or death. Inevitably, the doctors have to explain the one action they took that caused the harm. Of course, this leads to the conclusion that it was the doctor's decisions that caused the harm.

In the whole process, there is little discussion of the hundreds of other decisions that had to be made, given the available information. While in hindsight, it is often clear that the doctor in question could have made another decision, it is rare during complicated medical procedures, with limited information available, that the best decision is as clear during that time. There is also the matter of the culture in which the doctor is functioning and the staff, equipment, training, and other resources that have been provided. These investigations sometimes proceed without weighing such considerations.

The situation is similar with aviation accidents. In those cases, government bodies meet to decide why accidents took place, and of course, the first thing they start with is pilot error.

This is particularly clear in the case of the National Transportation Safety Board (NTSB) hearing of the landing of US Airways Flight 1549 in the Hudson River by Captain Chesley "Sully" Sullenberger. Almost immediately after takeoff from LaGuardia Airport in New York City, Flight 1549 flew through a flock of Canadian Geese, and both engines were essentially destroyed. Sullenberger was left with seconds to make critical decisions. While Sullenberger did safely land the plane in the Hudson River, which was a remarkable feat, Airbus test pilots using a simulator found that if Sullenberger would have followed procedures, he could have safely landed the plane back at LaGuardia Airport.

Essentially, despite all of the complexities, the NTSB protocols focused on questioning why Sullenberger didn't act perfectly according to protocol. Sullenberger was cleared of pilot error because the Airbus simulations did not take into account the amount of time that was necessary to gather information as to what may be wrong, as the simulator pilots, in hindsight, knew immediately that both engines were inoperable and immediately returned to LaGuardia for an emergency landing.

This is sadly the same strategy that Boeing claimed regarding the crashes of 737 MAX aircraft. Investigators attempted to say that if the pilots of the 737 MAX aircraft reacted perfectly to the conditions, they should have immediately shut off the automated controls and safely returned to the airport. Of course, in this case, nobody ever informed the pilots about the potential problem (that safety indicators had been removed) or what the perfect reaction should be.

As you can tell in the cases regarding both the doctors and the pilots, the tendency is to focus on the proximity of the people directly involved in the incident as the primary cause. While Flight 1549 was fairly straightforward in that there were no contributing factors to the incident, besides the geese, the fault with the 737 MAX aircraft, as well as most medical procedures, involves issues well beyond the control of the "operators" in the immediate vicinity. With the 737 MAX, the pilots were clearly left to their own devices with limited information. The root cause of the problem occurred in the whole design of the airplane, the removal of safety indicators, incomplete training documentation, etc. In old-school investigations of safety-related incidents, these issues are typically considered secondary.

Essentially, old-school safety science used to take the position that the system is generally sound and that it is the unreliable and erratic users who cause the problems. These beliefs were reinforced by the investigative process itself, which began with perfect hindsight into knowing what happened. This allowed for a linear investigation of why a person did not behave the way they should have, removing consideration of all of the forces that pulled an otherwise competent person away from perfection. In short, there is always something different a user could have done to avoid any incident, according to traditional beliefs, even when you lose power to both engines immediately after takeoff.

Most UIL Prevention Programs Are Old-School

The primary problem with most user risk reduction programs is that they mirror old-school thinking. Ironically, though, one of the major problems with many existing risk reduction programs is that they do not look to blame the users. Most security and risk reduction people believe that users make mistakes because they are unaware of the risk issues and that making them aware of the issues would prevent the mistakes from occurring. This is the mantra that the user is your first and last line of defense.

Paradoxically these risk reduction professionals avoid blaming users for their initiation of potential loss, while at the same time proposing to make the user more aware as a solution. This implies that proximity is the primary and most critical method for stopping a loss.

Yes, users can likely perform better, and they can be trained better. But from a safety science perspective, focusing on the user as being your first or last line of defense is an extremely old-school way of looking at the problem.

The real problem is that users have the ability to initiate a potential loss, not that a lack of awareness can result in a loss.

The good news is that there are improvements in the understanding of human cognition and limitations of learning, as well as how to enhance learning and improve behaviors. There are periodic breakthroughs in perception within a given field, and safety science is no exception.

The New School of Safety Science

Fortunately, safety science has moved away from the concept that the system is otherwise perfect and that erratic users cause the problems. If we could summarize the concept of the new school of safety science in one sentence, it would be:

> *Human error is a window into trouble inside a system.*

While safety science practitioners typically strive to proactively mitigate harm, the reality is that a larger portion of their work is the investigation of incidents. Using new-school thought processes is a good way to be proactive.

When you consider that human error shows you where your system is weak, you can begin to strengthen the system to protect the users. You are not looking to see how users can make better decisions; instead, you strive to create an environment where the right decisions are a default as a result of the system.

In modern safety science, human error is not the cause of failure. Instead, human error is a symptom of a troubled system that caused the person to make a mistake. When user error occurs, it is important to focus on *what* caused the error and *not* who caused the failure.

Similarly, in safety science, there is rarely a case where there is malicious intent in accidents. Therefore, you work with the assumption that when a user makes an error, the action seemed rational to the person at the time, and you work toward understanding how and why the user made that choice.

User error should never be considered a random event. In safety science, this assumption is that the conditions had to be ripe for an accident or error to occur. Even if something appears to randomly happen, such as a stack of boxes falling down, there are a variety of questions to ask to find the systemic problem. Why was the user stacking the boxes? Were the boxes balanced? Did proper guidelines for stacking boxes exist? Were there limits to the number of boxes that could be stacked on top of each other? If the user did do something improperly, what could have prevented that action? Was the user properly informed of the guidelines? Were there conditions driving the user to do something against the guidelines that the guidelines did not account for?

While the list can go on, a smart safety professional realizes that there is often a major difference between the way work is imagined and the way work is actually performed given the circumstances that the users encounter on a regular basis. It is important to identify any conflicts between planning and performance as soon as possible to reduce potential errors. In many ways, a user error represents how users have adjusted to working conditions while performing their work. While an error might be anomalous, the error should still be considered as resulting from work procedures in practice.

W-2 fraud, where criminals attempt to get the HR department to send personnel data to them, is common in the United States around tax season. Applying a safety sciences perspective to that scenario, you would ask how the messages were able to get to the users. Then ask if the process the users were supposed to follow accounted for verifying identities. If they did verify identities, did the system potentially identify the message as coming from an outside party? Even if that happened, you then have to consider whether the user required access to the information in the first place. Then you determine whether technologies were in place, or should have been in place, that could have prevented the information from being sent to the criminals, such as data leak prevention (DLP) software on outgoing email systems. It would, of course, be great for the user not to initiate the sending of sensitive information to a criminal. However, the user, in this case, would be just one in many points of failure.

To identify the cause of an error, you step back and consider the circumstances that put the user in the position to make the error. Where did the process begin? Was there anything at the beginning that made the possibility of error inevitable? What were the contributing factors to the user making the error? What were the decision points along the way that led to the eventual error?

When you consider the medical and aircraft error examples we provided in the discussion of old-school safety, the investigators looked at the single path that the pilots or doctors took to get to the point where they made the error. With modern safety science, you consider the entire decision tree that the user took to get to the point that they did. You need to understand the cascading decisions made that took the user down the path of the error. If the user did not take a path where the error could have been avoided, why didn't they take that path? Were there systemic issues that led the user to make the wrong decisions?

These are the kinds of questions that determine how you perceive a situation and what you can do to address it. Consider again the case of Flight 1549. Ultimately, the NTSB looked beyond the Airbus analysis of Flight 1549 to conclude that while the simulator pilots were able to make a safe return to the airport, Captain Sullenberger did not have sufficient time to gather data, analyze the situation, and decide to return to the airport. The simulator pilots never had to take the time to gather information before making decisions, so their situation was very different than that faced by Sullenberger. This is also a clear example of the gap between the way work is conceptualized and how it is actually carried out.

User error is the starting point of an investigation, not the conclusion. This is such a critical factor to understand. The error is systemically connected to the conditions that led to it. It is not the result of a random user decision. The work conditions lead the user to take the action that seemed rational and proper at the time.

Putting Safety Science to Use

In the process of creating awareness programs for organizations, we frequently work with safety practitioners to determine how they get their safety awareness messages across to the users. In one instance, they looked at accidents, such as a person walking into a forklift. Clearly, this caused significant injuries and a great deal of cost with the resulting lawsuits and increase in insurance premiums. The safety practitioners said the organization used to blame the forklift driver or the person for being careless.

Then they started to ask themselves how they could make the environment safer to reduce or eliminate such accidents, and they essentially came up with the concepts of sidewalks inside their factories. They did not want to actually create raised floors for pedestrians, so they painted lines throughout their factories, with the expectation that pedestrians would stay to one side, while the forklifts and other equipment would stay to the other. A few cans of paint saved the company millions of dollars a year. The number of accidents resulting from driver or pedestrian carelessness became significantly fewer. Beyond just creating the painted lanes, the safety officer had contingency plans in place to make some aisles solely devoted to equipment, in case such accidents remained a major problem.

There are many other environments where safety rules have already become proactive. For example, students in chemistry laboratories know they have to wear safety goggles. Steel-toed boots and hard hats are mandatory for most construction workers. Food service workers have to wash their hands after using the restroom. There is a myriad of errors that these safety precautions proactively mitigate, and they are independent of any specific user errors, and even protect people when other users make errors.

Safety Culture

Safety practitioners realize that safety has to be embedded into the culture, and that for the most part, the culture has to be driven from the top down. Safety practitioners have two tremendous factors supporting them in getting leadership to agree to establish a safety culture. One is that they often have the weight of laws and regulations dictating safety. The other is that the costs of safety failings can be extremely high. Workplace injuries and accidents not only cost money resulting from fines, lawsuits, equipment replacement, and so on, there are also operational concerns such as loss of skilled labor, disrupted workflows, and entire processes shutting down. Beyond these concerns, there is a moral imperative to provide a safe workplace and customer experience.

There is a major difference between a "Should" and a "Must." A safety culture works when it is a Must, and the potential costs drive executive management to make it a Must. This can empower the safety practitioner to define alterations to work processes that will be implemented. There will always be pushback, but when you have executive support, driven by a tremendous desire for cost avoidance, you can much more easily overcome that pushback.

Clearly, you need safety to be practiced from the bottom up. However, changing processes from the bottom up does not happen easily or consistently without some form of enforcement or motivation, which often is better driven from the top down. Again, the risks and costs are very clear when you are talking about workplace injuries or outages.

For people in operations, physical security, cybersecurity, and similar environments where user-initiated loss is important but sometimes not well-defined from a cost perspective, it is important to show how awareness programs relate to the safety culture. While you can have awareness programs that play to the well-meaning nature of most users, efforts to achieve a bottom-up risk reduction program will achieve only limited success, at best. Safety practitioners who achieve a true safety culture know that they can achieve and maintain such a culture only with top-down support.

The Need to *Not* Remove All Errors

While this may sound completely counterintuitive, safety practitioners know that they cannot eliminate all errors. In many cases, they even purposefully leave the opportunity for error. The reason is that when there is no error, or more specifically consequences for bad actions, people lose their skills and motivation to practice safety principles. This concept is often referred to as the *compliance budget*, which is the degree to which users do or do not see the benefit of safety measures and their correlating likelihood to follow them.

Consider again that the pilots of the ill-fated Lion Air and Ethiopian Airlines Boeing 737 MAX airplanes never had training to deal with the failure of the AOA sensors. Because there are rarely major failures on airplanes, regulations require pilots to undergo a certain amount of flight simulator training where they can experience such problems, albeit artificially. This way, they are better equipped to deal with problems when they do actually arise.

If you remove all opportunity for error in an environment, users become complacent and are more likely to ignore important safety rules. The users essentially see the safety practices as pointless busywork. It is, therefore, preferable to provide users with opportunities to utilize skills that deal with inevitable errors.

Author Ira Winkler is a master scuba diver trainer and drills into students the basics of scuba diving. He also realizes that when students go on real diving trips, where boat crews frequently take care of putting together all the diving equipment, they are less likely to personally check their own equipment. It is not until divers experience situations where a boat crew does not properly turn on the airflow, check equipment for leaks, and so on, that students learn the hard way why Ira spends so much time training them to perform such tedious tasks as ensuring that a fresh air tank actually provides air.

When all risk is taken out of a situation, it not only results in complacency but a loss of critical skills to handle unsafe situations.

The scuba example demonstrates the importance of ensuring that equipment has been properly maintained, despite that things rarely go wrong. The same scenario is applicable for all workplace equipment. Preventative maintenance is time-consuming, boring, and costly. However, should a company truck break down because regular oil changes were not performed, deliveries might not be made. People can potentially be stranded in dangerous situations. If it involves factory equipment, all production may stop, and people can be injured.

Regarding complacency, crosswalks actually become more dangerous for pedestrians, as they don't believe that they have to check for oncoming or turning cars. They believe that the crosswalk itself provides them some safety, while ironically people who jaywalk will be more careful, as they realize that they do not have the right of way.

From the opposite perspective, a driver who expects people only to cross at crosswalks becomes less attentive to jaywalkers and potentially children who run into traffic. There has been more than one case on the TV show *Judge Judy* where an elderly driver hits another car out of carelessness and their sincere defense was that they drove the same road for several decades and they never had an accident before, so the accident couldn't be their fault. While the claim is clearly ridiculous, this same attitude makes its way into every environment where there are few accidents.

All of these factors relate to the compliance budget. It is, therefore, imperative to try to leave the opportunity for limited error in business processes. Of course, you should do this where the consequences are not severe. If you cannot do so safely, attempt to proactively create simulations where the application of safety principles can be implemented in a secure manner.

When to Blame Users

As you read through this chapter, you might get the impression that there is no place to blame the user, as the user is essentially just a symptom of problems within the system. This is not entirely correct.

It is true that a safety culture is a "just culture" and blame is never to be assigned to users as the default action. However, there is a major difference between an *error* and a clear *violation*.

If an act is an error, you need to first understand why the error occurred. There is a spectrum from error to violation, and you need to figure out where a particular action may fall.

On one end of the spectrum, the system itself is the problem. Did you build competence and trust on the part of the user? If the user was put into a position where they were not competent, it is clearly the system's fault for placing such a person in a position to cause harm.

At the other end of the spectrum, you might be faced with a user who was completely derelict in their duties. They knew what was expected of them, and they failed to meet those expectations. Perhaps, on that particular day, they were distracted for a variety of personal reasons, and their personal compliance budget did not lend itself to performing their job properly.

It is rare for someone to perform their job perfectly. In the course of investigating an incident, if you find that a user was simply derelict in performing their duties and not making reasonable decisions throughout their personal decision tree, it is appropriate to consider assigning blame and punishment. However, you must be certain that the user was properly trained and assumed to be competent and still failed to perform their job functions properly.

Even if the user was clearly to blame for given violations of established procedures on their part, it does not mean that the system is without fault. Both the user and the system can deserve blame. Even if you have a user who was clearly at fault, there are likely some systemic countermeasures that should be in place to mitigate violations that either are malicious or create unintended loss.

We Need to Learn from Safety Science

Unfortunately, regarding UIL, most risk reduction practitioners seem to be practicing old-school safety science. Instead of blaming users when they make an error, we need to make them more aware of the right way to do things. The user is a valuable partner whose potential needs to be maximized in reducing UIL.

The users are, of course, in proximity to where errors can be made, as well as stopped. However, they can only make the errors you put them in the position to make. You need to create their workflow in such a way that they are in less of a position to potentially initiate loss.

Safety science is not the only discipline that advocates such principles, but it is clearly one of the most applicable on the subject. While most UIL circumstances do not involve life and death issues, there are tremendous parallels between user errors in safety-related circumstances and those in other disciplines.

It is old-school to look at the user as anything more than a symptom of your system, and throughout this book, we will keep coming back to this principle that the user is just one cog in a larger system where UIL occurs. Users may be an important cog, but they are not the pinnacle of the loss.

8

Applied
Behavioral Science

As you can see from the safety science discussion of Chapter 7, if you want to mitigate UIL, you need to look beyond the user's proximity to the actual initiation of the loss. Addressing only user proximity results in allowing the root cause of the loss to continue to exist, which results in further opportunities for both errors and malicious actions to occur.

Obviously, you also continue to attempt to reduce errors at the proximity of their occurrence. While most of the work is to reduce the opportunity for users to initiate the loss, users will inevitably still be in a position to do so. Therefore, a comprehensive strategy requires that you do target improvement of user actions.

Note that "target improvement of user actions" is not synonymous with "improve user awareness." Awareness is just one tactic in the overall substrategy of improving user actions. Chapter 5 addresses the limitations of awareness programs and relying too strongly on them.

An extremely relevant expression is, "All that is necessary for evil to win is for good people to do nothing." When good people are aware of what they should be doing but are not doing so, that is just as useless as if they were not aware of the expectations in the first place. You don't care what people know as much as you care what they actually do. In other words, you care about their behavior.

There is a wide variety of sciences that you can use to try to get people to behave as desired. When it comes to addressing UIL, some sciences are more effective than others. Psychology is the study of the human mind and behavior. It is a broad field that addresses many things, including functioning well in society and coping with mental health matters. While it addresses clusters of similar thought patterns and behaviors, it often tailors awareness efforts to each individual, which isn't generally the focus of an organization trying to effectively drive behavioral change across all of its users.

Mental models are an outgrowth of psychology that attempt to explain someone's thought process about how something works in the real world. Frequently, practitioners attempt to apply mental models in awareness and related efforts to reduce human error. Generally, you want to try to match user expectations with how things work. For example, people expect green to represent "go" or generally something good, while red represents "stop" or something potentially bad. It would, therefore, be a bad idea to use these colors in a way that differs from those widely accepted norms.

The problem with mental models is that they are often inconsistent. Some users may have the wrong mental model for some concepts. Other users might have an incomplete or inconsistent mental model. And different users come from different experiential or cultural backgrounds, resulting in differing mental models. When you are dealing with loss-related issues, you can take it for granted that there might be some basic concepts in a mental model that are appropriate, such as the use of red and green. (Of course, even these models can be ineffective. For example, using red and green isn't helpful with people who are color blind.) But you need to accept that there is generally no universal truth. If there was, you would not have a problem with loss in the first place.

In essence, you want to create the mental model for your users and not rely on the varying mental models that they already possess. This is ironically against the general principle of mental models, which is to work with the users' current understanding and expand it. Mental models can be helpful when the users are your customers and you're providing them a service or product. But they are less useful in scenarios where the users are your organization's employees and you are trying to guide their consistent behavior.

On the other hand, an approach that we have found to be quite effective, is applied behavioral science (ABS). ABS works with the fact that people come with different mental models, different personalities, different learning styles, and so on, and intends to create whichever behaviors you desire. While the other sciences have their purposes, they tend to support one-on-one interactions and not consistent organization-wide behavioral change.

The ABCs of Behavioral Science

To get people to exhibit the organization's desired behaviors, you have to understand what motivates behaviors. When you look at people who promote awareness training, for example, they give you the impression that they make awareness training the most memorable and, therefore, their materials are the best tool to get people to behave properly. As we explain in Chapter 5, that is insufficient.

To a certain extent, information only helps people behave better if it connects with what motivates them. Consider the example of a company rolling out new technology. If a user believes that the old technology is worthless and the new technology should improve the situation, they are likely to enthusiastically begin using the new technology when you tell them it is available.

On the other hand, if you have a user who likes the current technology, telling them that they should use new technology simply because you think it is better is not going to compel the user to convert to it. Even if you use a funny video to get the point across, the user may choose not to use the new technology.

Behavioral science uses terminology to address this phenomenon. In particular, we are interested in antecedents, behavior, and consequences (the ABCs). Information is an Antecedent intended to create the desired Behavior. The Behavior then results in Consequences. The Consequences then serve to reinforce or detract from the Behavior. Figure 8.1 depicts the relationship of the ABCs of behavioral science.

Figure 8.1: The relationship between antecedents, behavior, and consequences

These behavioral science terms apply directly to the previously discussed technology example. The information about the technology is the antecedent, their choice to use or not use the technology is the behavior, and the impact of their choice is the consequence.

When someone does not like the technology currently in use, the consequence of adopting the new, desired behavior is that they are switching away from technology that they dislike. That is a positive consequence, which is why they are adopting the behavior.

Conversely, when someone likes the current technology in use, the consequence of adopting the desired behavior is a negative one, specifically losing the use of something that they like.

In both instances, the consequence of the person's happiness and investment in their own personal interests feeds back into determining their behavior. Of course, if the organization orders the user to adopt the new technology and noncompliance would result in termination, that is an antecedent that identifies a specific consequence, which affects the user's behavior as well. Depending on the circumstances, either persuasion or a command might be a better antecedent.

In essence, the goal of awareness is to be an antecedent that influences behavior with information, while you can use consequences to engineer behavior from the other direction.

Antecedents

An antecedent is anything that theoretically precedes a behavior. For practical purposes, an antecedent is information provided that is intended to influence a user's behavior. An antecedent can take just about any form you can imagine, such as videos, newsletters, posters, commercials, coffee cup sleeves, squishy toys, instructional books, and so on. The key is that it is essentially something independently created or available that can influence a future behavior.

Consider health-related matters, where you have different awareness efforts created as antecedents to drive fitness behaviors, smoking cessation, and so on. It is important to note that people are generally well aware that they need to eat less and exercise more to lose weight, be healthier, and live longer. Likewise, people know that smoking can lead to a range of illnesses and an early death. Yet in both of these cases, despite the clear risk of death, obesity is at record levels, and millions of people still smoke tobacco products.

The reality is that antecedents are generally responsible for 20 percent of behavioral change at best. Antecedents appeal to the users' logic or emotions to encourage them to change their behavior. Antecedents attempt to get users to believe that there are positive consequences for following the recommended behaviors and negative consequences for not following them.

Security awareness programs typically focus on providing antecedents intended to influence behaviors. Security awareness practitioners distribute videos and other forms of media to warn people about the potential threat of hackers and other issues involving computer crime and loss. Yet, there are computer loss stories all over social media and the news, and there is little apparent progress in correcting behaviors.

When you consider any type of UIL, it is important to note that users are frequently provided with some form of information regarding how to avoid initiating a loss. While there might be a decrease in the behaviors likely to potentially initiate a loss, the behaviors are not eliminated to the point that awareness can consistently be declared successful as an antecedent.

Training is a form of antecedent. Training intends to get people to perform their jobs properly by providing them with some form of information that specifies the performance criteria. Training can have varying effectiveness depending upon the form and quality of the training. One form of training is known as hands-on training. In hands-on training, the observation coincides with the user actually exhibiting the behavior and being subjected to the consequences.

The culture of an organization can also be an antecedent. When you observe how everyone behaves, you are likely to behave the same way by default. If everyone wears their badge, you are likely to wear your badge. If co-workers leave their work areas clean, you are likely to keep your work area clean. While deviations from the cultural norm lead to consequences, the behaviors surrounding you are an antecedent.

Passive Antecedents vs. Active Antecedents

There are two types of antecedents: active and passive. Active antecedents directly engage a person in an unavoidable way, such as business meetings that the person is required to attend. Passive antecedents don't require direct interaction, such as a poster on a wall that a person may or may not observe. Let's look at both types of antecedents more closely.

Passive antecedents can be used either as a reinforcement of a desired message or as a trigger to initiate the appropriate behavior. Regarding serving as a trigger, consider the signs that remind people they can't smoke within a certain distance of a business's entrance. Those signs are clearly a blatant trigger to initiate the specific behavior of not smoking near the doorway.

Safety signs are another example of passive antecedents intended as a trigger. These signs warn people of potential hazards, such as hot surfaces, dangerous intersections, electrical hazards, and a variety of workplace safety hazards. They represent information intended to get the targeted audience to avoid or engage in a specific action.

Ideally, a passive antecedent is put in as close proximity as possible to where an act is to be made. This places the potential trigger for the desired action where it should be most effective. Should the person be wrestling with their personal Compliance Budget (as discussed in Chapter 5) and there is a passive trigger in the proximity, it may be the deciding factor that influences their behavior.

Consider a restaurant worker who takes a break that is longer than expected and finishes using the restroom. They are obviously in a hurry to get back to work and might be penalized for being late. At the same time, if they don't wash their hands, there is little likelihood that anyone will know. However, a sign to wash their hands might remind them that it is required of them, and they might determine that being an extra 30 seconds late is something that they should do.

While such antecedents are not typically implemented from such a scientific perspective, they serve to interrupt the Forgetting Curve (the rate at which people forget information over time that is not reinforced or otherwise put into practice). Anything that can get people to behave in a desired way can be a trigger.

Antecedents that serve as reinforcements can appear as frequently as possible. The more pervasive they are, the more likely they will be observed. The purpose is in theory to reinforce active antecedents that were previously provided to the target audience. They likewise serve to interrupt the Forgetting Curve by triggering a reminder of the intended behaviors.

ADDRESSING BACKGROUND NOISE

An important consideration for antecedents, and especially passive antecedents, is that you don't want your antecedent to essentially become background noise. For example, consider that if I ask a person to describe the pictures in a given room of their home, they might not be able to remember them. Similarly, if a person sees a poster on a daily basis, they stop noticing it. They forget it is there, and the poster becomes useless.

Similarly, you need to consider that even if you change a poster and the poster looks stylistically the same as the previous poster, few people will notice the change in the messaging. Unfortunately, we see many awareness programs that try to have a common look and feel across all of their materials. We have found that this is ineffective in engaging people with antecedents. We recommend that you try to make each antecedent as noticeable as possible.

Sometimes, there is an organizational requirement to use a specific format for all materials distributed within the organization. While we try to get exceptions for our materials, there are some realities that have to be accepted. Whatever your circumstances, the threat of your antecedents becoming background noise should be addressed proactively.

Active antecedents interrupt a person's typical functions and provide information intending to influence the person to take a specific action. To better understand the difference between passive and active antecedents, consider a typical web page that contains ads. An ad on the side of the page is a passive antecedent that attempts to influence you to buy a product, which you may or may not do. On the other hand, if an image or video covers the entire web page and you have to click to close it, you are being forced to take an action by that active antecedent.

Clearly, the previous example of active antecedents requires minimal engagement. Simulated phishing messages are another example of an active antecedent. (Note that we are talking about simulated phishing messages for training, not general phishing messages.) If a person does not interact with the message, there is no consequence provided. In that sense, the antecedent might seem passive. However, if the person clicks on the message or takes some other action related to it, they are provided with training. It is important to note that the training can be considered a consequence. In other words, as a result of the behavior of clicking on the antecedent message, the resulting consequence is user training.

Other active antecedents include formal training, meetings, presentations, or any other activity where a person has to take time away from other functions to receive such information. Different types of antecedents have different levels of effectiveness. Those levels of effectiveness vary by the personality types of the receivers, the quality of antecedent, the time of day, management attitude to the antecedents, and countless other factors.

Remember that any time you are taking people away from their other responsibilities, you are costing the organization valuable resources. While passive antecedents take no time away from other responsibilities, active antecedents should provide a clear return on investment (ROI) for the time spent to engage with them.

The Importance of Motivation

Generally, an antecedent can potentially convey three aspects of the problem: its nature, its solution, and why the user should implement the solution. The last one essentially provides people with the motivation to behave as defined, and it is the most important of the three.

For example, consider how those three aspects apply to training that instructs people on how to properly maintain equipment. The problem is that equipment can break down, the solution is that proper maintenance to prevent equipment breakdowns, and the reason to implement the solution is to avoid injury and death. The potential for death is clearly motivating and is likely going to get people to pay more attention to performing proper maintenance.

In theory, you can also state that properly maintained equipment can save the organization money. Compared to death, that is less motivating. Also, a well-meaning employee may consider that maintenance is required too frequently and costs the company more money than it saves. When weighing this concern in their compliance budget, the employee might decide that although they are expected to perform the maintenance, it is not worth the short-term loss in productivity. As you can see, there can be potentially unintended interpretations of any antecedent.

Antecedents can contain the perception of negative or positive consequences associated with the desired behavior. While many awareness practitioners are hesitant to talk about anything negative, it is important to realize that people will do exponentially more to avoid a negative consequence than to achieve a positive consequence. Either way, remember that motivation is the most important characteristic of antecedents, and you need to consider promoting all types of potential consequences.

Behaviors

Obviously, our goal of applying the concepts of behavioral science is to have the users behave in the desired way. For our purposes, we focus on user behaviors that potentially lead to UIL. The reality is that almost any behavior can initiate a loss, and getting users to behave in specific ways can sometimes be difficult to achieve.

From a practical perspective, when you want to mitigate UIL, you should begin by focusing on a few key behaviors that will have the most impact. Those behaviors should be specific, reasonable for an individual to enact, and measurable.

For example, one of the most daunting challenges in mitigating UIL has been that users click on phishing messages. At first glance, specifying the desired behavior seems easy and reasonable: users should not click on phishing messages. However, to perform this behavior, users must first recognize that a message actually is, in fact, a phishing message. Being able to discern a regular message from a phishing message is essentially the root behavior required to not click on the phishing message. Learning how to efficiently and effectively make this distinction can be hard. As the Verizon's Data Breach Investigation Report states, 4 percent of people will click on a given phishing message on average. This 4 percent of the population has already been resistant to your best efforts. Consistently changing their behavior requires a conscious choice of how you spend your efforts; either you can continue to invest in attempts to change their behavior, you can allocate more resources to other behaviors, or you can try to do both. For the existing behavior, you can consider changing antecedents such as training and consequences such as punishment. If you want to change where you allocate resources, you have to consider what new behaviors to focus on. Perhaps having users engage in proper reporting of phishing messages is the behavior to focus on. Measuring phishing attacks can be difficult as well.

You can use user reporting. You can try to track phishing schemes with software and IT professionals, but they likewise cannot recognize every phishing attack. You can use simulated phishing attacks and measure those results, but again that won't mirror every type of phishing attack and how people react on different days. It is not a simple task.

When it comes to behavior, you cannot turn people into robots, but you should be able to have reasonable expectations of your users. And there is a range of techniques you can use to influence their behavior. These include awareness, training, technology, consequences, and more. Regardless of how you choose to attempt to influence a behavior, it is critical that you try to measure the behavior to gauge the degree to which your efforts are working.

Obviously, you cannot get everyone to completely behave as you wish. The goal is risk reduction. You want to improve behaviors as much as reasonably possible, but there is no such thing as a perfect countermeasure. Even if you can bring the behaviors to 99.99 percent successful compliance, that still leaves more than enough risk for you to address. You should continue to provide an overall environment that reduces the opportunity for users to behave in ways that create UIL, and mitigate the loss when UIL inevitably occurs.

Consequences

When it comes to mitigating UIL, many risk practitioners fail to adequately consider the value of consequences in influencing user behavior. There is a common misperception that a lack of user awareness causes UIL, so risk practitioners focus on providing antecedents. That might be an outgrowth of the fact that awareness practitioners have a mandate that limits them to providing awareness training. It also could be that the concept of consequences implies blaming the user, and they are reluctant to do that. Either way, while antecedents should be used wherever possible, consequences have a greater potential to create the desired behaviors.

Referring back to Figure 8-1, antecedents impact behavior. Behavior creates consequences. Consequences then impact future behavior. For example, consider a restaurant server warning customers that a plate is hot. Many people see that the server can comfortably hold the plate, so they still instinctively grab it themselves. If they burn their fingers while grabbing the plate, they are more likely to heed future warnings. If they do not get burned, they are less likely to heed future warnings.

In a business setting, organizations tell people that they should not use the same passwords for both their personal accounts and their business accounts. The reality is that many people do use their passwords across multiple accounts. In other words, people behave contrary to the antecedents provided to them. Unfortunately, there is no way for their organizations to actually know what their personal passwords are, so the user perceives no consequence for not complying with the antecedents. At the same time, the user does not have to remember a new password, which they perceive to be a positive consequence. Seeing that the positives outweigh the negatives, the user is more likely to not behave as instructed.

Even if the users are aware of specific cases where attackers compromised personal passwords and reused them to compromise business accounts, as happened with the infamous and devastating attack by North Korea against Sony, it never happened to them, as far as they know. They never personally suffered a negative consequence as a result of the behavior. In such a case, the antecedent of being aware of consequences that others have endured is, by itself, insufficient.

As you can see, consequences are significantly more impactful on influencing behavior than antecedents generally are. According to Steve Jacobs in his book *The Behavior Breakthrough*, studies showed that antecedents had a maximum of 20 percent influence on behaviors, while consequences had upwards of an 80 percent influence on behaviors. Consequences are four times more effective than antecedents such as traditional awareness programs, yet there are comparatively few established consequences-focused efforts to create behavioral change.

THE ANTECEDENT WHO CRIED WOLF

In the popular fable "The Boy Who Cried Wolf," a mischievous boy keeps shouting for villagers to come save him from a wolf that doesn't exist. The villagers eventually get tired of his games, and they ignore him. Then, when a real wolf finally attacks him, the boy calls for help, and no one comes to save him. That same problem can happen with antecedents, behavior, and consequences.

When an antecedent warns of a threat that does not materialize as expected, it gives the user the impression that efforts were wasted, which is a negative consequence. This perception results in the user's behavior not following the antecedent's recommended advice for the matter in question. It also influences other behavior, encouraging the user to ignore other security recommendations as well.

Another concern is that sometimes too much discussion of a threat generates negative behavior. For example, one security awareness company touted that after people completed their training, users were afraid to check their email. That is clearly problematic. The goal of good awareness training is for users to be able to confidently and securely check their email and not be afraid to do so, which would negatively impact their ability to perform their work.

Clearly, it is important that antecedents properly motivate users to implement the recommended solutions. However, that must be achieved in a way that doesn't create fear to perform their job or skepticism of the motivation itself.

Consequences can be positive, negative, or neutral. Positive and neutral consequences are likely to cause a user to continue the causal behavior. On the other hand, negative consequences are likely to cause the user to change the causal behavior. A person will make more effort to avoid a negative consequence than to gain a positive consequence. While we do not advocate designing a program solely around creating negative consequences, negative consequences are significantly more powerful for creating behavioral change than any other means and should be included in your overall behavioral science approach.

It is also important to consider that there can be positive, neutral, or negative consequences for exhibiting both desired and undesired behaviors. For example, if you want your workers to maintain their equipment properly, you might perform inspections and grade the equipment as being well-maintained, adequately maintained, or poorly maintained. You can reward people for well-maintained equipment, take no action on adequately maintained equipment, and punish workers for poorly maintained equipment. That creates a mix of positive, neutral, and negative consequences.

By contrast, some organizations simply expect that equipment is properly maintained, resulting in limited incentive for workers to spend the extra time to ensure proper equipment maintenance. Typically, though, these organizations measure the workers' productivity regarding other responsibilities. Consequently, there are the negative consequences related to decreased productivity and no consequences for poorly maintained equipment. So, workers who are focused on their productivity receive positive consequences for not properly maintaining the equipment and a negative consequence for doing so. It is obvious where the workers will, therefore, allocate their energy.

As you can see, there are frequently conflicts where the desired behaviors can generate positive and negative consequences. In such cases, the compliance budget concept kicks in, and users will likely take the action that has the more immediate impact. All too frequently, that action is not the behavior you are attempting to create. This seems especially true when there are short-term considerations, such as productivity, while UIL is not immediately realized and behavioral programs do not have an obvious return on investment.

It is, therefore, important to consider the consequences for the behavior that you are trying to change. People have a reason for engaging in the current behavior, and simply telling them to change their behavior is not going to work. You need to understand the consequences for the behaviors that you are trying to change so you can determine what you are up against and how to improve the mix of consequences to replace the current behaviors with the desired ones.

On a positive note, one organization that we worked with wanted people to report all safety violations, including those they were responsible for, regardless of whether there was an injury. Consider how counterintuitive this is. However, for the company to best mitigate injuries, they had to have data about all potential injuries, including "near misses." To do this, they implemented a reward system that rewarded all reports of safety incidents. They also implemented penalties for not reporting incidents. Reports of safety violations went up, and all were happy with the results.

It is clearly preferable to implement positive consequences for people exhibiting the desired behaviors. However, you need to acknowledge and implement both positive and negative consequences wherever they are appropriate and effective.

Gamification

Gamification, when implemented as intended as a solution to business problems, and not as a buzzword, is the implementation of a system of rewards. To implement gamification, you need to determine what the desired behaviors are and then how you can measure and track those behaviors. You then determine the appropriate rewards (positive consequences) for the behaviors. Such an implementation is not easy.

Frequent flier programs are an implementation of gamification. Specifically, the airlines target customer loyalty and other profitable ventures, such as branded credit cards, as behaviors to reward. We were once on an airplane where the pilot came out to the first-class section and joked that the top-tier clients in first class were mostly Diamond status fliers who represented .5 percent of overall passengers but generated 25 percent of the airline's profits and 75 percent of the complaints. A top-tier flier minimally has to spend $15,000 per year, and the rewards have to entice that customer to stay loyal to the airline. Airlines constantly calculate how to reward fliers to balance out the passenger's cost of changing to another preferred airline versus the rewards that the airline can offer. These rewards include upgrades, cash certificates, gifts, companion tickets, entrance to airport clubs, and so on.

The example of the company previously mentioned that rewarded people for reporting safety violations is an excellent example of a gamification program.

To implement gamification yourself, you need to determine a simple and finite set of behaviors to reward. You then need to make your users aware of those behaviors and begin tracking those behaviors.

There is a more thorough discussion later in the book, but for now it is important to understand that a good gamification program can implement a set of positive consequences that should be strongly effective in achieving the desired behaviors.

Analyzing Consequences

By analyzing what makes an effective consequence, you can best design your UIL mitigation program, at least specifically where it involves the initiation of the actual loss.

Well-meaning people choose consequences that are counterproductive or don't motivate or otherwise work. For example, consultants once created a reward program for productivity that involved free food. However, the organization had a staff that was primarily remote, so offering a free on-site lunch was meaningless to people who never came into the office. Another organization wanted to incentivize employee retention, so they offered bonuses based on longevity. However, the incentives were paid on the employees' anniversaries as they occurred, with the reality being that employees could achieve a better financial gain by taking higher-paid jobs with other organizations.

The average person is constantly bombarded with personal and business consequences. The question then becomes how you can best determine the consequences that will best balance the desired impact with its side effects.

E-TIP Overview   E-TIP is a reliably effective consequence analysis methodology. E-TIP stands for Effect-Timing, Importance, Probability.

- **Effect** is simply whether a consequence will positively or negatively motivate a behavior. Ideally, you can determine the extent of the motivation.
- **Timing** is whether a consequence will be immediate or delayed. Immediate or delayed can be a relative time depending upon the perceived importance of a reward, among other factors. For example, going through the process of authenticating people whom you release information to can be time-consuming, and over the course of a normal workday, you will not be dealing with a criminal. Authenticating the recipient takes time, and you may not know for weeks, if ever, that on one occasion you released information to an unauthorized person. Consequences that are immediate have more impact than those that are delayed.
- **Importance** specifically refers to how important the consequence is to the targeted users. Importance can take on any characteristic. It could equate to fear of punishment or something similar. It could be financial. It could be esteem. Importance can be cultural as well. For example, in many Asian cultures, the opportunity to be acknowledged by a senior executive can be more important than money. In comparison, American workers almost always prefer the money. However, there are some exceptions in American organizations where the CEO is highly revered. For example, at one investment bank where we were designing an awareness program, the CEO was very well-respected. We implemented a gamification program where the reward was a round of golf with the CEO. We had great participation for the program.
- **Probability** is the likelihood of experiencing the consequence. Users' minds are more likely to assign a relative probability than a mathematical probability. It might be a simple Boolean probability of yes or no. For example, wearing seatbelts is a desired behavior for drivers. Awareness efforts, telling drivers how seatbelts can save their lives, were unsuccessful. The problem was

that awareness efforts did not generate any consequences, and the probability of a consequence, such as injury or death in a car, was small. As the fear of death was not shown to increase the behavior of wearing seatbelts, fines were implemented, as getting pulled over by police is more likely than a deadly car accident. This increase in the probability of a consequence worked.

The components of E-TIP work together in different configurations for almost any scenario. Let's look at a couple of examples.

Fundamentally, consequences can encourage or discourage behaviors. That being said, not all consequences have equal impact. Paradoxically, some consequences can even simultaneously discourage and encourage a given behavior. For example, if a person goes to a casino and learns that there is a big prize on a slot machine, that might motivate them to play that slot machine. However, if the person learns that the probability of winning is extremely low and there are no other rewards, they are not likely to play that machine for long, if at all. Now apply E-TIP's concepts of effect, timing, importance, and probability to this. For the player, the importance lies in the thrill of believing that they might win a certain amount of money within a period of time. However, the positive effect of the large prize is outweighed by the negative effect of its low probability and the time and money necessary to potentially achieve it. The discouraging consequence of investing time and money for no reward outweighs the encouraging consequence of a large prize that will likely never materialize. So, the player decides not to play the game at all.

On a more practical matter, if you reward your users for properly maintaining their workspace by sending them a thank-you letter, in general, you will not likely have success in significantly changing behaviors. Workers often tend to perceive the "paper praise" of gold stars and thank-you letters as a cheap ploy of their employers to save money. The workers would understandably rather receive a financial or other meaningful reward. Applying E-TIP's effect, timing, importance, and probability components to this scenario is fairly intuitive. The worker's probability of receiving the reward is high, but its importance and timing are relatively low for them. The effect is that the reward does not encourage the consequence of properly maintained work spaces. On the other hand, the worker now knows they are being scrutinized, which might result in better maintained workspaces. Even so, if the workers feel they are under surveillance and are offered hollow rewards, it will undermine their morale and have a negative effect on productivity, even if the workspaces are better maintained. As you can see, there are unintended effects and consequences in any endeavor.

It is valuable to be able to apply a process, like E-TIP, for your own purposes of determining the consequences that will support you, figuring out how to make the consequences more effective, and being able to explain the logic of the consequences that you want to implement to gain approval.

Applying E-TIP   We previously discussed the need for restaurant workers to wash their hands. There can frequently be incentives for them not to do so, especially given the time constraints and lack of immediate consequences. Consider, however, surgeons who have to wash their hands before an operation.

Surgeons don't just have to do a cursory hand wash but are required to scrub their hands for a period of time, with antiseptics. Not only is the process burdensome from a time and effort perspective, it can also irritate their skin. So, performing the desired behavior has a more significant impact to them, while they also have a great deal of other concerns to ensure a successful surgery. In theory, the only positive consequence of hand washing is avoiding an infection for the patient, which is something that is actually extremely rare.

Now apply E-TIP's effect, timing, importance, and probability components to this scenario and consider the encouraging effects. The only perceived encouraging effect of washing hands is not timely. It may be important, but it is not probable.

Conversely, apply E-TIP to look at the discouraging effects. Discouraging effects include the hand irritation, which has an immediate impact. Irritated hands are important to a surgeon, as hands are their most valuable tool. There is a high probability of the irritation. Likewise, washing the hands is time-consuming, while there are other things the surgeon is concerned about. It is an immediate consequence. The loss of time and focus is important. The probability is certain.

You, therefore, need to do something to increase the likelihood of implementing the behavior. Some hospitals resorted to requiring nurses to observe doctors washing their hands and performing other safety protocols. If the surgeon does not follow the procedures, they are not authorized to operate. Therefore, the effect of not washing hands is discouraged, because the impact of the surgery being cancelled is immediate and important. The probability is certain when the nurses are instructed to watch the surgeons wash their hands.

From a cybersecurity perspective, as well as just from a general operational perspective, backups are critical. They are ironically very much like a surgeon washing their hands. Backups only seem to matter when everything goes wrong, and they are time-consuming. This is a case where E-TIP would dictate that there needs to be oversight to ensure that employees back up all critical information that is not on systems that are already backed up, such as their mobile devices.

Whenever you are trying to change behaviors, you need to first understand the consequences of their currently existing behaviors. Remember, these include both the encouraging consequences that lead to the behaviors and the discouraging consequences for why people are not doing the desired behaviors. Why are they driven to do what they do? Why are they driven away from doing what they should be doing?

There are likely several reasons on both sides. If it helps, you can create a table, such as that in Table 8.1, to list the desired behavior along with the consequences in the E-TIP format.

You can develop similar tables for all behaviors that you want to change.

For more information on applying E-TIP, we recommend the book *The Behavior Breakthrough* (Greenleaf Book Group, 2013).

Engineering Behavior vs. Influencing Behavior

By understanding the difference between traditional awareness programs and applying ABS, you can begin to understand why awareness programs have limited impact. Awareness programs are valuable. However, they are not going to create the desired behaviors. At best, they attempt to influence the perception of the consequence of the behavior.

Until a user actually experiences a consequence, that consequence is merely a theoretical concept for them. By applying ABS and analyzing and creating consequences, you can begin to engineer the behaviors you want. Remember this applies to the phase of UIL where the user is actually taking an action via applying technologies to engineer away the ability for the user to initiate the loss.

Table 8.1: E-TIP Table Example

Behavior	Consequence	Effect	Timely	Importance	Probability
Hand washing	Patient infection	Encouraged	Delayed	Important	Not Likely
	Irritated hands	Discouraged	Immediate	Important	Likely
	Time away from other responsibilities	Discouraged	Immediate	Important	Likely

However, the user will inevitably be put into a position where they will exhibit behaviors that can initiate loss. Your goal is to engineer that behavior to the best of your abilities through the use of consequences. What those consequences are and how to create them requires a great deal of analysis and will likely require a significant effort to institutionalize. This is further elaborated in Part IV. For now, though, you should at least be able to start understanding why the users are not doing what you want them to do, even if you think their behavior is against their own interests.

9 Security Culture and Behavior

Culture reflects the shared values, experiences, and norms of a group, which in turn influence and drive the behaviors of that group. Consequently, behavior is sometimes indicative of the underlying culture in a workplace. When you go into your workplace, people behave rigidly, at ease, or somewhere in between. They socialize a great deal, or they don't. They dress formally or casually. It is the typical environment that they walk into every day and know how to behave.

Similarly, people's consistent behavior regarding security practices can reveal things about the security culture. Does everyone wear their badge? Do people keep clean desks? Do people log out of their computers when they leave them unattended? Do people properly maintain and track their equipment? Are they on the lookout for strangers? Will they regularly stop strangers? Will they call security if something is out of the ordinary?

These questions and their answers are revealing. You can observe a culture. You can sense the culture. When someone new enters the culture, they will pick up the habits naturally and attempt to fit in. If they do not fit in, they will generally be corrected or correct themselves so they can fit in better. There may be a few rebels who will not fit in and perhaps might even affect the culture, but the reality is that such people more likely either will decide to leave or will be pushed out.

As author Ira Winkler regularly performs social engineering penetration tests, he says the reason he is good at it is because he can walk into an organization, and within the first 30 seconds, he knows exactly what 95% of the problems likely are. Having been in hundreds of companies, he gets a sense of organizations that have strong security cultures and weak security cultures. If there are relatively weak security cultures, he knows, and you should assume that it will be easy to enter the facilities. Sensitive materials will be left on desks. Unknown visitors will be helped and not challenged. People will give away information with minimal prodding. Computers will be left unlocked.

With strong security cultures, there has to be a more disciplined and cautious approach to performing social engineering penetration tests. Credentials have to be obtained. Multiple people should perform the social engineering test, if for no other reason than to provide legitimacy and act as a lookout.

> **NOTE** We want to specifically acknowledge that there are many more facets to culture than just behaviors. However, for UIL we are primarily concerned about those facets that impact the initiation of loss, and those are driven by the combined behaviors of the culture. When we talk about changing or influencing the culture, we are focusing our discussion on the intent of the book, which is to address UIL. Should you have an interest in a more thorough discussion of the intricacies of culture, we strongly recommend research into the fields of sociology, anthropology, and similar subjects.

Of course, the outliers may change the culture, but that takes a long period of time. It is an uphill battle. Even when the person trying to change the culture is the management, it is extremely difficult and requires a massive effort to do so.

Culture is an extremely powerful force. The rest of this chapter describes culture and behavior further, but one of the main lessons you should get out of this is that culture is the best awareness program and simultaneously your greatest countermeasure and your greatest vulnerability.

BEHAVIORAL MOTIVATION

While we discuss culture as a motivation of behavior, we do not address the motivation of the culture. For the most part, it is not relevant to this discussion. For example, while it is true that a new person will wear the badge if everyone wears a badge, you might want to consider why that is happening.

For example, if the company is an airline, there are legal requirements to wear a badge at airports, and that requirement typically is embedded throughout the entire company. People may be detained and arrested for not wearing a badge. A company might have had a serious incident, where for example, an outsider entered a facility to assault an ex-spouse. A company might have spot checks and punish people who do not wear a badge. We have worked with organizations that have experienced all of these circumstances.

So the behaviors within the different cultures are the same, but the motivation is very different. For our purposes, we care about the end behaviors themselves. While we hope none of our readers have to deal with the aftermath of a workplace violence incident, we want you to understand the motivation behind your culture so that you can determine how to best implement loss prevention improvements.

In the future, you may have to work toward creating a motivation, such as obtaining management support to provide a proverbial carrot or stick.

ABCs of Culture

Much as with awareness, there is an ABC acronym for culture. Awareness creates Behaviors. Consistent behaviors practiced within an organization are the Culture. Most important, the Culture is itself Awareness, and it also reinforces Behavior.

Figure 9.1 depicts this relationship.

Figure 9.1 The ABCs of culture

Culture is essentially a consequence. This is how it reinforces proper behavior. When author Ira Winkler worked at the NSA, at one time, he worked shift work and would work late shifts. On one occasion, he took off his badge to work on something as it was dangling and would get caught in things. Ira then left the office, forgetting to put his badge back on, to go to the restroom. He ran into a security guard doing rounds in the hallway, who confronted him about not wearing a badge. The guard escorted him back to his office and waited by the door as Ira went to retrieve his badge. However, the badge was nowhere to be found.

One of Ira's co-workers then said, "Are you looking for something, Ira?" implying that he took the badge. Ira started yelling at him, as the guard then said, "Is there a problem?" The co-worker finally gave Ira the badge, and he showed it to the guard. Ira says he never forgot his badge again.

Clearly, there was a culture that reinforced the wearing of a badge. There was no need to watch videos regularly about wearing a badge. If someone was seen not wearing a badge, they were confronted by guards or other workers. If someone forgot their badge while inside the facilities, their co-workers would taunt them about it. You could not enter the building without wearing a badge. You did not need to watch an awareness video about the importance of wearing badges to know you needed to wear a badge.

At the same time, consider that if nobody wore a badge and did not remind others to wear a badge, videos would be useless to get people to wear a badge. Culture creates consequences that are more impactful than the best awareness videos, or any awareness effort.

Culture can be an awareness tool in that it provides a live demonstration as to how to behave. Culture is also a consequence in that culture corrects behaviors when they do not conform to the norms of the culture. This is a powerful weapon that can be your greatest resource or your worst enemy.

The fact is that people generally look to others around them to see how they should behave. There was a classic *Candid Camera* segment from the 1960s where a person got on an elevator as they normally would, and then actors got on the same elevator and faced backward. The people caught in the segment all eventually turned around to face backward, despite the cultural norm of facing forward.

At this point, it is important to consider the Peter Drucker quote, "Culture eats strategy for breakfast." In the original context, the implication is that deeply embedded norms, practices, beliefs, and so on, will hamper attempts to implement new efforts that require creating change. Extrapolating this to UIL, a UIL mitigation strategy that expects users to change their behavior solely because they are told to do so, despite the behavioral norm providing an ongoing example otherwise, is doomed to failure.

Consider that no matter how much you tell your employees to secure equipment at the end of the day, for example, if nobody actually does it, it is extremely unlikely that watching a three-minute video is going to change that. Even if you tell people it is critical that they do it, without some form of enforcement and consistent practice among co-workers, it will not become a lasting habit.

So for example, if you tell a user to wear their badge and they are initially inclined to listen, that user is not likely to continue to wear the badge if they are the only people doing so. After all, wearing a badge is not typically convenient and can be actually annoying.

As we already insinuated, clearly you need to create an environment around user behavior that mitigates the loss initiated by the behavior. However, improving behaviors is still worth pursuing to reduce risk and loss. To do that, it is infinitely more effective to change the culture than to improve awareness. It is, of course, much more difficult to do so, but it is worth the effort.

Types of Cultures

When you consider what cultures are, you have to look at them beyond a monolith of an organization. There are likely cultures within cultures within cultures within cultures. In Chapter 3, we discussed how the *USS Fitzgerald* and *USS McCain* crashed into other ships and formal investigations determined that there was a breakdown of leadership and communications within the ships themselves and the entire U.S. Navy 7th Fleet. When there is a criticism of leadership, there is a criticism of the overall culture.

In this case, there is a recognition that there are several cultures within a single culture. In general, you can argue that the United States has a culture. However, people in the U.S. military are perceived to have more discipline and have certain characteristics. Within the military, the different services, such as the Navy, Army, Air Force, and Marine Corps, each have their own cultures. Within the Navy, there are different divisions, known as *fleets*. Each fleet has its own chain of command, with each having its own culture. Then each ship within a fleet has its own culture. Then each department within the ship would have a culture of its own. For example, on an aircraft carrier, pilots would have a different culture than mechanics, because of the different functions, training, job expectations, working environments, etc.

We do not mean to imply that one group or culture is better than another, but they are still likely to be different. However, there are expected to be some common elements between the different cultures. For example, throughout the military, you expect discipline. You expect people to be competent and professional at performing their function. As the *USS Fitzgerald* and *USS McCain* incidents prove, a lack of discipline and professionalism resulted from an overall poor culture and led to disaster.

Culture can fail at any level. However, it is ultimately dependent upon the organization's leadership to allow a cultural failing to exist. What we mean by a "cultural failing" is consistent behaviors that are detrimental to the organization.

Likewise, a strong security culture, with consistently strong behaviors by its members, results in fewer losses. You do not hear about well-run ships crashing into other vessels. This is not to say that a well-run ship will never experience a negative event, but major events happen significantly less frequently in strong cultures.

NOTE Obviously, there are many types of cultures, and many aspects to them. For example, some airlines, hotels, and other organizations make a point of providing excellent customer service. From a perspective of product branding and driving sales, that is part of a strong culture. Conversely, because it helps social engineering attacks succeed more easily, it also provides for a potentially weaker security culture.

In the movie *Heartbreak Ridge*, Clint Eastwood played a U.S. Marine Corps master sergeant who is assigned to lead an undisciplined Reconnaissance platoon. The movie is about Eastwood's character instilling a sense of discipline that takes his unit back to elite readiness. It was clear that a lot of small, undisciplined acts, such as not wearing proper military dress, was a sign of lack of military readiness.

Heartbreak Ridge was released in 1986, but the message was extremely relevant in 2019. The commanding general of the U.S. 2nd Marine Division sent out a letter to his subordinates regarding a lack of overall discipline. Perhaps the triggering event was when the commandant of the Marine Corps visited the mess hall and ran into a Marine who went to breakfast in his pajamas. The letter noted how trash was strewn about, there were overgrown weeds in gardens, and many Marines did not display the proper dress code, among other issues. The implications for the Marines are that if basic discipline is sloppy, then fighting skills are sloppy, and equipment is poorly maintained and not combat ready. A lack of personal discipline in general implies that there will be a lack of discipline on the battlefield. The general wanted a complete reset on his division's overall discipline.

The implication is that strong leadership influence in culture creates an environment that does not tolerate poor behaviors on a consistent basis. They create a culture where strong behaviors are the norm, and weak behaviors are discouraged and potentially penalized. These are the consequences, and these consequences are handed out formally, or informally, as in the case of Ira's coworker, who hid his badge.

It is the same in nonmilitary settings. Consider that Disneyland gets approximately 44,000 visitors a day, yet the grounds are consistently immaculate. There are also approximately 23,000 employees for the park, who behave consistently from one day to another. This includes the proper wearing of uniforms and other behaviors to ensure consistent customer service. While problems will always arise, Disneyland has provided a consistent guest experience for more than 60 years.

Likewise, consider the quality of service and experience that you expect to get in different businesses. Walmart and Tiffany & Company both sell engagement rings. Walmart sells many more engagement rings than Tiffany & Company. However, you expect a very different experience when you buy from Tiffany & Company than you do from Walmart. You expect a much more knowledgeable staff and higher-end experience when you purchase from Tiffany & Company. You expect a more comfortable and elaborate in-store experience. You expect the staff to dress more formally. You expect more personalized treatment. The culture creates those expectations. If for any reason the culture at Tiffany & Company begins to decline, they can no longer justify premium prices, and their entire business model will fail.

Perceived culture is significant. Clearly, Walmart serves an important role for a wider range of people. At any point in time, should the Tiffany & Company culture falter, they are losing what justifies the premium pricing they take in and will likely lose their clientele to other upscale jewelry brands.

In his book *The Tipping Point*, Malcolm Gladwell discusses when things begin to either improve or go downhill. It is clearly easier for things to begin to go downhill than to improve. For example, Gladwell maintains that what it takes for a neighborhood to begin to go downhill is for two broken windows to go unrepaired.

The thought is that in a "good" neighborhood, a broken window is perceived to be an embarrassment, as it is below the standard of the house and the neighborhood as a whole. If one neighbor does not fix a broken window, for whatever reason, it remains an aberration. When two neighbors allow broken windows to remain, it means other neighbors can lower their own standards. Perhaps it is due to not being able to afford repairs readily, but either way, it means that other neighbors can choose to maintain their properties at a lower standard.

While many people may not appreciate the work of community associations and municipal inspectors, their work to maintain standards, when reasonably enforced, are incredibly valuable in maintaining the quality of the neighborhood.

Subcultures

Even within supposedly homogenous organizations, like the military, there are unique subcultures. Again, the Marines have a different culture than the Air Force. There are a variety of reasons for this. However, the important aspect to understand is that there is a difference, and that difference needs to be accounted for in the expectations, management, ways to manage change, etc.

While organizations generally want to perceive themselves as a cultural monolith, the reality is that within any organization of more than trivial size, there are distinct subcultures. This is especially true regarding UIL.

Each subculture has its own communications styles and business drivers. The business drivers determine the types of UIL you may be dealing with. Consider, for example, that a retail chain, such as Walmart, has a variety of major subcultures. The retail stores have employees who operate the registers and maintain the stock. The distribution centers have employees who receive bulk goods and redistribute those goods to stores. The headquarters facilities maintain accounting processes, among other traditional, white-collar functions. The IT organization maintains the computer systems that keep Walmart able to function. This, of course, is in addition to their online sales business.

The workers in each of these subcultures have different access to information, materials, computer systems, etc. Workers in the different subcultures have different abilities to initiate loss. The workers in the distribution centers primarily use handheld computers, and the ability for an individual worker to create a major loss is significantly limited. The workers at headquarters likely use PCs and cell phones, make regular use of emails, and have access to sensitive information. Some have access to financial assets. They can cause much more devastating losses than the distribution center workers. Theoretically, a headquarters worker can initiate millions of dollars of losses, if not significantly more.

Besides the potential scope and types of loss created, the subcultures have very different methods for communications. Distribution center workers have team meetings, break room posters, etc., and cell phone access. Communications is mostly person to person and limited to tactical responsibilities. Office workers have real-time communications and communicate electronically on systems with critical operational data.

If you are going to mitigate UIL, you need to accept that there are subcultures and that each subculture requires a different effort to mitigate the UIL, in both types of potential losses and methods to communicate relevant information.

Depending upon your organization, there might be more than just business units to consider when evaluating potential UIL. Demographics may be as important as job functions. While it is normally associated with younger workers, social media exposure is a function of people with different usage levels. Workers have posed a variety of risks due to social media–related issues. In some cases, sensitive company information has been posted on social media. In extreme cases, leaders have compromised sensitive information. In one infamous case, Netflix CEO Reed Hastings posted usage information on his Facebook account, which was a potential SEC violation at the time. In a more critical compromise, U.S. President Donald Trump posted highly sensitive satellite imagery on his Twitter account, exposing U.S. intelligence capability.

You need to understand that any group with unique communications styles and potential to initiate loss should be considered a unique subculture that might require a unique UIL mitigation program.

What Is Your Culture?

Before moving on, you need to consider your own culture. It is easy to talk about the Marine Corps and Disneyland, but odds are good that your organization does not have such a defined culture that expects specific behaviors. That being said, you do have a culture.

Culture involves many aspects of behavior throughout an organization. However, with regard to considering UIL, you need to focus on behaviors that increase or reduce potential loss. Admittedly, there are indicators that might not seem obvious but are very telling. For example, a Marine who is negligent in the proper shave and haircut is likely to be negligent in properly maintaining their rifle or fitness. Both clearly impact military readiness. Undisciplined acts in unrelated behaviors are likely to indicate a lack of discipline in behaviors related to UIL in any field.

While there are a different set of questions that each organization should be asking, and a lot of them are dependent upon the industry that they are in, the following is a list of general questions to at least get an idea as to whether you have a strong or weak culture. This will impact how you choose to move forward, should you decide you want to actively improve your security culture.

- How do people communicate?
- Do you have a culture where strong behaviors are expected?
- Are those behaviors well defined?
- Do people practice what is expected of them?
- Is there a general discipline when following company guidelines?
- Are policies generally enforced?
- Do employees enforce policies on other employees?
- Is loss prevention and mitigation considered a priority?
- How have past efforts to change culture succeeded?
- Do you believe that you have a weak or a strong loss prevention culture

The last question is usually the most important. If you are honest with yourself, you know whether your losses are a result of isolated incidents or symptomatic of the culture as a whole.

When we spoke about safety principles, we likened users who initiate loss to canaries in the coal mine. They are part of your system, and indicators of where your organization has failed to mitigate loss. That being said, a failure to mitigate an individual loss is not an indicator of weak loss prevention or security culture.

There will always be a loss in one form or another. The question is whether those losses are the exception or the rule. If the losses are the exception, they are rare, and losses are limited. More important, every loss is analyzed as a symptom of a problem, and a risk-based decision as to whether additional countermeasures should be made. In other words, there should be a specific and purposeful process for accepting, avoiding, mitigating, or transferring a risk. In a weak culture, losses are accepted as a given, and the organization suffers the proverbial death by 1,000 cuts.

Again, using safety programs as an example, some companies require even near misses to be reported. They go as far as rewarding people for reporting near misses. They understand that injuries are bound to occur, and they would rather consider the near misses as the canaries, and reward the fact that every report has the chance to make the organization safer, even if a person reports themselves. While this may seem counterintuitive, a strong safety program recognizes that when anyone potentially has the opportunity to injure themselves, others likewise have the same opportunity to injure themselves. Even in the case of outright stupidity, the company would rather reward a proactive reporting of the potential incident, as they can analyze the incident and potentially prevent it from happening in the future where the injury was not avoided.

However, it is important to consider that just because an organization is strong in one element of loss prevention, it does not mean that they will be strong in all loss prevention elements. For example, it is unfortunately common for an organization to have a strong traditional safety program and a weak cybersecurity program. We will talk about this more in Part IV, but for now you should at least know that if there are other strong loss prevention efforts, it does make it significantly easier to improve weaker elements of loss prevention.

Improving Culture

As culture can be your greatest tool or your worst enemy, it is important to consider how to change culture. Again, the consequences created by the culture can promote either good *or* bad behaviors. To that end, the goal is to improve the culture, or, more specifically, to improve the consistency of good behaviors.

Clearly, changing the culture is not an easy thing to do. It is actually one of the, if not the, hardest aspects of loss mitigation, which is why it is rarely addressed. It is easy to say that you want to implement an awareness program. While many professionals will say that they intend to change culture through awareness, it rarely happens and is naïve at best. Improving culture requires embedding changes within the fabric of the organization.

Determining a Finite Set of Behaviors to Improve

When people hear that you want to change culture, they assume that the entire organization has to change. While it may seem that way from a functional perspective, the reality is that as your goal is to reduce UIL, at least in the context of this book, you can at least begin by focusing on a finite set of behaviors. If you can improve the consistency of key behaviors, you can begin to achieve measurable improvements.

If you determine the key behaviors correctly, you should begin to see that most, if not all, related behaviors improve. It is a behavioral version of the phrase "A high tide raises all boats."

For example, from a physical security perspective, if you can get people to secure their desks, turn off their computers, and wear their badges, it should also increase the likelihood that they will report strangers, close doors behind them to prevent tailgating, and better secure mobile devices. After all, they are making it a habit of physically protection in general. Physical security becomes a default for many behaviors, and the carryover to other behaviors will come naturally.

For cybersecurity-related behaviors, if you can get people to secure their passwords, question email messages, etc., they will be more likely to question social engineering attacks coming over the telephone or in person. Likewise, this improvement in behavior should extend to their personal life.

Using the example we cite earlier, where a company wants to improve the safety culture by having people report, and even self-report, potential safety violations, the act of reporting violations implies that they must first know what behaviors are safety violations. The fact that they are rewarded for safety violations gives employees incentives to learn more about what is a violation. This makes it more likely that they will behave safely, given that they are aware of safe behaviors.

To that end, we recommend that you determine the losses that you are trying to mitigate and determine the behaviors you believe would likely improve the culture as a whole. Again, you need to ask yourself a series of questions that will help you determine the key behaviors that you can likely improve that would also have the highest likelihood of improving the overall culture. While there are countless questions that you can ask to determine the behaviors you choose to focus on, the following list represents sample questions that are a starting point:

- Which behaviors are fundamental to the desired behavioral improvements?
- Which behaviors are practical to observe?
- Which behaviors are practical to measure?
- Which behaviors can you readily track?
- Which behaviors can you reward?
- Which behaviors are the easiest to promote?
- Which are the three to five behaviors you believe best represent the improvement you are trying to create?
- Will your organization support the efforts required to improve the behaviors?

You are trying to determine actual behaviors that can improve the organization. As important, you are trying to determine behaviors that are practical to improve. Applying the behavioral science principles from Chapter 8, it can be difficult to change the E-TIP dynamic for certain behaviors. For example, some desired behaviors may be too burdensome to focus on as you have to change the overall perception of the importance of the behavior.

As implied by the list, you want to determine three to five behaviors that you believe you can improve consistently across the organization. Generally, you want to choose three behaviors to start. However, you want to have more than three to initially consider.

Once you have those three behaviors identified, you can then create a plan to implement the desired behavior changes.

Behavioral Change Strategies

When you identify the strategies you need to change, you need to create the appropriate plans that at least have a chance of succeeding. We specifically say "chance of succeeding," as we acknowledge that consistently changing a behavior, let alone a culture as a whole, is difficult. There are many variables in place that you can never predict. Support for your efforts can change. People may be more resistant to change than you anticipate. There might be factors you never considered. You might not have the right resources to begin with.

However, the appropriate strategy can at least make success more likely. A good portion of success depends upon the organization's willingness to change. There are countless change strategies that you can choose from, depending on the difficulty of the task and the level of resistance that you expect to have. Two common popular strategies are traditional project management and change management. There are many helpful books, websites, and other resources that explore these strategies in great depth, but the following sections will give a brief introduction to them.

WILL BEHAVIORAL CHANGE STICK?

A behavior can be driven by a variety of motivations, and the motivations are specific to the culture. Throughout this chapter, we imply that if you can make consistent behavioral improvements, you can change the culture. There are potential limits to this statement.

For example, if you change behavior by implementing penalties for bad behaviors, in other words, increasing specific motivation, you can change the behaviors and, by our definition, the UIL culture. However, this does not mean the overall culture has changed, and the behavioral improvement may only be temporary. If you stop enforcing the penalties, it is possible that behavioral improvement will end.

Consider the example of the COVID-19 pandemic. Many people adopted strong personal safety behaviors, such as frequent and thorough handwashing, social distancing, and so on. Clearly, frequent and thorough handwashing has strong benefits for a variety of reasons beyond preventing COVID-19 transmission and infection. However, over time, some people became less motivated to continue some of their behaviors, such as social distancing. Even so, some people probably improved their overall handwashing behaviors for years or even the rest of their lives.

While we advocate you use the tools available, be aware that some of those tools provide primarily short-term motivation. When those motivations are removed, you are hoping that the habits they introduced became engrained within the overall culture, and the temporary motivation is ideally a moot point. Obviously, you need to follow up and monitor to determine to what extent this may or may not be the case.

Traditional Project Management

Traditional project management is essentially a rollout of desired behaviors. You create a plan where you tell people what you want them to do, provide the information on how to do it, and track progress. You track adherence to the behavioral change and make adjustments accordingly.

The critical issue is that this approach assumes that people want to change and welcome the change. The strategy essentially assumes that people will adhere to guidance provided to them. There are many ways to implement a traditional project management strategy.

You can inspire people, and their enthusiasm will get them to both adhere to the guidance and encourage others to likewise change their behaviors. You can be more straightforward and then provide the guidance and the reason for the desired change and assume that people will make the appropriate decisions and follow your guidance, because they understand how important it is. Similarly, you can tell them that something is simply an expected part of their job, and therefore they will do it. Along the same vein, you can tell people that management says they have to do it, and therefore they will do it. Finally, you can implement training and expect that people will implement the behaviors specified in the training.

While there is some overlap between the strategies, they all fundamentally rely upon people being provided with the appropriate information and acting on that information. If the behavior involves replacing an old, outdated system with new systems that everybody wants, yes, people will follow the guidance. On the other hand, if you expect people to change how they actually do their work and they do not see an immediate benefit to changing their behaviors, there is little hope that such a strategy will be successful.

This is how most awareness programs are designed. They essentially provide antecedents and expect people to follow the guidance. The only hope is that the consequence of implementing the desired behaviors actually encourages the behaviors. While traditional awareness programs are not necessarily doomed to fail, they do have to somehow address problems the target audience believes need to be addressed.

Change Management

A change management approach works when you anticipate there will be strong resistance to the change. In a change management strategy, leaders assume there will be resistance and plan accordingly. This involves engaging with users and proactively addressing the concerns.

Simultaneously, you are engaging a bottom-up strategy, where local managers are engaged in the process and are leading the change. Frontline managers must ensure that the desired changes are being implemented and implement the appropriate consequences, either as a reward or as a discouragement for behaviors, as appropriate.

In this process, you are constantly monitoring the metrics and adjusting the program accordingly. As you expect, there will be hesitance to implement the desired changes, and you are constantly looking for successes and failures.

Is Culture Your Ally?

It is admittedly frustrating to us to watch security and other loss prevention experts believe that if you tell people what to do, they will do it, and that if you make it funny or entertaining, people will definitely do what you want them to do. The reality is clearly different.

Even assuming your organization demands that users do the right thing, if the culture does not enforce the right thing, it will not be done. We frequently hear people say that you should encourage the right behaviors and not demand them. Yet at the same time, nobody bemoans a zero tolerance for sexual harassment. Nobody bemoans a zero tolerance policy for not watching pornography at work. Nobody bemoans a zero tolerance policy for unsafe work practices. Yet, when you say you want a zero tolerance policy for violating security practices, such as bringing in USB drives, logging off of computers, or keeping sensitive materials locked up, we hear complaints that you need a gentle hand, and you shouldn't be overbearing because people will rebel.

As we discuss, accounting and HR teams implement rules, without exception, that require employees to follow specific practices, or they do not get paid. The justification is that good practices are required to mitigate losses and implement sound business practices. Yet, when it comes to security and other loss prevention practices, professionals in these disciplines seem to believe that their recommendations are not as critical to the business as accurately tracking payroll, for example. The reality is that they are as critical, if not more critical, as demonstrated by incidents such as WannaCry, which took down major hospital systems and cost businesses billions of dollars.

The reality is that the accounting and HR functions demonstrate that any culture will support loss prevention behaviors that are deemed as not optional. Again, nobody complains that they will not be paid if they do not follow the required time reporting procedures. However, the professionals involved in other loss prevention efforts fail to make the case to the overall organization that this line of thinking likewise applies to their endeavors.

If your organization requires any specific behaviors for employees, they can require other specific behaviors. However, if they are not doing this with regard to mitigating UIL that is under your responsibility, it is a sign that the culture can accept requiring behaviors; you have just not made the case that they should require your UIL mitigation behaviors. You need to make your organization's culture your ally. It can be accomplished. The issue, however, starts with you believing that your areas of loss prevention are as critical to the organization as others.

10 User Metrics

When the costs associated with business loss are clear, reasonably competent organizations find a way to justify the appropriate countermeasures. Because safety failings have clear costs to an organization, there are serious efforts to reduce losses from injuries and death. Unfortunately, the costs of technology and security failings due specifically to users are often not as clear. This is why efforts to mitigate losses due to poor user security awareness and related user actions have been largely trivialized. Unless you can demonstrate how reducing user-initiated loss (UIL) will save the organization money, awareness and related programs will likely remain inadequate in your security and IT programs.

While there are many vectors to measure UIL, here we look at metrics related to awareness. It can sometimes be difficult to separate actions due to a lack of awareness from those due to malicious or accidental reasons. However, for the purposes of examining the overall loss due to user action or inaction, awareness-related metrics suffice.

The Importance of Metrics

Chapter 4 discusses the importance of making strong risk-based decisions where you invest resources wisely. Few organizations truly understand the risk, but more specifically the potential loss, associated with user actions. UIL is a cost of doing business. Recognizing and addressing it is a soft skill that is not really understood by technology professionals. This again is one of the main reasons why there is little coordinated focus on awareness and mitigating UIL.

To gain executive and broader organizational support to comprehensively address UIL, you need to identify metrics that matter to the organization and that demonstrate a clear association with user actions or inactions. To a large extent, most metrics currently used by organizations do not adequately address issues important to the people who are responsible for allocating and approving budgets.

In the safety field, injuries result in increased insurance costs, outages, paid benefits, additional regulatory oversight, and other costs. Beyond organizations caring about their people's health and happiness, when there are injuries or even deaths in their operating environment, the associated costs matter even more to the organizations. Although many of those costs might seem intangible, their costs are the driving reason why there are specific, long-term programs implemented to reduce the injuries and deaths.

Unfortunately, most awareness efforts rely on compliance-related metrics. Although compliance in and of itself is not a bad thing (assuming the compliance standard is useful), if you only need to ensure people receive training to ensure compliance, it doesn't matter what that training is, and you can just find the cheapest training available. However, if you instead want to improve behaviors and reduce losses, you need to justify the additional expense to management.

The justification can take many forms. Clearly, the most logical justification is cost savings. If you can prove there is a return on investment, it is a powerful metric. Sometimes metrics can relate to other issues that are important to the organization. In Chapter 4, we discuss value and cover a variety of values that may be important to an organization. Ideally, you will be able to tie metrics back to whatever value is deemed important to the organization.

In this chapter, we delve into metrics so that you can make a better business case for deserving more resources and the authority and ability to coordinate across different departments.

The Hidden Cost of Awareness

There are financial costs associated with awareness efforts that most technology and security practitioners do not acknowledge or even know to consider. Even more than the cost of the materials necessary for the awareness efforts is the cost of the employees' participation.

Beyond the cost of providing any computer-based training (CBT) and phishing simulations, the development or contracting of collateral materials, the expense of bringing in paid trainers, and so on, there is also the cost of lost productivity when employees spend time taking awareness training. In some unionized organizations, training must be compensated. In some cases, the amount of time an employee is allocated for taking training may be limited by corporate contracts or policies.

For example, in working with an airline, we learned that contracts had specifically limited the amount of training time that could be assigned to flight attendants and pilots. This included training related to operations, safety, equipment, and other critical functions. Adding technology-related training requirements meant that some other training had to be removed.

In some factory environments, there might not be as stringent limitations, but workers often have fixed schedules for performing their specific duties and have little available time for training. Training has to be worked in to existing time slots that are already allocated for group meetings and similar functions. Training is competing with other responsibilities for these highly limited time resources.

Even assuming you are in an environment where time can be more flexibly allocated as required, you must consider that training still diverts employees from doing their actual work. This time can add up. For example, if an employee spends a short 10 minutes per month on awareness training, it equates to 2 hours per year. For every 1,000 employees, that equates to the equivalent of one full-time person per year devoted to awareness training.

Regardless of whether an organization tracks this type of expense, you must be ready to justify it, although you don't necessarily have to highlight it. In environments where time is tracked, you need to proactively address the issue. Where time is not typically tracked for training, you should at least be ready to address this expense. This is where a smart manager, who is not supportive of your efforts, will challenge you. The way you respond is with metrics that justify the cost of the program.

From a compliance budget perspective, many users may feel that their participation, if not a waste of time, conflicts with other more critical responsibilities. Even if you believe the hidden cost of training is acceptable, your users may feel that your efforts to mitigate UIL are themselves creating a loss. This impacts user morale and enthusiasm for your efforts.

Types of Awareness Metrics

To demonstrate that you deserve more consideration and resources from your organization, you need to determine metrics that show true business value. Toward that end, you need to understand the metrics most relevant to measuring the user actions in question. In being involved with awareness efforts for more than 30 years, I've worked with a variety of metrics, and I've divided them into five categories: compliance, engagement, behavioral improvement, tangible return on investment (ROI), and intangible benefits. Some of them clearly demonstrate deserving more resources. Others are easy to collect and demonstrate positive impact to your organization.

As you review these metrics throughout the following sections, you should consider which categories you are already measuring, which ones you should start measuring, and which metrics you could measure better. You should collect metrics from multiple categories.

Compliance Metrics

Compliance metrics involve ensuring that an organization satisfies third-party compliance requirements. Those third-party requirements might take the form of government regulations, industry organization standards, customer requirements, vendor requirements, or others. In some cases, you might only need to conduct and document a self-assessment that can be archived as future proof of compliance. In other cases, independent auditors may come in to verify your compliance. The penalty for failing to meet compliance requirements can vary greatly and can include warnings, fines, demands to cease operations, and, in extreme cases, prison.

For example, employment laws require that you post information regarding employee rights. Compliance just requires the posting of information, which is generally done in physical workplaces and on websites and internal portals. Another example is safety standards, which generally require some type of formal training for employees.

Security standards, such as Payment Card Industry Data Security Standard (PCI DSS) among others, often have vague awareness compliance requirements that in one way or another state that you need to ensure employees' complete awareness training. In this case, ensuring and documenting that everyone in your organization has completed the assigned training is sufficient.

When you are trying to satisfy compliance requirements, it is hard to justify more than the minimum budget required to provide training for your employees. In many cases, auditors state phishing simulations are a best practice and require them as a condition of compliance. In these cases, phishing simulations can be justified as well.

Given the potential penalties for failing to be compliant, it is easy to justify the budget for those efforts. It also justifies the hidden costs associated with the time to take the training. As we move onto the discussion of other forms of metrics, realize that any awareness efforts that cost more than compliance alone may require appropriate metrics to justify them.

Engagement Metrics

After compliance metrics, engagement metrics seem to be the most common category of metrics that we see used by awareness practitioners. These metrics involve the general use and acceptance of the components of awareness training. Engagement metrics can be further broken down into attendance metrics, likability metrics, and knowledge level.

Gamification is a type of activity that is sometimes associated with awareness programs. From a formal, business perspective, *gamification* is a program that rewards desired behaviors. In its true business sense, gamification involves rewarding demonstrated behaviors, frequently including systems that award points, badges, and leaderboards. Airline frequent flier programs are an example of gamification. In a strictly business area, sales compensation plans frequently incorporate gamification to reward sales of particular offerings, to reward achieving sales goals, etc.

The term has become bastardized to also include game-based training. *Gamification*, applied as a game, is a method of education and knowledge transfer.

The different uses of the term involve the use of different types of metrics. Gamification can drive behavioral improvement, but only when it is true gamification. Chapter 15 addresses gamification further.

Attendance Metrics

Attendance metrics are generally straightforward. How many people completed the mandatory training? How many people showed up for a given event? How many people watched an optional video? How many people opened an emailed newsletter?

Attendance metrics can also overlap with compliance metrics, assuming there is a compliance requirement. Frequently, organizations have a learning management system (LMS) that manages and tracks CBT. LMSs create reports that can show compliance and course completion. When you are tracking compliance, you clearly need to ensure that everyone takes the required training.

Attendance metrics also have many uses beyond applying them to compliance metrics. They may include voluntary engagement with supplemental materials, such as identifying whether a user voluntarily takes extra awareness training, attends an event, and so on. If there is an internal knowledge base, such as on a security portal, you can measure optional views of that content.

When you provide optional training, for example through guest speakers or newsletters, the attendance or viewership implies whether you are reaching your intended audience. Engagement metrics should be examined to determine the extent to which communications tools are being consumed. For communications tools that have poor engagement, you want to consider either improving them or dropping them and putting your efforts into other tools.

It is difficult to determine the engagement of some materials. For example, it is hard to know how many people read a poster or monitor a display. You can potentially place QR codes on posters for scanning by people, but it is not a given that people will scan the code. Even if they do, they might still not sufficiently review the information provided. For this reason, you may have to resort to surveys, if you believe it is worth the effort to gather this information.

Keep in mind the hidden cost of awareness training discussed earlier in the chapter and that more engagement could be problematic for an organization.

Likability Metrics

Sometimes people are surveyed about how much they like the content presented. This is typically accomplished through a questionnaire delivered soon after training. Frequently, likability is collected on a Likert scale, which typically asks people to rate how much they liked the materials on a scale of 1 to 5.

This type of metric has varying usefulness. Obviously, you do not want to force unlikeable training on people. Consequently, there has been a recent focus on "funny" videos in industry. While humor is great in the right places, when you are attempting to convey important messages involving safety, security, risk reduction, legal issues, among other topics that have serious consequences, you risk trivializing the issue by adding a comedic tone to it.

Beyond that, the reality is that likability does not equate to effectiveness of training. Even if a user loved a training experience, it does not mean that the training materials were well-designed, that the user adequately understood them, and that the user will retain and use that knowledge in the future.

However, if you have no other metrics to provide, likability is at least something with a positive implication.

Knowledge Level

While an increase in knowledge does not equate to a change in the desired behaviors, it is a good potential metric that the messaging is getting across to your user base. Testing for knowledge level usually involves a short quiz covering the relevant knowledge. Taking into account the forgetting curve (see Chapter 5), these tests should be independent of training quizzes, where you provide the information immediately before the quiz. That becomes a test of short-term memory, as opposed to actual knowledge a person possesses and may act upon.

To determine what to test for, you need to identify the essential knowledge required for an individual to perform their functions properly. You can then develop a quiz that best tests for that knowledge. Multiple choice tests are a popular option because grading and administration is easily automated. One of the downsides to multiple choice tests is that users often choose random options when they don't know the answer so they can get a higher number of correct answers. For purposes of testing true knowledge level, that can reduce the accuracy of the test by 20% to 25% (assuming there are four to five options for each question).

Gamification, when implemented as an instruction game, could potentially be used to test knowledge level. However, this type of gamification may just create an improvement in short-term memory, as opposed to more practically retained in long-term memory, thus driving a change in behavior, which often is the desired result of awareness training.

Behavioral Improvement

One of the main goals of awareness is to create desired behaviors. Behavior is very different than knowledge. Just because people know something doesn't mean they will act upon that knowledge. For example, everyone generally knows that to be fit, they need to eat healthier and exercise more. Given the prevalence of obesity, it is clear that people do not act upon known information.

Metrics that demonstrate changes in actual behaviors are best. Some simulations create scenarios where people have to behave properly. Sometimes the collection of actual behavioral metrics can be difficult and expensive. However, with creativity, it can also be simple and inexpensive.

For example, to test security awareness in practice, a company might hire consultants who make telephone calls to their employees and attempt to get them to divulge their passwords. This can cost a great deal of money and cannot be performed regularly. A different approach for testing security awareness might be to track security-related calls from employees to the help desk. It is relatively easy to track employees who detect and report incidents, and over time you can see whether that behavior is improving.

A key way to measure behavior is to track the number of UIL incidents. Depending upon the environment, this could include the number of injuries, system outages, malware incidents on a network, lost USB drives, data compromises, and other types of UIL.

Phishing simulations have become common for security awareness metrics. The one problem with this metric, and all simulations for that matter, is that such simulations can be manipulated and misleading, because you can show tremendous success by testing with highly complex simulations at first and then easy-to-detect simulations later. Also, people sometimes learn to detect the simulations. Although these metrics are synthetic and subject to manipulation, they can be useful as they are relatively easy to collect.

As gamification, in the true sense of the word, involves rewarding desired behaviors, it can be one of the best methods for tracking behavioral change. To implement gamification, you have to identify the desired behaviors and set up a system that tracks them.

Behavioral metrics are more useful than attendance, likability, and even knowledge-level metrics. They show actual behavioral improvement, and not just inferences of improvement. They are even more effective when combined with the cost savings associated with the behavioral improvements, which is known as tangible ROI.

Tangible ROI

Tangible return on investment (ROI) is the metric by which you provide a specific monetary figure that demonstrates the reduction of loss based upon your efforts. You can use tangible ROI to clearly demonstrate why you deserve more resources to further improve your work.

When you determine the cost savings associated with the behavioral improvement, you can create a specific figure for your tangible ROI metrics. In the safety field, if the average injury costs the organization $30,000 and you demonstrate that your efforts have reduced the number of injuries from 20 to 10, you have saved the organization $300,000. In the security field, if the average data breach costs organizations $1,300,000 and you can demonstrate a reduction in data breaches, you can demonstrate a significant ROI.

It is also important to understand that you can demonstrate value even if losses increase. For example, if operations double in scope, but losses increase by less than 100%, that is a reduction in the expected loss. Given the proliferation of computer-based crime, if your organization's increase in loss is comparatively less than the industry average's increase in loss, that can still be considered a demonstrated reduction of loss.

Some organizations and industries have a better understanding than others of measuring UIL costs. They expended a great deal of effort to obtain the actuary data to understand exactly what potential losses are and where they can arise. However, that wealth of data is admittedly not easy to obtain or determine. If you don't have the data available from your own organization, you can potentially obtain it from others in your industry. Depending upon your field, there may be readily available studies on the costs of incidents.

Intangible Benefits

It is important to acknowledge that not every improvement in awareness will have a clearly tangible benefit. There are cultural aspects to consider as well. For example, in one company where we implemented a security awareness program, we integrated a security library into the corporate knowledge base. It turns out that the materials we provided were the most read content in the entire knowledge base. This was a source of pride within the organization, as while there was no specific reward, the CEO believed it was a critical indication of the security library's contribution to the organization.

Some of the security library's most accessed information included how employees can better use and secure their personal computers and devices. Such information might not be directly related to the employees' everyday work, but it has an indirect impact. It improves morale by showing the employees that the organization cares about them and their families. It can also reduce identity theft among employees, thereby reducing stress and distractions. Improved morale and reduced stress can translate into increased productivity and better employee retention.

Similarly, holding in-person security-awareness events may make employees feel both more comfortable reporting concerns, as well as behaving more conscientiously in general.

Although workplace productivity and retention can be measured, it can sometimes be difficult to attach reliable metrics to some of the factors that affect them. Regardless, these factors should still be considered when highlighting the value of awareness.

NOTE Sometimes it can be difficult to measure intangible benefits. If you can measure them in a limited capacity, that's great. If you can use outside research or studies to bolster your points, that can help as well. Even if you can't provide any hard metrics for seemingly metricless, intangible benefits, it is still important to include intangible benefits in the awareness metrics program and address the impact they can have on the organization.

To understand what might have intangible benefits to the organization, you need to understand the organization's culture. You need to talk to stakeholders and people running other behavioral change programs to determine what they believe is important besides the obvious. In some cases, you might find the intangible benefits are easy to achieve and even more valuable than some tangible benefits to the organization.

Day 0 Metrics

Be sure to collect metrics before you begin any behavioral modification or awareness program. These are known as Day 0 metrics. If you realize you have made the mistake of beginning to implement a program without collecting Day 0 metrics, you should immediately collect them.

You are providing a business function, and you must demonstrate the value you provide to the organization. By collecting Day 0 metrics before you begin a program, you can then compare them to later metrics and determine the impact your program has on the desired behaviors. If you see no improvement as you compare your ongoing metrics to your Day 0 metrics, you can make changes as quickly as possible to improve the situation. Ultimately, you can demonstrate the ROI provided by your efforts.

How frequently you collect metrics to compare to your Day 0 metrics depends upon logistics and resources available to you, as well as the logical times to collect the metrics. For example, say you are addressing the number of malware incidents that occur in your organization. You can go to the appropriate administrators who manage the anti-malware software and ask for the existing statistics before you begin any efforts. These form your Day 0 baseline data. Malware generally gets on a network through phishing, infected USB drives, and unsafe web browsing.

You can complete a round of phishing simulations and collect metrics from the administrators. Then you can provide training on phishing, USB safety, and safe web browsing, and then collect further metrics. Comparing your Day 0 metrics to your metrics collected throughout your ongoing efforts can indicate their effectiveness.

Day 0 metrics can be used in the vast majority of situations. Regardless of your specific needs, Day 0 metrics are critical for measuring your success and failures.

Deserve More

Many organizations need to maintain compliance and, for that reason, will always have an awareness program. While demonstrating compliance has a clear business value, you should strive to do so much more. There is a clear risk associated with user actions, and that risk needs to be quantified so that the appropriate resources can be devoted to mitigating UIL.

Every mature business function collects metrics that show their efforts have a clear ROI. Sales and marketing are supposed to demonstrate higher revenues. Accounting is supposed to demonstrate tighter controls that reduce costs. Operations is supposed to demonstrate improved efficiency to increase profitability. Safety efforts demonstrate decreased injuries. The security department should return less loss associated with security-related incidents.

When we speak to security and technology executives, we highlight this belief:

> *You don't get the budget you need; you get the budget you deserve. You need to deserve more.*

While there may be some benefit to having likable training or demonstrating that people show up, you need to demonstrate that your efforts provide a real benefit to your organization. After all, your job is to reduce loss, not entertain. Only through providing metrics that demonstrate that your efforts are providing the organization with a clear ROI do you demonstrate that you deserve more.

11 The Kill Chain

Attacks of any type call for defense, and an approach to defense can span a multitude of methodologies. Ultimately, protection comes from anything that stops an attack. Unfortunately, in many cases, defense methods are heavily reactive. We posit that a deconstructed review of various methods can provide a proactive approach in fighting adversaries. To begin, we consider how the attacker succeeds in launching an attack.

Hollywood has led many to believe that an ominous person in a hoodie can infiltrate a network in moments to navigate or control it, at will. Despite the Hollywood hacker's glorified moment of triumph with a tap of the Enter key and gratified whisper of "I'm in," an initial successful intrusion is not that easy. Well, for the most part, it's not. Planning an attack campaign takes time in identifying a target, researching vulnerabilities, and determining the best course of action to achieve objectives. It is through these phases that an attack is successfully carried out.

It is important to understand how an attacker's phased approach can expose vulnerabilities that may facilitate intrusions and result in data exfiltration. Knowing an attacker's motives and methods better prepares you to form a security strategy and specifically an approach to defense.

An attacker may bypass any single defense. Be it a physical, technical, or other type of control, limiting a defense approach to a single form will, more often than not, lead to disaster. Therefore, a robust defense strategy is required. The purpose of a layered, defense-in-depth approach is not to stop an attacker, but rather to increase the number of barriers across each phase of an attack that the attacker must navigate during a campaign.

Let's say you have a malicious accountant. Your job is to anticipate or predict what could be done to mitigate any malicious activity from that bad actor. For example, if the malicious accountant attempted to wrongly access money or data and an incident occurred as a result of the malicious accountant, this is considered user-initiated loss (UIL). The accountant took time to identify a target, plan an attack, implement the attack, and successfully complete the desired objective. Each phase of an attack represents a point of protection, failure, and detection, as well as provides an opportunity to stop the attack while in progress. This leads us to consider what could be done, at any phase of the attack, that would mitigate loss.

If planning an attack occurs in phases, it stands to say deconstructing an attack is a valid method for establishing defenses. Enter the kill chain, which is a concept that is used to identify how attacks occur and how to defend against them. In this chapter, we discuss how to deconstruct a kill chain to identify in which phases we could implement countermeasures, predict where a malicious act could occur, and intervene and mitigate the risk of UIL.

The kill chain is particularly useful in deconstructing how attackers function, which also helps you mitigate UIL and reinforces your security strategy. You can also often use it in conjunction with other frameworks, some of which we will explore later in the Chapter 12.

Kill Chain Principles

The kill chain is a military principle defining the structure or phases of an attack and is ultimately used to anticipate and predict an adversary's operations. The initial concept of find, fix, track, target (FFTT) was adopted by the U.S. Army, Navy, Air Force, and Marine Corps and later expanded to F2T2EA adding *E* for "engage" and *A* for "assess."

The Military Kill Chain

The most well-known military kill chain is known as F2T2EA. Let's look at the F2T2EA kill chain phases:

1. **Find:** Identify the target using information gathered via intelligence or reconnaissance.
2. **Fix:** Obtain detailed coordinates of the target through existing data or by acquiring additional data.
3. **Track:** Monitor the target's movement until you can determine whether to engage it.

4. **Target:** Assess the target's value, select appropriate measures, and determine the availability and capacity of resources to engage it.
5. **Engage:** Implement the measures.
6. **Assess:** Review and evaluate the after-effects and effectiveness of the measures and resulting intelligence from the scene.

The end-to-end kill chain method of the F2T2EA kill chain is considered to be an integrated model because any interruption within the cycle has the potential to interrupt the entire process. Collectively, all of these phases are how a malicious actor attacks your organization. They might not consciously label their actions according to these steps, but they generally follow them.

Understanding this can help you apply countermeasures against their efforts. Also, you basically employ a similar model in establishing countermeasures. For the find phase, you identify the types of attacks that might take place, such as phishing or malware. In the fix phase, you determine where such attacks might be directed at your organization. During the track phase, you actually spot attacks as they try to enter your system. In the target phase, you determine the seriousness of the threat. During the engage phase, you employ countermeasures to reduce or neutralize the threat. Finally, during the assess phase, you review the success or failure of your countermeasures and the potential damage done, and you plan for the future.

Various other military processes exist such as decide, detect, deliver, and assess (D3A) and find, fix, finish, exploit, analyze, and disseminate (F3EAD). However, regardless of the process you choose to follow, the concept of deconstructing the process to identify gaps and provide countermeasures remains the same.

The Cyber Kill Chain and Defense in Depth

Lockheed Martin, a large defense contractor, developed the Cyber Kill Chain to help defenders identify and stop cyber attacks. Initially, the Cyber Kill Chain was meant to address malware, ransomware, and advanced persistent threats (APTs), and allow defenders to recognize and predict attacks.

However, the Cyber Kill Chain also applies well to UIL. Attackers consider the human a target choice vector because of the potential for human error at any point within the attack process. Most users' security awareness is poor at best, as are controls on users' actions. Awareness and controls are part of an overarching strategy. The Cyber Kill Chain intrinsically addresses the human factor by recognizing internal threats, social engineering, and APTs.

Let's look at Lockheed Martin's Cyber Kill Chain phases.

1. **Reconnaissance:** The research phase for obtaining detailed information for a successful attack, typically gathered through means of social engineering
2. **Weaponization:** The development phase for combining an exploit or backdoor with a deliverable payload
3. **Delivery:** Delivering a weaponized bundle via email attachment, malicious link, or portable storage device or media
4. **Exploitation:** Exploiting a vulnerability to execute malicious code on a vector's system
5. **Installation:** Infiltrating or installing the intended payload on to the target system or asset
6. **Command and control (C2):** Remote command to control a victim's system or asset
7. **Actions on objectives:** Actively obtain access to accomplish the malicious actor's intended goals

There are several similarities and differences between the military kill chain and the Cyber Kill Chain. See Table 11.1 for a side-by-side comparison of the kill chain phases.

Table 11.1 Kill Chain Comparison

Military Kill Chain	Cyber Kill Chain
Find	Reconnaissance
Fix	Weaponization
Track	Delivery
Target	Exploitation
Engage	Installation
Assess	Command and Control
---	Actions on Objectives

Let's examine some of the similarities and differences between these kill chains.

In the first three phases of the military kill chain, you find, fix, and track the target to help you determine whether you want to attack it. That basically correlates to the reconnaissance phase of the Cyber Kill Chain.

The military kill chain's target phase and the Cyber Kill Chain's weaponize phase both focus on mobilizing resources to make an effective attack.

The military kill chain's engage phase is divided in the Cyber Kill Chain into five separate phases: delivery, exploitation, installation, command and control, and actions on objectives.

The military kill chain's assess phase, where an attacker reviews and analyzes their results, doesn't formally exist within the Cyber Kill Chain. However, it will still implicitly take place once the Cyber Kill Chain is completed.

In addition to the Cyber Kill Chain, Lockheed Martin also recommends implementing layers of control to reinforce defense in depth. At each phase within the chain, protections can be implemented that detect, deny, disrupt, degrade, or deceive an attack in progress.

- **Detect:** Identifying when or how an attack can take place using tools such as analytics, firewalls, or intrusion detection technologies
- **Deny:** Stopping an attack by preventing exfiltration, lateral movement, or unauthorized access
- **Disrupt:** Interrupting or changing the process flow of an attack using tools such as antivirus or anti-malware
- **Degrade:** Minimizing the effectiveness, implementation, or efficiency of an attack in progress
- **Deceive:** Manipulating the attack in progress by intentionally providing misinformation including tools such as deception technology, DNS redirects, or honeypots

Deconstructing the Cyber Kill Chain

As previously discussed, the kill chain is the series of steps from start to finish that hackers perform when conducting a successful attack. Given the kill chain concept defines the structure of an attack, deconstructing the attacker's kill chain can be considered a preemptive or defensive countermeasure. This approach makes for a solid method for understanding where the potential vulnerabilities within any given process might exist. Let's take a closer look at the phases of the Cyber Kill Chain.

In the reconnaissance phase of the Cyber Kill Chain, an attacker is assessing a potential target and gathering information actively and passively utilizing the Internet, publications, social engineering, vendor information, systems access, and more. For example, an attacker calling employees under false pretenses or dumpster diving are all tactics for obtaining information to facilitate an attack. Effective security awareness training, physical penetration testing, and social media policies can be useful countermeasures in mitigating attacks and UIL.

The second phase of the Cyber Kill Chain is weaponization. Weaponization is where the adversary will create or acquire a tool for exploiting a found vulnerability. The tool could be a phishing email, malware, or some other payload. In this sense, the IT and security teams need to know what the current and emerging threats are so they can better employ countermeasures and educate users. Otherwise, the IT and security people are the ones who are indirectly responsible for UIL.

The third phase of the Cyber Kill Chain is delivery. This is where transmission of the attack to the intended target occurs, which could be actively implementing a spear-phishing campaign, virtually providing an infected PDF file, or physically leaving infected USBs in a break room or supply cabinet. User awareness training, email and Internet policies, and tighter controls on user behavior are some possible mitigation strategies.

The fourth phase of the Cyber Kill Chain is exploitation. This phase is when the weapon of choice is detonated. Educated users typically have choices to make that could stop the attack at this point, perhaps by not clicking a link or opening a suspicious file.

Installation is the fifth phase of the Cyber Kill Chain. Installation is when the attacker takes advantage of the exploited vulnerability to enter the system and begin their activities. If you are lucky enough that there is some indication to the user that installation is in progress, even training them to immediately shut down a device, disconnect from the network, and then contact IT can sometimes be helpful.

The sixth phase of the Cyber Kill Chain is Command and control. In this phase, the attacker is able to manage a system or navigate a network to conduct additional operations for accomplishing the mission. At this stage, you still can work on detecting and stopping the intrusion, and you can review all system activity for signs of what might have happened so that you apply lessons learned in the future.

Finally, the last phase of the Cyber Kill Chain is actions on objectives. When this phase occurs, the attacker is able to fulfill the desired outcomes by gaining access, destruction, data exfiltration, financial gain, or a myriad of other objectives. It is important to move into mitigation steps as rapidly and effectively as possible to counter damages, restore capabilities, and prevent future such occurrences.

Keep in mind that the IT department, department managers, the organization's top leaders, and other policy makers can affect your mitigation efforts at every phase of the Cyber Kill Chain. Thus, they themselves are all users who can potentially initiate loss.

Phishing Kill Chain Example

While we examine the Cyber Kill Chain as a framework to use for deconstructing attacks, it's safe to say that each type of attack will have its own kill chain. That attack will likely use phases of the military and cyber kill chains in some configuration that is particular to the nature of the attack. With that in mind, let's review an example of a phishing kill chain.

A phishing attack consists of 10 phases, which means there are potentially 10 opportunities to stop a phishing attack. In reality, nine of these are within your control. Seven of them are technological, and two are user-related. Here are the 10 phases of a phishing attack:

1. Pre-mail server
2. Mail server
3. Client mail application
4. User decisions
5. Client applications warns user
6. User confirms action
7. Client prevents damage
8. Network prevents damage
9. Network detects attack
10. Network mitigates attack

Let's examine these phases a little more closely. As you move through the phases, understand that at each phase, you have the capability to stop the phishing message in its tracks with the right countermeasures in place.

In the pre-mail server phase, Internet infrastructure should prevent some phishing messages, and your perimeter devices can potentially filter some illicit messages. Essentially, the phishing messages have to originate somewhere, and if you can proactively mitigate the botnets or filter out emails from known, malicious servers, you can stop the attacks from reaching your network. Implementing the DMARC protocol, which authenticates email messages across the Internet, can also stop spoofed messages.

Second, the mail server should detect phishing messages and quarantine suspect emails, while neutralizing payloads. Any reports of a phishing message should result in the unopened message being deleted.

The third step is the client mail application. Like the server mail application, it provides another layer of mail and anti-malware filters that can quarantine suspected spam and phishing messages.

In the fourth step, a user has received the phishing message and can review it. If the message is delivered to the user's spam folder, the user can choose to leave the message alone or to open it and act. If the message is found in the user's main inbox, the user can choose to perceive it as a phishing message and report it or open it. Notice that three layers of technology had to fail in order for the phishing message to reach the user.

If the user chooses to open the message, that leads to the fifth step, where the mail application asks for confirmation of the action from the user. Most mail applications will warn the user against taking actions on suspicious files, links, or opening malicious documents.

The sixth step is where the user considers the warnings provided from the mail application and can choose to confirm the action, report the message as spam, or delete the message. Users often become habituated and desensitized to warnings and still choose actions that result in UIL. For this example, let's say the user decides to confirm the action and open the file.

The seventh step resides with the user's computer preventing the attack. Typically a phishing message intends to download malicious software or solicit credentials from the user. Soliciting credentials involves sending the user to a malicious website. To stop such attacks, the computer can be configured to not allow the user to install software. This stops ransomware and other malicious software from compromising the system. Regarding the solicitation of credentials, web browsers frequently have the capability to detect fraudulent websites and prevent the user from connecting to the website.

If the action continues, the network can prevent actions in the eighth step. Web content filters can prevent the user from going to malicious websites. A secure network should prevent malware from impacting other systems. The network should prevent malicious behavior including file changes, connecting to malicious links, or other actions. Data leak prevention (DLP) can stop sensitive data from being sent out of the network.

The ninth step is the network detecting successful attacks. At this point, intrusion detection and prevention should detect indications of an attack by identifying data exfiltration, illicit logging activities, or other signs of an active, successful attack.

Once an attack is detected, malicious activity should be mitigated, which is step 10.

It's important to understand that detection does not stop the attack but requires action such as deleting messages in other user queues, blocking domains, blacklisting, activating antimalware software, or other actions.

Phishing campaigns are typically launched against many users simultaneously. However, not all messages are opened at once. It is common that a few users will open the messages almost immediately, while it might take most users hours, if not days, to get to the message. If one of the early recipients detects attacks and alerts the security team, the security team can remove the message from users' inboxes before they have the chance to open it. In other words, early detection can feed prevention by removing unopened messages earlier in the kill chain for some of the users.

Additionally, you can look for and review infections that were not prevented, so you can implement countermeasures to mitigate against future attacks.

In a non-cybersecurity example for a kill chain, consider the construction of a simple wood chair. The kill chain would be roughly as follows:

1. Ensure the wood is in good condition.
2. Ensure the wood pieces are shaped exactly as specified.

3. Drill holes in the proper places.
4. Ensure glue is properly measured and placed.
5. Assemble the wood pieces, ensuring the pieces are placed to the appropriate depth.
6. Measure the assembly of the chair.
7. Allow the glue to properly dry.
8. Stain the wood completely, with the appropriate amount of stain.
9. Perform final quality control of the chair.
10. Ensure the chair is packed appropriately to avoid damage in shipping.

If there is a mistake in any phase, the resulting chair may be defective. However, by ensuring that every phase is performed to exacting standards, the chair should likely be in mint condition.

Other Models and Frameworks

The Cyber Kill Chain is not the only framework to use when deconstructing an incident and refining a security strategy. We can use other frameworks to predict and prevent future UIL. A few include the following:

- Common Attack Pattern Enumeration and Classification (CAPEC)
- NIST Cybersecurity Framework
- Indicators of compromise (IOCs)
- Techniques, tools, and procedures (TTPs)
- MITRE Adversarial Tactics, Techniques, and Common Knowledge (ATT&CK) framework

CAPEC and NIST are widely discussed in many sources. Let's look at the latter three of these a little more closely.

Indicators of compromise (IOCs) are used for intrusion defense. These are known malicious behaviors that adversaries often use, such as domains, IP addresses, bio hashes, and more. However, the number of false positives that come from IOCs can be a hinderance to establishing effective countermeasures for mitigating UIL. While IOCs are still widely used, the sole use of IOCs in identifying an attack is reactive and insufficient as they rely on information against only known threats.

However, when IOCs are used in tandem with intelligence from multiple methods of discovery, the combination can contribute to a robust, in-depth approach to detection.

Let's quickly look at techniques, tools, and procedures (TTPs). Like the kill chain, TTPs consist of a sequence of events and identify how threat actors organize and administer attacks. In describing or profiling the behavior of an actor or APT, the levels of detail are categorized as tactics, techniques, and procedures. TTPs are a critical concept in counterterrorism and cyber security. Pattern recognition is essential in any critical defense methodology, particularly in examining and identifying activity by a specific threat actor or organization.

TTPs can help an organization learn and evolve attack detection. They can assist an organization with identifying gaps in the security strategy of their processes, procedures, staffing, controls, technology, and risk management. TTPs can also significantly assist with contextualizing risks and vulnerabilities while influencing research and response methods.

One disadvantage of TTPs occurs when multiple bad actors or organizations demonstrate common behaviors, which indicates collaboration, learning, and adoption. When multiple bad actors share similar attributes, that complicates identifying the source of a threat. Another disadvantage is that the TTP approach can demand a heavy budget because threat intelligence is required from multiple sources, which can increase expenses.

MITRE ATT&CK is a global community knowledge base of behaviors demonstrated by known attackers provided in a matrix format. The MITRE ATT&CK model is more of a list of TTPs, as opposed to the Cyber Kill Chain's model of sequential phases in an attack. Although MITRE ATT&CK may not be focused on an order of operations, it can still be used in deconstructing an attack by determining behaviors used by adversaries and identifying applicable countermeasures.

In the MITRE ATT&CK matrix you will see rows of tactics and columns of associated techniques. Any attack campaign will consist of a sequence of events that correlate to the progression in the matrix. At each stage of the attack, you can identify the tactics and techniques used and develop or implement relative controls to mitigate against future events, including taking steps to minimize UIL.

APPLICATIONS OF MITRE ATT&CK

MITRE ATT&CK is generally specific to computer-based attacks, but it does include non-technical attacks. It is a robust framework that allows you to map attacks as they have occurred. If you can track multiple attacks to a particular adversary, you can see that they have a pattern or, in other words, a signature. In the law enforcement world, it would be referred to as a *modus operandi* (MO). Once you have an MO and you see an ongoing attack, you can then predict future actions, and mitigate the attack.

If you are somehow involved in the cybersecurity field, you should become familiar with the MITRE ATT&CK framework. It is incredibly useful as it helps you understand how computer-based attacks evolve. It also provides for establishing a cybersecurity framework. Even if you are not in the cybersecurity field, it is valuable to at least appreciate how it methodically breaks down the phases of an attack and identifies the different ways that each phase of an attack may be realized.

Applying Kill Chains to UIL

When you intend to mitigate UIL, you step through every phase of a business process to determine where a loss may be initiated. Then you figure out what would prevent the initiation from happening in the first place or what happens after the initiation of a loss. This is essentially an analysis of a kill chain for that UIL. It can be rather dynamic and hard to predict, but when you understand this as a concept, you can start to address the problem.

Reviewing a past incident, identifying a framework, and collecting attack data will mature a UIL mitigation strategy by implementing new or different controls to mitigate or defend against future attacks.

Each attack has its own chain of events, so you can create a kill chain type model that fits an attack, keeping in mind that each phase of the attack is an opportunity to stop an attack in progress. Using a framework to deconstruct an attack provides defenders with a structured view of an attack to more effectively identify vulnerabilities in controls in technology, governance, security awareness, safety, and more. With this approach, you're better able to mitigate future attacks.

Part IV will step through the facets of applying kill chains to UIL. In the meantime, this chapter has made you at least familiar with the concept of using a framework to break down the process of an attack. In this way, you can implement countermeasures as an effective approach to strengthening your loss prevention strategy. Without employing the concepts we've discussed here, mitigation would otherwise play out very differently in your organization. How can you effectively approach mitigation without a methodology?

Part IV will step through the facets of applying kill chains to UTM. In the meantime, this chapter has made you at least familiar with the concept of using a framework to break down the process of an attack. In this way, you can implement countermeasures as an effective approach to strengthening your loss-prevention strategy. Without employing the concepts we've discussed here, mitigation would otherwise play out very differently in your organization. How can you effectively approach mitigation without a methodology?

12 Total Quality Management Revisited

We've visited the significance of process in multiple chapters, and as we stated in Chapter 2, users are pieces of the system. When users initiate a loss, we must address each potential point of failure and implement mitigating measures. Using an established framework will help across an organization by reinforcing involvement, boosting accountability, and using a process-focused method rather than a chaotic approach to fixing the system.

Waiting until an incident occurs, conducting a root-cause analysis, and piecemealing a resolution will only lead to variable processes and, over time, increase the potential for gaps, vulnerabilities, and costly user-initiated loss (UIL). All too often, when a loss occurs due to lack of security practiced by the user, we hear security awareness training is the cure. Author Tracy Celaya Brown is a well-versed educator and uses the Pareto principle (or 80/20 rule) to structure educational and behavioral change efforts. The Pareto principle simply states 80% of consequences result from 20% of the effort; this is also phrased as 80% of actions produce 20% of the results. Applied to adult learning, we would say 80% of employee behavior is a result of 20% training. While it is a generalization, the idea is to show the uneven distribution within a relationship. Not all employee behavior is a result of training. This perspective is not to be taken literally but rather to provide a perspective on how multiple factors contribute to behavior and to encourage using security awareness training as a tactic or component of an overall strategy when mitigating against UIL.

What we strive to show is that awareness training, though valuable, is not the key to implementing lasting behavior change. However, a structured approach to process identification and improvement in alignment with a solid security culture, as we discuss in Chapter 9, and security awareness, as discussed in Chapter 15, is a hearty approach to ensuring users are taking the right actions and minimizing UIL.

Implementing security best practices into business processes is no easy undertaking. Process identification and improvement alone is a challenge. In this chapter, we revisit Total Quality Management (TQM) and how a structured process improvement framework can bolster your security strategy in good times and during a crisis. The UIL you experience is not usually the result of a singular failure, but from small, seemingly innocuous issues embedded throughout the entire process.

TQM: In Search of Excellence

Total Quality Management is a customer-focused approach to management, process improvement, and quality by minimizing errors. Its origins date back to the early 1920s in statistical control and expand through manufacturing modifications until the 1950s when the concept was implemented in Japanese industry. The significant results demonstrated by Japanese applications were irrefutable, with drastic improvement in process, quality, and engagement. We explore ideas from founding experts, such as Walter Shewhart, W. Edwards Deming, and Joseph Juran, and how these ideas apply to improve loss prevention in business processes today.

Total Quality Management is inclusive of organizational culture and the attitude required by leadership and adopted by staff to provide quality in products and services offered to customers while minimizing waste in process and operations. The clinching component is the ongoing effort for continuous improvement in all areas of the organization and how work is done. To implement TQM, a management philosophy must be adopted to integrate and engage all functional areas of the organization (marketing, operations, engineering, sales, R&D, customer service, etc.). This requires everyone throughout the organization to be involved in moving the culture needle and showing improvement. Involving everyone at work requires total commitment from each person and with all activities conducted in the organization. The objectives of implementing TQM are to aim for zero defects, utmost efficiency, and highest quality with no waste. Ultimately, it is everyone's responsibility to improve quality, including frontline employees, mid-level management, and executive leadership.

In the security field, practitioners often struggle while creating a security-minded culture in siloed business units, much less across an entire organization. This is even more challenging across a global enterprise. We understand the importance, if not criticality, of establishing a strong security culture to implement a robust security strategy spanning the organization and embedded in the manner in which work is done. We want excellence, but sometimes we must take baby steps to minimize UIL. Much like the goals of TQM, a security-minded culture should strive to reduce the loss at each and every step in a process.

Exponential Increase in Errors

While working with a client in the financial/banking industry, we found multiple points of error when evaluating critical processes for optimization. In some cases, a true separation of duties was not conducted, automated processes faded into manual touchpoints that differed, based on the person doing the work, or unsecure paper trails were left in the wake. It was easy to see how sending a domestic wire transfer could be a security risk at numerous points in the process, but the ripple effect of those points was exponential.

For example, if a caller was not properly authenticated at the beginning of a call requesting a financial transaction, it made it much easier for the criminal to proceed with the criminal request, as the criminal established trust. If the verification of the requested transaction was not strong, that further facilitated the transfer. If the confirmation message for the transaction could then be rerouted, based upon the trust already established on the part of the criminal, the crime was less likely to be stopped in progress.

Let's consider TQM where errors are concerned. A 100% quality rating is required at every point in any given procedure; otherwise, there is waste within the process. Say a production process on a manufacturing line is considered to be perfect 99% of the time. The process will produce 10,000 errors for every one million products created. In this case, the yield of the product is a result of performance for every step within the given process. If a process consists of 20 steps and each step is completed to 98% of perfection, the errors or defects increase quickly, with the total output being approximately 40% defective.

Going back to the simple domestic wire transfer example, consider the risk and possible UIL. If a true separation of duties is not followed, opportunities for fraud increase if the same person receives, inputs, and approves a wire transfer. A bad actor could facilitate fraudulent activity causing the account owner and bank a substantial loss. If a manual process goes undocumented and requires the user to decide without explicit instruction, the risk of error and UIL increases additionally, which may result in employee training without undocumented processes. We see how every undocumented, manual, or decision-making point harbored risk. Thereby, each point facilitated an increase in risk.

For example, if there are 10 points where an error can be made, and each point has a 1% error rate, the total error rate is 10%. When humans are involved, you can definitely assume that there will be more than a 1% error rate.

Cloudflare, Inc., is a web infrastructure and security organization providing Internet security and content delivery services to enterprise customers. On April 15, 2020, planned maintenance was conducted at one of their two core data centers. A technician was to remove all equipment from a specific cabinet. While the cabinet contained old and inactive equipment, it also contained a patch panel providing external connectivity to other Cloudflare data centers. Armed with simple instructions to remove all equipment, the technician decommissioned the old hardware, also disconnecting the cables attached to the patch panel. The change resulted in a four-hour outage of customers to the Cloudflare Dashboard and API with restorative actions taking longer than needed due to the technical team working remotely required by COVID-19 restrictions.

A root-cause analysis of the four-hour outage revealed, while redundancy was provided via multiple carriers and data centers, this specific patch panel was a single point of failure (SPOF), additionally consistent cabling for quick identification was needed, and clear instructions with documented processes were required for anyone conducting the work.

Could one simply say the outage was due to a stupid user? The contributing factors would indicate multiple people responsible for the outage. This is an example of UIL, however; someone didn't provide proper labeling of cables or the patch panel, the panel was not identified as a single point of failure, and someone provided vague instructions, while a technician was following orders who likely did not ask clarifying questions. All of the enabling factors demonstrate how the environment led to the user actions and infer how each step could have been improved to prevent the loss, before initiation.

To Cloudflare's credit, the organization was more than transparent with customers, employees, and the public. No customer information was lost, and all configurations remained; however, a loss of time and productivity occurred, and the ripple effect to customers is unknown. Cloudflare conducted a root-cause analysis, identified the areas with opportunity for improvement, and made efforts to mitigate future risk. Additionally, no single employee was blamed or considered a stupid user. Cloudflare graciously and humbly reported the outage and the lessons learned for others to gain knowledge and apply mitigating measures to minimize UIL resulting from similar incidents in the future. So what does TQM have to do with any of this? With our simple wire transfer and Cloudflare examples, we see how errors in a process can have far-reaching repercussions and exponentially increase room for error and, thus, UIL. A structured approach to process identification and improvement could have mitigated against the initial outage and certainly provided a method for improving processes for future user action.

Principles of TQM

As we mentioned, TQM is a management strategy with an emphasis on customer satisfaction as an organization-wide effort through continuous improvement and high quality. The strategy requires committed engagement from all employees and leadership and customer feedback. From a loss reduction perspective, the approach is akin to a strategy that requires commitment and engagement from everyone throughout the organization with feedback on improvement from anyone involved in our processes, including customers, vendors, and frontline staff.

According to the American Society for Quality (ASQ), there are eight guiding principles of TQM.

- **Customer-focused:** The customer ultimately determines the success of TQM as improvements are made to product or process and the customer is satisfied.
- **Total employee involvement:** An organization-wide effort where every employee, at every level, is involved and committed to a common goal of continuous improvement.
- **Process-centered:** A focus on process thinking. Using a series of steps with input from internal and external resources (suppliers, individual contributors, etc.) for outputs delivered to customers.

- **Integrated system:** Interconnecting cross-departmental or cross-functional processes, including microprocesses with an organizational understanding of associated mission, vision, policies, standards, and objectives.
- **Strategic and systematic approach:** The formulation of a strategic plan that integrates quality as a core component.
- **Continuous improvement:** Ongoing and consistent improvement in efficiency and quality.
- **Fact-based decision-making:** Continually collecting and analyzing data to guide and improve decision-making.
- **Communications:** A clear and consistent approach to change management that provides ongoing, methodical, and transparent communication across the organization in a timely manner.

Exxon used TQM to rebrand the company after the Exxon-Valdez oil spill of 1989. Franchise fuel station owners were charged with embedding Exxon's corporate values into their branded stores, and Exxon reviewed customer and end-user desires as an opportunity to improve products, processes, and technology. The global effort was embraced throughout the organization, and it was able to positively progress.

Total Quality Management is a time-tested, globally instituted strategy across multiple industries including aviation, automotive, financial, healthcare, and manufacturing. For our purposes, we must consider how to use TQM for loss reduction. A fundamental concept for TQM is that mistakes can be made by users, but most are a result of poor systems and processes. The root cause of errors or UIL can be identified and mitigated by changing the process. Using a strategy such as TQM, turns the user into a valuable partner to be leveraged for insights and tribal knowledge. They often know where the bodies are buried and will have background as to why a process is conducted a certain way or how it can be improved.

What Makes TQM Fail?

The primary purpose of TQM is to cultivate a management strategy realized throughout an organization. Frequent failure factors include a lack of leadership commitment, poor change management, deficient communication, a lack of employee involvement, and insufficient resources.

Examples of small failures that lead to large loss include vehicle recalls due to random explosive airbags and author Ira Winkler obtaining a badge to server rooms for which he was not actually authorized. Errors in the process, no matter how small, require consistent review to create an environment where there is a proverbial canary lives and UIL can be eliminated.

The concept is applied across the company as part of implementing a permeating loss reduction strategy. We discuss culture and its importance in relation to creating a security-minded culture in Chapter 9, and we frequently work with organizations on process optimization, which is why culture is so embedded throughout this book. Despite our ongoing message to leaders, typically we find many have not adopted a loss reduction-minded culture or created a culture in which principles, such as those aligned with TQM, are pervasive, and this is often where TQM fails. This is inclusive of cross-functional collaboration between security and business leaders, as an integrated system using a strategic and systematic approach toward the common goals of loss reduction and continuous improvement.

Author Tracy Celaya Brown worked with a financial client, and all staff and contractors were required to badge into the main building. Everyone was encouraged to question tailgaters or ask to see an official badge if one was not properly displayed. As such, everyone entering the restricted area badged accordingly, and everyone was authenticated. One dreadfully stormy day, the roof leaked and flooded the carpeted entrance into the restricted area. As a result, facilities staff propped the doors open and placed fans at the entrance to hasten drying time. Imagine the plethora of risk and potential UIL had a malicious intruder accessed the restricted area of a large financial institution. A group of employees gathered in front of the entrance as if determining if badging was still a requirement. A few seconds later one employee badged in and continued through the entrance, and everyone else followed suit.

The example seems simple but is an insight to many of the TQM principles in action. The company chose to learn from the experience and improve procedures across the board, instead of chalking this situation to a one-and-done. Here we found the process was followed as a result of a solid security-minded culture. Additionally, the company made changes to how facilities should handle similar situations and provided security contact information, updated policies and procedures to reflect additional requirements, and further empowered employees by communicating recognition for maintaining a strong security-minded culture.

Other Frameworks

As we mentioned, TQM is the granddaddy of quality, but not the only game in town. Just as the right tools for process and quality improvement are required, so is the right framework.

A few others to consider include Six Sigma, ISO 9001:2015 Quality Management Systems (ISO 9001), and ISO 27001 Information Security Management Systems. Six Sigma is founded in the principles of quality experts Walter Shewhart, Joseph Juran, Dr. William Edwards Deming, and TQM as a method to measure quality. It is based on the concept of restricting defects to a perfection level of 99.99966%, focuses on continuous process improvement, aligns with ISO 9001, and emphasizes strong leadership with mutually beneficial supplier relationships. Six Sigma measures process quality with a data-driven approach that minimizes defects with continuous improvement. Two methods are used including the DMAIC and DMADV. The DMADV approach is used for new product or service development, which we will briefly visit in the next section. The DMAIC philosophy is used to improve or develop an existing process and stands for Defined, Measured, Analyzed, Improved, and Controlled (DMAIC). The method is considered a rigorous approach to process improvement, as you will define opportunities, measure performance, analyze opportunities, improve performance, and control performance. A tactic for mitigating UIL is ensuring processes are defined, documented, and distributed so users know explicitly the actions or behaviors to demonstrate that minimize risk and, ultimately, loss.

The ISO 9001:2015 is an international standard developed by the International Organization for Standardization (ISO). This standard can help organizations improve performance and product or service quality, by focusing on quality management principles and on process using the Plan, Do, Check, Act (PDCA) cycle and risk-based thinking. A quality management system is directly related to management with the objective of achieving customer satisfaction and, for the ISO 9001:2015

standard, using seven principles that affect outcomes. The quality management principles include the following:

- **Customer focus:** An emphasis on customer satisfaction and meeting or exceeding customer expectations
- **Leadership:** Establishing unity, accountability, and direction from leaders across the organization toward meeting quality objectives
- **People engagement:** Ensuring people from every level within the organization are actively engaged and empowered with competency in order to create and deliver value
- **Continuous improvement:** Consistently seeking betterment
- **Evidence-based decisions:** Gathering, analyzing, and assessing data to substantiate decisions
- **Relationship management:** Creating mutually valuable relationships with interested parties such as vendors

There are 10 clauses that make up the ISO 9001:2015 standard. Organizations that adopt the ISO 9001:2015 for certification must actively adhere to the requirements defined within the clauses with limited room for flexibility to achieve the desired quality. Management of the entire system is achieved using the PDCA cycle, as shown in Figure 12.1. The clauses include the following:

- **Scope:** An introduction to the process-approach of the standard
- **Normative references:** Identifies the importance of ISO 9000:2015 as a foundation
- **Terms and definitions:** Directly aligned with the ISO 9001:2015 standard
- **Context of the organization:** Identifies requirements for aligning business objectives with quality management systems
- **Leadership:** Defines requirements for accountability, quality policy and objectives, planning, communication, review, inputs, and outputs
- **Planning:** Identifies requirements for associated risks, opportunities, and changes
- **Support:** Defines requirements for people and infrastructure resources required to achieve objectives

- **Operation:** Determines requirements for planning a product or service including review, design, development, and monitoring
- **Performance evaluation:** Identifies requirements for assessing customer satisfaction, internal audits, and proper function
- **Improvement:** Addresses requirements for continuous improvement

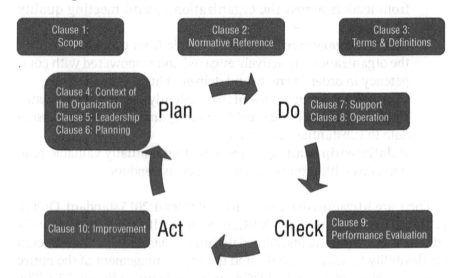

Figure 12.1: The PDCA cycle of the ISO 9001:2015 clauses

Capgemini is a leader of technology consulting and services. A strategic business unit of Capgemini is Cloud Infra, a cloud infrastructure services arm with locations in 14 countries with more than 80 sites and 22,000 employees. Cloud Infra adopted the ISO 9001 standard and achieved certification to ensure consistency in quality and productivity. Additionally, Cloud Infra was able to remove duplicate efforts in production, enhance business reliance, and create a more cost-effective management system.

Given this book is about security, it is important to mention ISO 27001. As security concerns and regulations increase, more organizations are implementing ISO 27001:2013, "Information Technology – Security Techniques – Information Security Management Systems." This standard defines the requirements for an organization to manage security risks, provides a framework for policies and procedures, and provides a framework to implement and maintain an effective information security management system. The foundation of ISO 27001 is based on ISO 9001, and you'll find commonalities within the 10 clauses with specifics relative to quality or information security. Organizations can create a holistic approach to managing quality and information security by considering using the frameworks of these ISO standards when focusing on a strategy that mitigates against UIL.

Ultimately, multiple frameworks exist that can assist in establishing a methodology for mitigating UIL and holistically integrating security-mindedness through process improvement, quality management, or through your specific objectives.

Product Improvement and Management

The concept of using continuous improvement principles holds true for product development as well. For example, the DMADV approach of Six Sigma shares some commonalities with the DMAIC approach we visited earlier but is used for creating new products or process designs. DMADV stands for Define, Measure, Analyze, Design, and Verify. The objective is to create products aligned with customer requirements and high quality while minimizing errors. For example, Apple Inc. does not explicitly use DMADV or TQM, but its approach toward product development and improvement is reflective of TQM principles. Apple relentlessly uses customer behavior to create beautiful design, practicality, and enhanced functionality. Manufacturing processes have grown to handle ever-increasing demand with faster delivery times. The values of the organization permeate throughout the company, products, and customer lifestyle. Employee and leadership engagement are undeniably creating a culture inside and outside of the organization. Apple has customized a management, quality, and product improvement framework as an organization and instituted it as a global brand.

Another option for product development, or more specifically application security, is the Open Web Application Security Project (OWASP) Top 10. OWASP is an international nonprofit organization that provides software developers with resources and education to create and maintain trusted applications. The OWASP Top 10 is an annually expert-reviewed list of the most critical web application security risks. Developers can participate in the community and learn how to counter against critical risks via education and the application of suggested methods. While the

Top 10 is not necessarily a process improvement methodology, it identifies the common risks to address, based on crowd-sourcing experts in the field who identify what they see as attack vectors.

Kill Chain for Process Improvement

In Chapter 11, we discuss the concept of kill chain and phases of the Cyber Kill Chain. Breaking down the Phishing Kill Chain is an example of root-cause analysis to facilitate process improvement and decrease UIL. The efforts span cross-functional operations, require involvement from people at various levels in the organization, must be supported by leadership, and undoubtedly can be reverse-engineered to support improving systems and processes. Other frameworks, such as MITRE ATT&CK, NIST Cybersecurity Framework, and IOCs can be used within the greater organizational management strategy of TQM. These methods only strengthen your tool belt for implementing strategy and mitigating loss as a security, or general business, practitioner.

COVID-19 Remote Workforce Process Activated

In late 2019 over the span of a few months, COVID-19 went from an epidemic with ground zero in Wuhan, China, to quickly crossing oceans and jumping borders, becoming a pandemic of a scale unseen since the Spanish Flu in 1918. In a matter of days, millions of people were required to practice physical and social distancing as a countermeasure to lessen the spread of infection and flatten the curve of medically assisted treatment. Suddenly, the global workforce had to move into a position to work remotely, with many companies unprepared for the infrastructure required. The situation was dire, with governments mandating only essential businesses remain open and only essential staff remain on-site. Organizations worldwide quickly activated remote-work policies, equipment, and infrastructure. In some cases, organizations dusted off business continuity plans, while others were left head-scratching, attempting to hastily pull a plan together to maintain business operations. In many ways, it demonstrated the lack of planning on the part of most organizations.

Electronic stores all over the world were inundated with purchase orders for any and all laptops, desktops, and webcams in an effort to activate work-from-home efforts and provide employees and contractors with the necessary equipment. Internet service providers were taxed with increased bandwidth demands, cloud services providers were flooded with requests for new accounts, and, oddly enough, bulk retailers were running out of toilet paper (and cleaning supplies) as quickly as they received inventory. Security for people, places, and things was never more important and never more lacking.

The majority of the world was not prepared. Limited processes were in place for handling a pandemic. At a minimum, the U.S. government did not have the proper agencies and experts in place due to changes implemented during the Trump administration. Medical supplies were improperly distributed, accurate and truthful information was challenging to obtain, and the definition of essential workers changed overnight.

It was a breakdown of many systems. Countless hard lessons were learned by organizations, agencies, administrations, and the people who run them, in process continuation, quality, and improvement. While no single framework or methodology could assist in perfecting the processes necessary to move and secure a workforce, all needed supplies, and data traversing international wires, a plan for continuous process documentation, review, and improvement would help at any time, even more so during a crisis.

Applying Quality Principles

How do we blame a single user for loss of inventory, poor infrastructure to handle remote workers, or lack of secure connectivity? How can we use people, process, and technology to minimize UIL and strengthen our security strategy? How can organizations implement a framework for continuous improvement and create long-lasting behavior change as part of a resilient strategy?

It's easy to point the finger at a single user when loss is experienced. A more challenging experience is understanding how points of failure can exist at any part of a process, leaving exponential room for error and increasing potential for loss. We must create an environment where users are encouraged to participate in refining and continuously improving how work is done. Leaders must support these efforts in providing users with specific guidance that promotes a security-minded culture with cross-functional collaboration. Lest we forget, mitigating UIL is a group effort, and providing a structured approach, such as TQM or another framework, can help create a more conducive environment.

As we frequently highlight, the greatest threat is well-intentioned users who want to work around problems. Per Deming, this is a symptom of a quality problem in the overall process:

> *People sometimes find themselves in a situation where things don't go right, the best employees find ways to "correct" the problem. I put the word correct in quotes because often the correction winds up making things worse. Not because of mal-intent or lack of follow-through. If the problem is caused by the way the process is designed (a management responsibility), the tweaking done by the employee may alter the system in such a way that future products or services are even worse. The correction addresses the wrong problem and winds up doing more harm than good. It's counter-intuitive to believe that your best workers, doing their best, could make things worse. Best efforts won't cut it; better management of the system is needed (Deming & Orsini, 2013).*

We spent this chapter of our book highlighting that where safety sciences developed their processes, operations have developed their own. Professionals with Six Sigma and other certifications are sought out to manage projects and programs effectively. Unfortunately, these people and the processes they bring have not been sought out to apply to UIL in security and other areas that experience regular loss due to user actions.

While Part IV of this book shows how you analyze each step of a potential loss, we strongly recommend looking into TQM, Six Sigma, ISO, and other quality processes. If you can develop your own skills and/or involve professionals who already have such skills on your UIL reduction efforts, it will help you immensely.

III Counter measures

Countermeasures are essentially the proactive aspects of a user-initiated loss (UIL) mitigation program. The various categories of countermeasures (such as technical, operational, personnel, and physical) are based on the countermeasure's actual effects. For example, a physical countermeasure restricts physical assets. Personnel countermeasures impact whom you hire and fire.

Our methodology requires a programmatic and holistic examination of mitigating UIL. We recommend an examination and consideration of every potential countermeasure to include in your loss reduction program. However, to mitigate UIL, you need to focus on an agnostic process that considers any required countermeasure, regardless of an area of specialization.

We advocate looking at any user's actions that might result in the initiation of a loss and considering whatever countermeasures would mitigate the loss, either proactively or reactively. This means you need to be free of arbitrary constraints, such as being assigned to operations or physical security, and need to focus on what is under your specific responsibility. You need to look at a potential user error and consider the string of events that leads to an action that initiates a loss (maliciously, accidentally, intentional but not malicious, etc.), as well as the string of events after the initiation of a loss, and then consider any countermeasure, in any category, that could mitigate the UIL.

We advocate mitigating UIL through a strategy that combines governance, technology, and awareness. We specifically use the term *governance* instead of *process* as governance is a control to implement and design process. We want governance to be the fundamental countermeasure that proactively prevents UIL and, as no countermeasure is ever perfect, mitigates losses after being initiated.

As technology requires specialized knowledge and expertise, we separate out technology as a distinct countermeasure. Technology implements a large portion of governance.

Awareness programs should focus on informing users of the governance and how they are to do their jobs. Unfortunately, that is not how most organizations perceive or use awareness. We advocate how to improve this situation.

The intent of this part of the book is not to provide prescriptive guidance on how to implement governance, technology, or awareness. We describe the purpose and format for these countermeasures so that readers can implement the countermeasures in a format specific to your unique concerns.

13 Governance

Governance traditionally establishes policies that guide how people are to behave. Governance is not the same as management—it is the decisions about what to manage and how. Many well-managed organizations have failed because they weren't managing against the right goals and objectives for their industry or purpose. That's a governance failure—you're successful at what you do, but what you do isn't going to be successful

While governance should effectively be synonymous with process, most organizations do not have sufficient governance to sufficiently define their processes to the necessary specificity. Governance is generally well-defined regarding some areas of an organization. However, when it comes to security and user actions, it often tends to be poorly defined and only at a high level. Poor governance leads to poor processes.

For example, it is a common security concern that there are unsafe websites. In response, companies issue what they consider to be governance, which amounts to statements and awareness training that broadly states that people should avoid unsafe websites. That sounds intuitively proper. However, that is not a clear process that people can follow. For example, what is an unsafe website? How does the user make such a determination? If a user gets a link to a website from a customer or supplier, what are they supposed to do?

Fundamentally, this is an example of a poor awareness program practice of telling people what they should be afraid of, instead of telling them how to do their job properly. A better handling of governance to inform your processes is to tell people that they should only go to known websites required for their business functions. It would be better to define the specific websites that are approved for specific functions.

There should then be guidance as to what to do if they have to expand their Internet search to unknown websites. It would also be appropriate to provide governance that systems must be configured to disable web browsing for people and computers who do not typically need web browsing capability.

As you can see, there is a fine but significant difference between providing a specific definition of process versus vague guidance of what to be afraid of. For this reason, we need to define how specifically people perform their particular work functions. This includes how they should make decisions. Ideally, there should not be any arbitrary decisions made by people within your organization.

Likewise, the work process should see where decisions will likely be made and determine whether those decisions can be taken away from the user.

When considering governance, we want to identify a process that reduces UIL by defining how users are to behave in their work functions. As important, we believe that we must analyze the process to reduce opportunities for users to be put in the position to initiate loss. This can involve removing users from the entire process when possible.

Governance defines the process and must do so on as finite a level as possible to remove random discretion from the process.

Defining the Scope of Governance for Our Purposes

Traditionally, governance would be an overarching definition of the entire process. However, we prefer to separate technology and awareness as distinctly separate functions. Technology is specifically the implementation of technological controls. The goals for those controls should be defined in governance.

Similarly, awareness efforts will be defined in governance as well. However, we do believe it is critical to separate it, as awareness should be used to promote the goals, strategies, accountabilities, and even specific user behaviors defined in governance.

Admittedly, we could also separate physical security controls, personnel security controls, and operational security controls as separate disciplines to discuss. We do acknowledge those controls as critical, and they should be performed by experts who are skilled in those disciplines.

Fundamentally, operational security is the establishment and practice of good governance. Personnel practices are frequently legally defined, and experts know they need to handle their job functions in a consistent matter. Physical security likewise has specific practices that define manual actions.

Technology takes away manual actions, and we prefer to treat it uniquely and more robustly. Awareness is a separate discipline for us in that its purpose is to promote the goals laid out in governance. Unfortunately, many, if not most, awareness practitioners do not acknowledge their job as essentially one of promoting compliance to governance.

Ironically, awareness regarding personnel security is extremely clear. It is typically clear that sexually harassing behaviors are wrong. It is clear that people need to accurately record their work time. They must accurately report financial spending. I am not saying that there are not periodic failings and abuses, but in most established organizations, HR and accounting practices are very well-defined. The process itself is the awareness effort, as failing to record work time or proper submission of expenses results in penalties, and those failings become self-correcting. This is not the general case with UIL.

Operational Security or Loss Mitigation

Operational security (or loss mitigation as appropriate) is traditionally what we are addressing here: the establishment of a repeatable process to mitigate losses. With specific regard to process, you traditionally look at processes and define those processes to proactively mitigate loss. Traditionally, this might include defining steps on the manual processes of the dissemination of information. It might include reviewing the receiving of shipments to ensure that everything arrives and is paid for as expected.

Operational security for our purpose includes any analysis of a business function and the resulting embedded practices. We are hesitant to call them security or loss reduction functions, as the intent is that those practices are as fundamental in the overall processes as the base practices themselves.

These practices are memorialized in the resulting governance. This governance must never be a paperwork exercise, but an embodiment of actual processes.

Physical Security

While we traditionally discuss physical security as a separate discipline from governance, the reality is that it is embodied in the same way. Physical security procedures and other physical processes should be documented, with the appropriate countermeasures implemented and embedded within the governance documents. As with all governance, all documentation should reflect actual practices.

There is usually a separate physical security function. However, remember that we advocate you analyze a given business process and determine where and how losses may be initiated within that process. While there will always be general locks, guards, access controls, file cabinets to lock up sensitive documents, etc., you need to be able to bring in physical security considerations when you analyze how to mitigate UIL.

For example, no matter how well you automate a function, there will inevitably be hard-copy documents that contain sensitive information, even if they are handwritten notes. While you clearly want to have general document handling procedures under the guidance of the physical security program, you also need to look at the individual business processes to see where and how hard copy documents may arise. General governance and processes are always important, but each process might involve a unique implementation.

Even if there is not anything unique about a given process with regard to physical practices, you need to ensure that the process is defined by the overall physical security governance. This is a critical distinction: While there are usually physical security governing practices, they are not distinctly embedded within each business process.

If you want to mitigate UIL, you need to embrace legitimate physical security governance and embed that governance within all business critical processes. This is one way to overcome the compliance budget discussed in Chapter 5. When a security, compliance, or other function is embedded within a process, the user will not have to make the choice as to whether they do their job or practice security and loss mitigation.

Personnel Security

In most cases, personnel security-related concerns should have already been accounted for in general processes. That would take place independent of any business process for which you are trying to mitigate UIL. That being said, you can never discount that there might be a need for specific personnel responsibilities. You might have to ensure that a given person involved with a process is properly trained. You need to ensure that people with only the appropriate qualifications are provided access to a system or are assigned to perform specific functions. You might need to ensure that people have background checks. If people need to have special qualifications and training, this must be accounted within the specific process in question.

The HR department, along with legal, physical security, and other relevant departments should set universal personnel processes. However, anyone involved in setting governance and specifying processes for any function, where a user can initiate a loss, must also consider what personnel requirements they must set for that business process.

Traditional Governance

While we may generally criticize traditional governance efforts, they are required. Even when they don't meet our newly proposed recommendations, they are the backbone of any security or organizational program. Even if governance is lacking, it still provides the formal justification for the program.

For example, you need some document to point to, blessed by the appropriate executives, to say that General Motors will make cars. It sounds intuitive, but it is not. This governance then goes down to what cars should be made, how they should be made, and the demand for the intellectual property protection to secure the sensitive information that provides General Motors with its competitive advantages. Governance should provide a justification for every dollar spent. It also gives stakeholders throughout the organizations the ability to demand a budget and support for their programs.

We are not going to claim that all organizations look to their governance in this way, but this is the formal purpose of governance. It is not supposed to be a random set of documents to pull from the shelf to appease some party that such documents exist, but a guiding process for how a business is to fundamentally function.

This being said, there is the traditional documentation that comprises governance. While there might be some variation in terminology among different organizations, industries, cultures, countries, etc., there is a commonality among the types of documents. We put these specific terms and definitions here, as they appear to be the most common from our observations.

Policies, Procedures, and Guidelines

With regard to a UIL program, effective governance consists of standards policies, procedures, and guidelines that define the expectations and impact of the loss reduction strategy. They may include the methodologies or frameworks used to outline any part of the program. A thorough approach to governance is inclusive of each component to prevent UIL. This section will examine the concepts of standards, policies, procedures, and guidelines more closely.

A *standard* is a widely accepted approach of determining what something should be. A standard is often developed by an agency of expertise and authority defining a minimum level of effort or result that will be acceptable. Standards are the high-level beginning to a strategy that may relate to industry or technical standards.

Some standards are required as a prerequisite for conducting business. These standards may be considered industry standards and impact security and other loss reduction programs in relation to laws and regulations. Data protection and privacy requirements include standards set by the Payment Card Industry Data Security Standard (PCI/DSS), Federal Information Security Management Act (FISMA), Health Insurance Portability and Accountability Act (HIPAA), and General Data Protection Regulation (GDPR).

It should be noted that not all standards are alike. Failing to abide by laws such as HIPAA and GDPR can result in substantial fines and penalties. PCI/DSS is an industry standard, and violations might have penalties associated with them, but they are civil penalties and much more up for negotiation. Some standards might just be considered best practices, and while they are helpful, they have no enforcement ability.

Technical standards will often describe a uniform practice or precise description of a technical method or component for typical universal implementation. Examples of technical standards include specifications and mechanical components of the National Institute of Standards and Technology (NIST) Cybersecurity Framework or the International Organization for Standardization/International Electrotechnical Commission (ISO/IEC) 27001 for Information Security Management

Systems (ISMS). Whether the standard is industry-specific or technical in nature, it will be the foundation for creating policy, procedures, and guidelines.

A *policy* can be described as a method of action enacted or proposed by a governing body that defines how security is enacted upon resources including data, assets, and expectations for compliance. A policy is typically a high-level statement of an organization's approach to an activity such as a travel policy, acceptable use policy, or remote access policy. Policies include a general level of detail and are the beginnings of procedures. It is important to note that standards are typically created by an external authority, while policies are created internally to an organization.

Typically, the standards drive policies, as there may be a compliance activity. The standards creation bodies have world-class experts who define acceptable practices that are made available to the world. Policies take those best practices and make them relevant and required for the organization in question.

A *procedure* is essentially a series of steps, actions, or detailed instructions for achieving a specific outcome and is often associated with enacting a policy. For example, an incident reporting policy may align with an incident response procedure that defines a step-by-step approach to handling a security incident. Procedures will include a low level of granularity and define user actions. While policies are often reviewed annually with few changes, procedures may change based on associated technologies, location, or some other dependency.

The last sentence is critical in understanding that procedures are essentially a how-to document and should identify every step and action to be taken. A procedure should specify how decisions are to be made. While many people may criticize that by saying it is impossible to know everything that must be done in unknown circumstances, the reality is that most actions do not have great variability, and it is merely a lack of will that stops organizations from attempting to go into detail. At the same time, every procedure should have exception handling embedded into it. The reality is that the long-term success and growth of any organization depends on their ability to make a science, in other words, a repeatable process out of everything they do.

For example, McDonald's serves hundreds of millions of people a year in hundreds of countries. Each of those countries has different suppliers, laws, builders, etc. Yet, McDonald's procedures enable it to deliver a consistent product and experience across the entire world. While it may, of course, be difficult to do so, your organization's loss mitigation efforts rely on a similar commitment to capturing the procedures accordingly. To further enhance McDonald's foundation in governance, they are known to model their quality program based upon ISO 9000, which is a family of standards for quality management.

A *guideline*, while similar to a procedure, is a suggested course of action typically used to streamline a particular process. For example, the Security Exchange Commission (SEC) 2018 Statement and Guidance on Public Company Cybersecurity Disclosures is essentially a set of guidelines for organizations regarding cybersecurity risks and incidents, and a procedure is described as a series of steps, or instructions, to accomplish a goal. To simplify the difference, a guideline can be described as a "should," while a procedure is a "must."

Additionally, we have frameworks and methodologies. We describe a methodology as a set of principles or rules to solve a problem and is systematic, often defining a set of specific steps or used when defining a procedure. On the other hand, a framework is an outline or an approach for achieving a goal or objective that often serves as a flexible guideline.

For a user to do their job correctly and effectively requires a process. Critical parts of the business will have a process that users are required to follow. We recommend a comprehensive governance program including standards, policies, procedures, and guidelines that may have foundations to specific methodologies or frameworks in order to minimize exposure to UIL and ensure a strong security strategy.

In the Workplace

Consistency is a fundamental human need, and as such, humans seek homeostasis to the point of resistance to change. As a result, habits are formed, and this is seen in everyday life. Think about one's typical day; one prepares for work (using a personal process), takes the usual route, stops at the same coffee shop, orders from a few favorite options despite the massive menu, enters the office, and continues with the day by following processes to conduct one's work duties. It's a process.

If we consider this concept in the workplace, users with specific instructions, guidelines, or procedures will maintain the process and reduce UIL associated with a lack of process. This should exist for all critical or important parts of the business. In many cases, the most critical activities of the business have associated processes, and the same should apply to any activity in which loss or damage is a risk.

For example, when a new employee is onboarded, there is a process. Specific legal documentation must be obtained, verified, signed, and stored. Orientation is provided to acclimate the new associate to the organization's culture, policies, standards, and processes for conducting work. If the employee is responsible for processing financial documents, there is likely to be a strict process to ensure monetary exchanges are properly handled, recorded, and audited.

However, this is not often the case with security and loss reduction. Rarely are user actions defined, documented, and followed with security best practices embedded into the process to minimize human error and potential loss. User behavior is left poorly defined and measures to ensure security are not considered.

Minimizing UIL requires a partnership between all lines of business to create and maintain alignment from strategy to procedure. Every function within an organization should have its own loss reduction strategies embedded within its governance. However, this governance can cross organizational lines to best reduce loss. For example, supply chain security is a critical business function. Supply chain security ensures not just the prevention of malware from getting into computer systems, but also that inferior parts do not make it into organizational products and systems, which can have devastating effects. Unfortunately, security is not frequently integrated into such functions. Thus, as guidelines and processes are created, the possibility for human error resulting in a breach and UIL increases.

Security and the Business

Protecting an organization from internal and external threats has its downside. Security is often seen as the inhibitor of business as people within the organization experience inaccessible websites, limited user access, and more policies around, well, everything. In one case, we were performing a security assessment and interviewed a product manager for a major pharmaceutical company. The manager did not want to cooperate with the assessment, because as he constantly repeated throughout the interview, he believed, "Security stands in the way of innovation." His resistance to security led to one of the largest losses in the organization's history.

There may be a mutual lack of understanding between people on both the business and security sides of an organization. In some cases, security controls are implemented that are perceived as inhibiting the ability for a person to do their respective job.

For example, some may romanticize the idea of a CISO with a heightened sense of distrust who implements excessive controls without consulting with business unit leaders to discuss strategy, policy, and process. However, the behavior does not support a long-term partnership, meaningful and deliberate strategy, or confidence among peers. Rather, the behavior is essentially the antithesis of collaboration and trust. For example, a CISO who denies developers access to platforms such as GitHub or does not publish security policy on an accessible intranet page to safeguard against publishing vulnerabilities may be a bit excessive if the company is an application development firm or employees can deny accountability for lack of knowing security policy.

There is no need for loss reduction efforts to butt heads with the business. Rather, they should support the business by partnering with operations and IT to create an inclusive approach to governance that specifies how people perform their jobs and make decisions in order to proactively mitigate error and UIL.

Employees require guidance to perform effectively in their respective roles. It is the leader's responsibility to ensure alignment to secure processes and performance. We do this by setting explicit expectations, providing the right resources such as guidelines and processes, and holding our team members accountable to performing with those expectations and resources. This is part of building a security-minded culture. In fact, we can't expect to create or reinforce a security-minded culture if we don't approach governance in this way.

Analyzing Processes

To create governance, you must define the process. We know all too well that most organizations, from a security perspective, determine the high-level policies that they need as a best practice and then have someone write (or usually copy from past assignments) those policies. If they consider that they then need some more detailed guidance, they may create procedures and guidelines to implement those policies.

Stop to consider that what we describe are basically vague and off-the-shelf documents that sound appropriate for the organization.

They are not, however, specific to any processes but are broad guidance on how people are to behave in common circumstances. It is no wonder that these documents are rarely used in practice, except to hand to auditors during an audit to prove that they exist and there is some governance in place.

Consider, for example, that there are laws that restrict the distribution of PII. Such documents say that PII should only be provided to authorized individuals, maybe for specific functions. In practice, however, it is trivial and useless guidance. Procedures should be specific about what is an authorized individual, should likely implement an approval process, and even more likely should restrict who can release PII, forcing most HR analysts to forward requests for PII to a more senior party.

From a less technical perspective, equipment maintenance is required and frequently vaguely states, "Equipment must be properly maintained." There needs to be a definition as to what is proper maintenance, potentially referring to manufacturers' specifications, who performs the maintenance, who verifies maintenance is performed, when is maintenance to be performed, and so on. Some people will contend, "What happens if a person isn't available or there is a business need to delay maintenance?" While those may be reasonable concerns, there must again be exception-handling procedures, while also realizing that some things must be done when required.

Many respectable standards and policies exist out there. However, instead of looking at some preexisting definition of required governance, UIL mitigation professionals must first analyze work processes. They must examine what loss users can initiate and then develop governance around that.

Each and every job function should be examined and analyzed. While you should assume that governance should be added to the process so that the process can be accomplished securely, removing decision points for a user, or even removing a user completely from the process, should be legitimate options. This is done for HR, accounting, and countless other processes throughout an organization. It must also become a standard practice for analyzing all functions throughout an organization.

This guidance may sound like a daunting job. However, there is no reason to not start with critical functions, with a goal of expanding the analysis and definition of job functions. You may want to especially consider starting with new functions being added to the organization.

Everyone loves to say that security and business efficiency are part of everyone's job, and that is true. The problem is that people seem to think this means they have special functions outside of their normal job functions. These functions are not something that should be considered additional to the job, but embedded within each and every job function.

For example, when driving, your primary job is to get from one point to another. However, as part of that goal, you know you have to look side to side to stay safe. You know that you need to obey traffic signals and laws. Safe driving is considered a fundamental aspect of driving.

Similarly, the job of a cashier is to facilitate transactions and provide customer service. It is also to ensure accuracy in the financial transaction. Author Ira Winkler had a summer job at a large department store while in college that sometimes involved serving as a cashier. The training as a cashier involved ensuring packaging was checked for alterations, ensuring customers didn't try to present separate items as a package (such as a cup and saucer for just the price of a saucer instead of two separate items), etc. There were a variety of loss mitigation functions that were embedded within the simple process of entering prices into the cash register and making the financial transaction.

Again, none of this is a special function in addition to the fundamental job, but the loss reduction responsibilities are embedded within the basic job processes. That is how each and every job should have the embedded security and loss reduction functions.

Grandma's House

Remember the discussion of Grandma's house from Chapter 5? Expectations for behavior are set in advance and expected every time we visit Grandma's. Our behavior is reinforced by the people around us, and consequences are to be had in the event our behavior is not as expected. Let's walk through this concept.

Your parents tell you how to behave at Grandma's house and give you *the rules*.

- Wipe your shoes before you walk in.
- Give Grandma a hug (yes, even if you think she's wearing too much perfume).
- Tell Grandma you love her.
- Don't sing or use your phone while you're sitting at the table.

- No running in the house.
- Watch all of her favorite soap operas if you want to watch TV.
- Give Grandma another hug before you leave (yes, even if you *still* think she's wearing too much perfume).

Now, your parents, cousins, aunts, uncles, etc. are all well-versed with the rules. There is a sense of peer accountability because they will reinforce the expected behavior. In the event a rebellious nature rears its little head, and the rules are not followed, then consequences ensue. Perhaps a timeout, grounding, or no phone access are part of the consequences. Either way, an action will occur to further reinforce the expected behavior.

The same holds true for the workplace. Let's follow the concept. The manager sets expectations for behavior and performance with the employee. The employee is provided resources of policies, procedures, and guidelines. The employee's peers are well-versed in the expectations as well. They will let you know when something is not completed correctly, such as if a computer was left unlocked, if someone left their badge unattended, or that they missed a step in a process. There are a multitude of ways the employee will be given guidance. Along the way, the manager provides opportunities to reinforce following the rules as part of managing performance. However, if the lack of adherence to the rules persists, then the process of consequences is followed, be it verbal or written warnings, performance plans, or termination.

You will be successful in mitigating UIL when you can say that your organization is like Grandma's house. In Grandma's house, the process is the culture. The culture is the process. You don't need to write it down. In the business world, there is a need to document your process as governance. However, the culture that you are looking to implement is one that doesn't need to read the governance documents to mitigate loss but that the desired process is followed consistently without a need to refer to the governance.

14 Technical Countermeasures

Typically, when we discuss technical countermeasures, we refer to computer security–related countermeasures. In other words, we are securing technology in some way. However, for mitigating UIL, we use it to refer to technology that is a countermeasure to more than just computer- and network-based attacks.

This means that even if a countermeasure intends to secure physical assets, such as a physical access control system, it is still a technical countermeasure. The reason we make this distinction is that the technical countermeasure is not itself a process issue, but rather a tool to implement a process.

Understanding the capabilities of technology allows you to understand what is and what is not possible. In many cases, you can introduce the appropriate technologies to mitigate the risks in ways not otherwise contemplated. At the same time, you might realize that your governance is not feasible, and you have to consider accepting more risk than previously anticipated.

So, you need to understand the tools available to you to better implement your UIL mitigation program. The remainder of this chapter covers many countermeasures. It is in no way an exhaustive list of potential and desired countermeasures, as the list would be almost infinite. However, these are tools that we have repeatedly found to be useful in a variety of contexts. We also acknowledge that other professionals would likely add and delete different countermeasures, which is expected. When implementing your own loss mitigation efforts, you have a responsibility to do your own research into what is currently available and appropriate for your conditions.

For this discussion, we will separate technical countermeasures into their primary operational disciplines. It is an easier way to conceptualize the integration into analyzing your kill chain for the potential UIL in question. These operational disciplines are personnel countermeasures, physical countermeasures, operational countermeasures, and cybersecurity countermeasures.

SOFTWARE AS A SERVICE

A great deal of the technical countermeasures in this chapter can best be described as software as a service (SaaS). While you can purchase software that fulfills a specific function, such as QuickBooks for accounting-related functions, you can also license a software tool that resides on the Internet, aka, the cloud. With a traditional software tool, you purchase or license software that you load onto a computer that you own. All data needed for that software is likely stored on the same computer. However, with a SaaS solution, when people access the system, they are essentially logging onto the system over the Internet. All data is stored on that system on the Internet.

There is likewise a cloud version of QuickBooks, called QuickBooks Online. All data is stored in the cloud, and while there might be software on personal systems that makes access more efficient, the critical functionality resides online.

There are clearly both benefits and downsides with a SaaS-based solution. One downside is that you are usually paying a subscription fee, which is cheaper than purchasing the software up front, but more expensive over time. Also, you have limited control over your own data, and there have been cybersecurity-related incidents with most of the major SaaS providers.

At the same time, there are also benefits. You do not have to pay for and maintain the computer and software yourself. You have automatic access to updates of the software. You can increase or decrease functions that you want. You can more readily integrate with other SaaS systems. You can provide access to your entire organization, customers, and providers with significantly less effort.

For example, QuickBooks Online allows for easy access for your accounting firm. You can create and send invoices, your customers can pay the invoices online, and the money can be directly deposited into your bank account. This is more costly in the long run, but it does help your business run more efficiently.

The important thing is to make a knowledgeable risk-based decision. Many of the countermeasures listed in this chapter involve SaaS-based solutions, while some also have traditional solutions. One of the main advantages of SaaS solutions is that they have focused on a specific problem and frequently, but not always, incorporate the best loss mitigation controls into their products that are not easily done with an "in-house" solution.

Personnel Countermeasures

Personnel countermeasures generally involve the hiring, maintenance, and separation of employees. They can also involve anyone who can initiate loss to your organization, which can include vendors, customers, and anyone with any sort of access to your organization in any way. Clearly that is a vague description, and admittedly you might have limited control over these individuals, if any at all. More important, you might not know these people actually exist. For example, we once found out a building inspector was flipping power switches to figure out what the switches were for. He didn't realize that he was turning off power to critical computer systems. While that might be a technical vulnerability to a certain extent, you need to consider that these unknown people need training, or to be otherwise prevented from causing harm.

You also need to consider that some people might be in what is best described as protected classes, such as union workers, and you might have limitations as to what you can do to monitor or protect against their initiating loss. Similarly, there may be laws or other regulatory concerns that limit what you can legally do to observe or control a person. For example, even if you suspect someone of malfeasance, you might have to go through extensive measures to remove that person from their position.

A key aspect of personnel countermeasures is applying them consistently. This means you have to go out of your way to treat everyone equally. You need to treat the most disliked person in the organization the same way you treat the most revered person. Otherwise, you can be accused of bias and are setting yourself up for lawsuits, legal investigations, bad publicity, and so on. Implementing technology that theoretically removes biases from the personnel process is one critical process. Technology that monitors activity and consistently reports any suspicious activity can take away claims of bias.

> **NOTE** Many of the countermeasures discussed in this section are technological. However, the purpose of this chapter as a whole is to define technical countermeasures that mitigate human error from various categories of vulnerabilities. The countermeasures we describe in this section mitigate personnel vulnerabilities. For example, data leak prevention detects and responds to employees attempting to send data to their personal accounts. Preventing UIL by preventing users from unnecessarily sending data is both a technological and personnel countermeasure.

Background Checks

Whenever you allow anyone access to your organization, background checks can be a critical process to implement. They can weed out people with criminal backgrounds or those who present other potential concerns. Background checks can also verify critical credentials and save you organization from liability.

For example, author Ira Winkler was a regular patient of a doctor. At some point in time, the doctor hired a physician's assistant (PA), and it was later learned that the PA was not licensed to practice. The doctor was otherwise a highly regarded physician and cardiologist, without an apparent malpractice complaint against him. This incident subjected him to a variety of lawsuits, despite that the PA, who treated Ira on several occasions, provided medical support without incidents or complaints. In another case, a CISO from a biotech company told us about an incident where an employee contacted the security team because they saw a co-worker featured on the TV series *Inside Edition* as "the drug dealer to the stars." Clearly, something was missed in the hiring process.

In general, people who lie about credentials, degrees, criminal records, and other general information have been found to be less trustworthy. While not everyone will be the drug dealer to the stars, if there are inconsistencies in self-reported information, you have to research whether it is an honest mistake or a sign of future trouble. Sometimes people leave an employer off their résumé if they left under troubling circumstances. Background check systems allow you to check for such things reasonably quickly.

You can perform certain levels of background checks by yourself, such as performing open source searches or paying for different search services. You can also hire companies that specialize in background checks. One critical word of warning is to ensure that you verify any negative findings. We previously served as an expert witness in a class action lawsuit that involved a background check company that included criminal records of people with the same name as those being investigated. Unfortunately, the hiring company did not even put thought into the review, as demonstrated by the fact that the criminal was a white woman who was 5'2" tall, and the employee was a black woman who was 6'0".

Continuous Monitoring

While background checks are important, it is equally important to ensure that there are no critical incidents occurring during the term of one's employ or access to the organization. The U.S. Department of Defense implemented a continuous monitoring program that ties into databases to find activity relevant to people with security clearances. If a position requires some form of licensing or certification, it is critical to ensure that the credential is maintained. For example, if a doctor or lawyer loses their respective credentials, they are not eligible to continue practicing their profession in the same capacity. A conviction for a violent incident or a crime relevant to a position of trust can likewise indicate a concern that threatens the organization.

Lyft, for example, had drivers who were guilty of sexual assaults. Ira's PA not having a license to practice his profession puts both the patients and the medical practice in danger. Large financial organizations have a policy of mandatory leave for up to two weeks, where a team of forensic practitioners goes through that employee's work activity, computer accounts, and emails, and performs updated background checks to ensure there is no malicious or concerning information. If the status changes during the course of employment, and you fail to detect it, that can create great loss to an organization.

Employee Management Systems

The hiring, maintenance, and separation of employees, or the equivalent processes for users and other people with access to your organization, should be a highly repeatable process with established systems. Everyone should sign the appropriate legal documents specifying the requirements for the protection of information. They should be granted access to all required computer systems with the least access required for their role. They should be provided with all required training.

Upon separation, there must be systems in place to revoke all accesses, collect all information, etc. This also implies that you need to track access to information while a person has access to it. We previously investigated an incident where a salesperson, who left the organization, would log into the proposal database to look for competitive proposals. The former salesperson would then approach the potential customer with a competing proposal and actually highlight why his proposal was better than the one that will be submitted by his former company. He was that brazen.

There must be a repeatable process that connects to, or accounts for, all relevant systems and information. Not only does this help contain potential losses, it provides for much more effective user management. Systems like Dayforce and SAP help in the automation of such functions, allowing for consistency in the implementation of HR functions.

Misuse and Abuse Detection

Misuse and abuse detection, frequently now referred to as *user and entity behavioral analytics* (UEBA), is a technology that can oversee user accesses to data and computers and determine whether there is unusual activity. Frequently, unusual activity is benign. However, it can be the quickest way to determine whether someone is doing something that can intentionally or unintentionally initiate a loss.

If someone begins to access excessive data, it should be looked into. An example of this is when Edward Snowden used his co-worker's login credentials to steal the bulk of the information that he collected. The co-worker's accounts could have been flagged by the NSA, and at least an investigation could have begun that would have caught Snowden before he fled the United States. Several UEBA companies claim that they can predict that an employee intends to leave an organization months in advance, because they can detect patterns of activity that indicate a person is consolidating all of their data.

Tools that examine user behavior can indicate patterns of activity that may be of concern, if not outright criminal. They should, therefore, be considered part of a comprehensive personnel security program.

Data Leak Prevention

Data leak prevention (DLP) systems scan outgoing information sources to indicate whether people are sending sensitive information out of the organization.

This can be intentional or unintentional. Even if it is intentional, it may not be malicious. For example, email tools autopopulate the sender field as you start typing a name. You might, for example, start typing a common name, such as Michael, and it might put the wrong Michael automatically in the recipient field. If you attach a file containing sensitive information into the email message, it is a data breach. Phishing messages claiming to be from the organization's CEO ask employees to send out sensitive information. If a person falls for the phishing message, they create a data breach. People sometimes send out data via a web page that should not be allowed out of the organization. Clearly, someone may also have malicious intent and send sensitive information out to a personal account.

These things happen. You need to anticipate that people will attempt to send sensitive information outside of the organization, for a variety of reasons, and DLP software has the ability to stop the potential loss.

Physical Countermeasures

Physical countermeasures, for the purposes of this chapter, are those technical systems that limit or track access to physical resources. Those resources can be facilities or tangible goods. Such systems are common and easily available. They also provide an obvious return and are frequently required by laws or regulations. There are countless variations of such systems, but they generally fit into well-known categories, as they are common in both homes and workplaces.

Access Control Systems

Access control systems limit entry into protected areas. Buildings have keys. Yards have gates with locks on them. These are low-tech physical access control systems. There are also higher-tech access control systems that allow for more finite access to areas, and less cumbersome versions of keys, such as access cards that can allow for access to multiple facilities, while allowing for the immediate revocation of access rights. Apps on smartphones can provide similar functionality via Bluetooth. A computer system controls such access remotely.

Such systems are common throughout industry. Hotels almost exclusively use this technology for room access. Homes and apartments now use similar systems.

Not only do access control systems limit physical access, but they can provide audit trails and detection capability. Alarms can trigger unauthorized or unusual accesses. We were once asked to help a company improve their security posture after a major data breach. They implemented a variety of countermeasures, many of which we were not aware of. One of them included access controls on server rooms. While we were getting a tour of the facility, we went into the server room. As we walked around the server room, a guard came running in, as an alarm went off, because the door to the room was held open for more than 30 seconds.

These systems are mainstays of traditional security programs, and you need to understand their capabilities that you are both using and not using. They can be used for prevention in that they restrict access to facilities. They can be used for detection in that they can proactively detect when people are attempting to gain access to facilities where they do not belong. As important, they can be used historically to examine who was, as well as was not, in areas where an incident might have gone on. In case of actual emergencies, if access controls are used, you may be able to determine who is actively at risk and what their approximate locations are.

Surveillance and Safety Systems

Surveillance systems involve equipment such as cameras that monitor facilities and employees' physical accesses and locations. These are traditionally the video cameras that you expect. There are also motion detectors to tell when people are in different facilities. While access control devices such as cards and keys can be used by anyone, a surveillance system can be used to visually confirm who used the access control devices.

When there are major incidents, it is not uncommon to seek video from surveillance systems throughout the entire region. For example, cell phone videos were used to identify the bombers involved in the Boston Marathon bombing. Likewise, it is common for law enforcement to use license plate readers and toll tags to potentially identify and locate subjects of interest in investigations.

Although it is unlikely most organizational loss prevention efforts will go to the extreme of involving outside parties, the use of video and other surveillance systems can be invaluable in all phases of protection, detection, and reaction.

In a controversial move, governments started using cell phones to track people's movements during the COVID-19 pandemic. In the United States, cell phone usage in general was used to see where people tended to stay in place and where people tended to ignore stay-at-home orders. For example, a study out of the University of Maryland found that when Georgia opened up its economy, people from neighboring states began traveling to Georgia. This was accomplished without tracking individuals and helped state governments make policy decisions. In more controversial uses of the technology, South Korea, Israel, India, Singapore, and other countries used cell phone tracking to assist in contract tracing, in attempts to alert people who came in contact with infected individuals.

Safety systems can and should frequently be integrated with surveillance systems. Combining the two categories of technologies can make them both more effective.

Safety systems are a broad category of countermeasures that provide a wide variety of functions. Fire alarms and suppression systems are the most prominent and are usually required by law. Robust systems are integrated with other surveillance systems to ensure the safety of people within the affected areas.

There are many systems to consider. Besides fire, you need to be concerned with water damage, temperature and environmental controls, and any other systems that might be used to alert you to problems within your facilities. It would benefit any person involved in preventing and mitigating loss to think through all potential scenarios and look to the countermeasures that would best benefit their organization.

Any form of surveillance system should be used responsibly. The first aspect to consider is that you have a right to perform surveillance of your facilities and systems, but you need to have the deference to the rights and laws involved with surveillance. When used without regard to what is reasonable and legal, surveillance can be more harmful than good.

Likewise, responsibility includes operating those systems securely. We have heard of countless cases where baby monitors and home surveillance systems were attacked by hackers who log into those systems to torment the residents. Likewise, while criminals breaking into corporate surveillance systems have been fodder for many movies, it is a possibility for real-world abuse. These systems must be secured as well as any other computer system.

Point-of-Sale Systems

Point-of-sales (POS) systems are critical elements of an inventory system and, therefore, are critical for accurate tracking of physical assets. We separate them out because they require special attention in the access that they have, the level of refinement that they can add to a physical loss prevention system, and other aspects that lead to a more effective environment.

Clearly, the ability to efficiently purchase goods and services at accurate prices is critical. However, POS systems can also assist with facilitating customer service and reducing loss. For example, if people cannot find their receipt, but they are a member of a loyalty program or there are other transaction tracking tools in place, the receipt can be found within the POS, and people can, therefore, get refunds, warrantee services, etc. As important, there is a detailed record of how much someone purchased an item for, so you do not have to worry about sales prices, discounts from coupons, etc. This can significantly reduce losses related to returned goods.

In a real case involving author Ira Winkler, his mother bought his wife a ring as a gift. His wife already had a similar ring and wanted to return it to a store within the same chain but within a different state. He did not have the receipt, but he was able to go to a store within the chain and find out exactly what the ring was purchased for, and they actually applied the return to the engagement ring. This not only made for a very happy client and reduced the stress of asking an elderly woman to find the receipt for a gift purchased months before, but it led to an even larger purchase within the chain. Without knowing the specific purchase price of the initial ring, there was no way to know what type of credit to offer, and there would be otherwise no reason to have shopped for the ring specifically at that store.

Inventory Systems and Supply Chains

Physical inventory systems are required in many retail environments. Just-in-time deliveries and shipments require accurate tracking on what is in stock and what is sold. Retail stores can completely turn over their inventory five times during the month before Christmas.

Manufacturing also requires complicated technology that ensures that composing parts arrive when required, while also not arriving before actually being needed and thus, straining limited storage space. Automation of this process, which takes a user out of the loop, allows for a more seamless system, where user error is proactively eliminated. Manufacturing is just one example where a detailed supply chain is required. Any breakdown in supply chains can cripple most organizations.

Both electronic and physical documents require tracking systems. If documents are critical, they should be logged and recorded in a document library. Anyone reviewing the documents should be logged. Document controls are especially critical in legal and HR environments. Only authorized people should be granted access to such documents. They should also be locked up as appropriate and stored in rooms that are secured. While this may sound more related to physical security, as appropriate, electronic tracking can optimize the security. It can identify when someone might be accessing excessive and unnecessary amounts of documents. It can also be used as a forensics aid when investigating how information might have been leaked or abused. Ideally, there might be a system that scans and stores documents. However, whether the documents are soft or hard copy, they need to be tracked.

Computer Tracking Systems

Loss of computers and their associated media and equipment is a problem that plagues all organizations. Thefts of computers happen while people are traveling and even when in the office. For example, there was one case we became involved in where laptops were being stolen from people's desks overnight. It turned out that video surveillance found that a cleaning person would periodically take a laptop while cleaning late at night. He would put it in a trashcan and wheel it out of the building. This type of situation is not unusual.

In a somewhat similar case, we investigated an instance where someone stole components out of computers. It took an alert employee to notice that their computer system had less RAM one day than it did the day before. An audit was performed, and it was determined that tens of thousands of dollars of computer equipment was stolen from the organization, and nobody else noticed the issue.

Technology can be used to track computers and other devices. For example, the FindMyiPhone app runs across the entire Apple product line. It makes it easier to track stolen and lost computers, and it can potentially delete the data on the device. Similar technologies are available for other computer technologies and devices.

USB drives and other portable storage media should be tracked. Ideally, they should be eliminated in organizations as not only are these storage devices easily lost and the data not tracked, they are one of the best ways to steal information. In several organizations we worked in, USB ports were either removed or intentionally damaged so they could not be used.

While we want you to protect computing assets because they are physical assets that have innate value and provide critical functionality, the fact is that they also store data that can dwarf the value of the physical equipment.

Operational Countermeasures

Operational technical countermeasures are those tools that you use to track processes and workflow. Many of these tools are those that you acquire, or perhaps license, to automate workflow. While they might be computer based, the purpose is not to automate a computer-related function but to automate a work function. They are, therefore, unique to the cybersecurity functions that are likely required to secure these tools.

For example, accounting systems are critical to proper financial controls. They are, therefore, an operational countermeasure to mitigate fraud and other financial losses. However, you likely need to layer on cybersecurity controls to ensure the veracity of the data, as well as proper access to the systems.

Whenever you implement a process, you need to determine whether there are tools you can use to automate the process. The more common the process, the more likely there are tools that can simplify your systems. Many of these will be SaaS-based systems. The following sections, while by no means exhaustive, discuss a representative range of operational controls.

Accounting Systems

Every organization requires accurate accounting to maintain control of losses. Accounting systems can provide tremendous insight into your organization and can tell you when and where your losses arise. Ideally, you can determine what causes those losses. A poor accounting system is itself a major risk. In general, the more you automate and integrate the accounting systems, the lower the likelihood for the introduction of user error and fraud. Even in the case of a UIL, such systems can more quickly identify the potential for loss and begin mitigation procedures, or at least send out the appropriate alerts.

As we stress the importance of metrics, robust accounting systems provide a plethora of metrics that can allow you to dive into your finances and see where you should and can make financial improvements. The more robust the accounting system, the more visibility that you have into all of the processes. This insight can help you not only decide where the improvements can be made but can allow you to delegate responsibilities to others.

Accounting systems can potentially be burdensome to organizations in that they typically create an excessive amount of paperwork. However, they can also automate payments and streamline processes, allowing for a more efficient organization that is less likely to fall victim to financial fraud. For example, we are consultants, and we frequently have to travel for work. This involves having to pay for potentially thousands of dollars of expenses and then hoping we are reimbursed before our credit card bills are due. Clearly, we don't like the burden of having to provide a receipt for each and every trivial expense. At the same time, assuming we submit a properly completed travel expense report, we can likely receive reimbursement in a timely manner.

At the same time, too much focus on accounting can lead to an environment that is proverbially penny smart, pound foolish. For example, there are some organizations that require so much documentation in employee expense reimbursement that it costs more to satisfy the accounting requirement than the money it saves. For example, while many organizations allow for a fixed per diem reimbursement for meals and daily expenses, other organization want a detailed accounting with receipts. We can personally attest that compiling receipts, entering each and every charge onto a form or into a system, and then having an accounting person verify each and every charge takes hours for a trip of more than a couple of days. Then if the accountant finds a problem, it can take even more time to correct the issues. If you consider a consultant's billable rate is hundreds of dollars per hour, the amount of money potentially saved by requiring all employees to account for every expense is far outweighed by any fraud that may be incurred due to providing a fixed per diem.

At the same time, few organizations have ever complained that they have too much financial insight into their organization.

Customer Relationship Management

Customer relationship management (CRM) is critical for tracking sales and customer interaction. While this may seem like a basic and obvious function, customers are the lifeblood of almost all organizations. Without an ability to track and cultivate customers, you cannot ensure current and future income.

Salesforce is one of the largest technology companies in the world, based solely on its excellence in providing CRM functionality. It has figured out how to integrate CRM throughout the lifecycle of customer identification, tracking, management, sales, billing, and renewal. The value is so clear that Salesforce has become a major Internet driver.

CRM provides the ability to optimize your revenue potential. It is relatively easy to look at the operations of an organization and not look at customer acquisition as critical, since it is not part of the overall fulfillment of an organization's mission. However, without customers to purchase products and services, the organization's products are irrelevant.

Operational Technology

While people are familiar with the concept of information technology (IT), the concept of operational technology (OT) has not yet achieved the notability that it deserves. Both IT and OT are essentially computing assets. However, IT is specific to information processing and traditional computer services, while OT are those computing resources specific to running the operations of an organization.

If you are in an information-based company, such as Salesforce, where IT is essentially the deliverable, the point is moot. However, if you are in an operational environment where the computer assets control the operations of equipment that produces other goods and services, it is important to understand OT as a unique discipline.

For example, power generation systems, such as nuclear reactors, generators, transformers, and so on, rely on industrial control systems (ICS) and supervisory control and data acquisition (SCADA) systems to operate the equipment that produces the power. ICS, SCADA, and the equipment involved in the production of electricity are all considered OT. Likewise, factories that produce goods are essentially composed of OT.

OT automates business processes and should ensure consistency and reliability across all production efforts. While many systems can be implemented manually, automation provides for control that cannot be as easily achieved. If your systems are not yet automated, and it might be possible to do so, you should clearly explore the process. One of the benefits of doing so is that it removes multiple vectors of UIL that can potentially be quite costly. This is obviously the case when it comes to major power facilities, but it applies to many other organizations as well.

Workflow Management

When processes cannot be automated and must be performed manually, implementing workflow management systems is an alternative. To ensure loss is mitigated as effectively as possible, you must ensure that each and every step in a process is followed.

If you cannot use workflow management software, you should attempt to otherwise document and enforce the process to the best of your ability. While you clearly want your people to be able to enhance the process as reasonable, you cannot ignore that establishing a process to ensure consistent and optimal output is critical to success. If you have not defined the process that you need to implement, you have fundamental problems.

Cybersecurity Countermeasures

While all of the previous sections contained computer assets, they did not provide for security of those computer assets. They involved technologies that can be implemented to prevent and mitigate UIL. Those technologies, however, have to be protected against traditional cybersecurity-related attacks.

For example, accounting software is an operational control, but you need to ensure that only the appropriate people be allowed to manipulate information. Therefore, you need to have embedded security controls that verify identities, while also tracking and limiting access as appropriate. This is true for all technologies.

While the other categories of countermeasures are relatively static, cybersecurity countermeasures can be dynamic. There are new types of cybersecurity countermeasures that didn't exist a few years ago. While passwords have existed for decades, they are being enhanced with other technologies, and sometimes replaced. Behavioral analytics is emerging as a mainstream category of countermeasures.

We are going to stick to broad descriptions of cybersecurity countermeasures. As with the previous sections, it cannot be a comprehensive list and intends to cover the most notable categories of countermeasures. The goal for the discussion is to highlight the potential uses of the countermeasure and to help you decide if a particular category of countermeasure is relevant for you to implement in your organization. Should you choose that you have a potential use for the countermeasure, we recommend that you perform further investigation to determine the available features that are most relevant to you so that you can choose the best products or solutions that best fit your needs.

A good portion of this section is derived from Ira Winkler's *Advanced Persistent Security* (Syngress, 2017), and we recommend that you review that book for a specific detailed discussion of the cybersecurity field.

The 20 CIS Controls and Resources

The Center for Internet Security has been managing a list of best practices for computer systems and networks for many years. The 20 CIS Controls and Resources is a high-level list of best practices for the implementation of organizational technical security practices. The guidance is a starting point for organizational security programs. The controls map well to a variety of technical standards, such as ISO 27001, so they can be used for a variety of purposes.

The controls are not specific technical tools but assist in the identification of those tools. Using our previous discussion of governance, the 20 CIS Controls and Resources would qualify as a standard. While there is some overlap with the other categories that we discuss, the 20 CIS Controls and Resources list lays out the foundation for a strong technical security program. The individual controls overlap with some of the content in the remainder of this section. The countermeasures that follow are among the more critical technical countermeasures.

For more specific information about them, visit www.cisecurity.org/controls/cis-controls-list/.

Anti-malware Software

Antivirus, antispam, and related malware prevention software is a fundamental requirement in any environment. Anti-malware software should be placed on all end-user systems. While viruses are typically associated with Windows systems, there is plenty of malware targeting Macs and other machines, so all end-user systems should have anti-malware software.

Anti-malware should also be considered for servers as well. Many servers are based on Windows and other common software operating systems, which are vulnerable to malware. While many people assume, for example, that ransomware attacks end-user systems, one of the most critical issues is that when a user initiates ransomware, it not only attempts to encrypt the user's PC but all data that the user has permission to access. Frequently, that shared data is on one or more file servers. Since the spread of malware is largely through spam and targeted emails with attachments, it is important to ensure that anti-malware is integrated into your email servers and clients. However, malware can also be spread through malicious websites. Additionally, there are worms, which spread and infiltrate systems through system ports.

While anti-malware software should perform periodic scans of a computer, it should also be memory resident to actively prevent the installation of malware.

Traditional anti-malware software on a system is important, but it has to receive regular updates for the latest malware signatures. This means that licenses must be kept current, and automatic updates must be enabled. We realize that there have been some problems related to periodic updates; however, the risk is too great not to enable the auto updates.

There are also anti-malware products that can operate without signatures. These tools constantly examine the behavior of programs running on systems and then stop any activity that could potentially be malicious. These types of tools incorporate behavioral analytics, machine learning, and/or other forms of analytics, and are frequently referred to as *endpoint detection and response* (EDR).

The two types of anti-malware are not necessarily mutually exclusive. It is not uncommon for an organization to use traditional anti-malware, as well as EDR. While traditional, signature-based anti-malware can stop a majority of known attacks, it is useless against unknown attacks. So, given how hackers are essentially in an arms race, constantly developing new attacks as the security industry tries to stop them, EDR that looks for unknown attacks is a powerful enhancement. This can be a very effective combination.

Whitelisting

Whitelisting is a software application that stops anything except for specifically allowed software programs to run on a system. If an application is not specifically enabled, it will be blocked. In the infamous Target hack, one of the cited failings of Target was that they did not implement whitelisting on the POS systems. It is considered a standard practice for retailers to implement the function.

This functionality significantly limits the versatility of a given computer, and in a large environment, it can be burdensome to maintain. However, for some critical systems, such as industrial control systems (ICS) or POS systems that have a very limited purpose and that can be significantly harmed if compromised, whitelisting should be mandatory.

Firewalls

A firewall is a perimeter security device that limits the ingress and egress of data, primarily based on the network services. That is an oversimplification of the functionality, but for the purposes of this chapter, it is sufficient. Firewalls can be very useful in easing the security burden on individual systems.

While a firewall is often used for isolating an internal network from an external network (frequently the Internet), it should also be considered for isolating segments within an internal network. If an adversary gets into a network, they will use trusted systems to compromise other parts of the network. A firewall also prevents malicious insiders from exploiting systems outside of their immediate access.

Intrusion Detection/Prevention Systems

Intrusion detection systems (IDSs) and intrusion prevention systems (IPSs) are generally being combined into a single functional system. Generally, they intend to monitor network traffic to detect and block traffic that could be associated with malicious actions. Frequently, the functionality is integrated with a firewall. As with firewalls, the technology should be considered for deployment at network perimeters, as well as within a network at appropriate network choke points.

Again, the detection of malicious activity is at least as important as prevention. Even if malicious activity is prevented or you don't know that the malicious activity is occurring, the attackers will keep trying to get in until they are successful.

Managed Security Services

While firewalls, IDSs, and IPSs are very useful perimeter devices, it can be difficult and time-consuming to manage the devices, investigate potential concerns, and update the systems as necessary. For these reasons, there are companies that manage the devices for organizations.

The better providers also analyze incidents and collect intelligence to prevent attacks proactively. They search a variety of Internet sources and compile incidents from all of their clients to protect each of their clients. The more capable organizations will have extensive intelligence capabilities and provide an added value well beyond solely managing the devices.

Backups

As a critical focus of our philosophy, the one inevitability of security is that something will go wrong. This especially includes the loss or destruction of data. Disks can crash. Data can be destroyed by ransomware, and USB drives can be misplaced. Malicious insiders can delete or alter data. While you can never prevent all potential situations, backups provide a reactive capability to mitigate the loss of data.

If you have hot sites and real-time backups, there is the possibility that no data may be lost. This can be expensive. Automatic, periodic syncing of mobile devices can also prevent significant data loss. A process of manual periodic backups might not save 100% of all data, but it does reduce the amount of loss.

Various services in the continuous data protection category, such as Carbonite, iDrive, Google Drive, and others, provide automatic backups over the Internet. They can be a valuable service to consider.

Secure Configurations

For a system to be secure, it should be secure with a default configuration that is implemented with security in mind. Organizations should have security configurations so that when a new system is installed, the configuration of the system is predefined to be secure by default. The configuration should define the services the computer runs, the default user permissions, file sharing, versions, standard applications with the appropriate settings, and so on.

When an administrator installs or delivers a new system, that system should be essentially identical to all other systems of the same type in use within the organization. Not only does this provide strong security, it also eases administration and maintenance. Vendors and industry associations typically provide guidance for securely configuring applications and operating systems. The Center for Internet Security maintains benchmarks for different systems that are readily available for reference.

Automated Patching

As software vulnerabilities are discovered regularly, and ideally vendors release patches, it is critical to install those patches as soon as possible. Both Macs and Windows operating systems provide an automated patching capability, as long as you allow them to do so. The average person should allow that capability to run as designed. Organizational administrators might want to first test the patches to ensure that they don't cause any negative effects. It is possible that some updates might cause other software not to work. However, if an organization cannot perform the testing in an efficient manner, it is safer to allow automatic updates.

As previously mentioned, automatic updates should be enabled for anti-malware software. Operating systems are regularly updated. Applications are frequently updated. Given the common usage of the products, Microsoft Office and Adobe Flash and Reader applications should be updated as rapidly as possible given the fact that attackers rapidly create and use exploits of those software products. But generally, unless you have extensive knowledge in the area, you should enable automatic updates of all software.

Vulnerability Management Tools

Vulnerability scanners check systems for known weaknesses. They look for outdated components of operating systems and applications that are known to have security vulnerabilities. In other words, they look for software versions that have known bugs. Depending upon the access of the vulnerability scanner, it can also potentially find configuration errors, such as improper file sharing and similar issues.

There are network-based vulnerability scanners that scan systems that sit on a network. They can detect the vulnerabilities that are exploitable by network-based attacks. There are also vulnerability scanners that run on individual systems and can do an extra level of scanning to find vulnerabilities that can be exploited by someone with system access.

There are some tools that look for changes in systems and critical system files. For example, Tripwire detects whether monitored files change and alerts the administrator of a potential compromise. While most vulnerability scanners are a form of protection, to the extent they detect modification of system files, they can be considered a detection tool.

Behavioral Analytics

Behavioral analytic tools are a form of detection that looks for unusual activities. They can look for that activity by either examining actions on an individual system or checking network traffic for unusual patterns. These tools are programmed to either look for known patterns of unusual activities or study activity to determine what is normal activity and then report activities that fit outside the norm.

Depending upon the nature of the tool, it can look for user actions, such as excessive file accesses, activities at unusual times, and so on.

Some tools look for unusual network traffic that might indicate the presence of attack tools used by advanced persistent threat (APT) actors. Whatever the target, these tools can be useful in finding activities that would otherwise be missed.

Data Leak Prevention

Data leak prevention (DLP) software looks for potentially sensitive data being sent outside the organization. These tools can be used on individual systems to look for data that is being sent intentionally or unintentionally by an individual user. There are also network-based DLP tools that sit on mail servers or network egress points and watch for data that is being sent over the network.

The tools allow organizations to set criteria for what data should be stopped from exiting the organization and what to alert the appropriate staff about. They can identify certain types of data, such as PII, or look for key phrases that are tied to sensitive project data.

In some cases, the egress is due to malicious software planted by APTs. Sometimes employees send out this data before they quit so they have it available when they leave the company. In one case we know of, a well-meaning employee sent customer data to his personal account so that he could do some extra work at home, which would have benefited the company. Regardless of the reason, these tools can stop information from leaving the company, where they would have little control of it.

Web Content Filters/Application Firewalls

Web content filters can be considered a form of DLP to some extent. They intend to prevent users from sending out sensitive data to other websites, while also filtering out potentially harmful or malicious data or information from a website. They can also prevent access to sites that have content that might be deemed unnecessary or harmful. For example, it is common for organizations to prevent connections to pornographic websites and web torrents. Many organizations ban social media sites on work computers. We have worked with several organizations that also ban access to hacker websites, as they don't want malicious tools downloaded onto their network.

There are also more broad application firewalls that filter out other types of data and attacks. They can prevent malicious software from getting to an organization's website. These tools should be considered for any organization with more than a trivial Internet presence.

Wireless and Remote Security

With more employees using mobile devices, more employees connect to wireless networks that are outside the control of the organization. Hackers can spoof a legitimate access point. Even if there are legitimate access points, data can be sent in the clear, and it becomes accessible to anyone else who has access to the networks.

When possible, organizations should distribute virtual private network (VPN) software that sets up a secure and encrypted connection directly to a trusted network. In the absence of a VPN, individuals have to attempt to ensure that they are using legitimate networks. They then should ensure that they use encrypted connections through their web browsers and hope that end-to-end encryption is enabled. There should also be a purposeful attempt to reduce the amount and type of data that is accessed remotely. Admittedly, any unknown wireless network can be malicious, even if they appear trusted. Even if your web browser uses encryption, you can fall victim to a man-in-the-middle (MITM) attack, where the attacker sets up servers that establish secure connections and then decrypts the traffic in a middle point before forwarding the information to the intended website.

When traveling to known hostile areas, it is recommended that you take a new system with minimum amounts of data and use it for purely tactical purposes. When network access is used, there is a conscious attempt to access as little data as possible. The system should then be "scrubbed" and no longer used upon return to a trusted area.

Mobile Device Management

Mobile device management (MDM) software provides security tools for cell phones, tablets, laptop computers, and related equipment. It allows organizations to control certain functions related to system configuration, data storage, and data access. MDM software can enforce software updates, look for malware, and perform other basic security functions.

MDM software also provides for control of the data on the devices. It can remotely delete data, if the employee leaves the organization or loses the device. It can potentially selectively delete emails on the device, reset the passcode, and perform other data and system administration functions.

MDM software can be deployed as part of a bring-your-own-device (BYOD) strategy, where organizations let employees use their own devices for work-related purposes. In such instances, employees agree to allow the MDM software to run on their mobile devices so they can work more efficiently. It is a standard practice at many organizations.

Multifactor Authentication

Multifactor authentication implies that you use more than one method to authenticate yourself to a computer system. There is a general rule that authentication can involve what you know, what you have, and what you are. Multifactor authentication frequently means you are using at least two of those methods.

In multifactor authentication, "what you know" is a piece of knowledge, like a password. It can also be the answer to the ideally more challenging authentication questions that ask for what is supposed to be more obscure information, such as your mother's maiden name, favorite movie, and so on. While not perfect, it does make it significantly more difficult for an attacker to compromise an account.

While passwords can be compromised, because they are easy to guess, criminals rarely need to guess a password as they are compromised via phishing attacks, password sniffing, or reusing passwords from compromised websites. For example, in a series of incidents in 2019, criminals were using account information, posted on the Internet, compromised from hundreds of websites. The criminals went to the Ring website and were able to log into home cameras of Ring users, who reused the same email addresses and passwords across multiple accounts.

In multifactor authentication, "what you have" can be token-based authentication, such as a SecureID card, or other access device that provides a one-time password. It can be a software token on a computer, and it is frequently your mobile device, where organizations send you a text with a one-time passcode that has to be entered to access the account. The assumption is that you need to be in possession of the account holder's cell phone to compromise the account. This is much more difficult to compromise than compromising a person's password. Google Authenticator provides a passcode on a mobile device so that the person does not actually have cellular access and the passcode cannot be compromised in transmission.

In multifactor authentication, "what you are" usually involves biometric authentication. Retina scans, fingerprint readers, hand geometry scanners, and similar tools provide a detailed layer of authentication and are much more difficult to compromise. Due to the perceived invasiveness, as well as the difficulty to collect the information, while it may be the strongest form of authentication, it is currently the least used. The common exception is the fingerprint reader on iPhones and other mobile devices that can be used to unlock the device, as well as for activating mobile payment systems.

Like all other security tools, no method of multifactor of authentication will be perfect. However, it is exponentially more secure than traditional password mechanisms and may allow for reducing password complexity, as the password is not used as the final tool of authentication.

Single Sign-On

Single sign-on (SSO) facilitates a user moving seamlessly across a network to access required systems and files. There can be many individual systems on a network that require authentication, and having a user be required to have individual accounts for each and every system can be extremely burdensome. SSO tools allow a user to log on once, and the SSO then authenticates the user to all required systems on the network as necessary.

It can save a great deal of administration effort, as well as frustration for the user, who may otherwise be required to create and maintain dozens of passwords. It does, however, require that the authentication to the SSO tool be accurate and secure. It also provides for a single point of failure. However, the assumption is that if you are using SSO, you are aware of this issue and implement stringent authentication, which would include multifactor authentication, heavy monitoring of activity, access from specific domains, etc.

Encryption

Encryption is a fundamental element of data protection. Encryption involves making data unreadable to anyone who doesn't have the decryption key. For example, if you look at a file that is encrypted, you cannot tell what you are looking at as it appears to be just a random collection of bits. Web browsers can encrypt data while it is being transmitted to a web server, which enables most activity on the Internet, such as ecommerce. Hard drives can be encrypted by default, so in case a computer is lost or stolen, the data on the computer is unreadable to anyone who is not the owner. Encryption is built into most storage devices. Most standards require the encryption of sensitive information.

Encryption is available in many applications and computing hardware. You just have to know how to activate it. For example, a major controversy occurred when Apple refused to help decrypt the iPhone of a dead terrorist. If encryption is available, you should consider using it. If encryption does not already exist in your devices, networks, or systems, you might want to consider acquiring encryption, depending upon how sensitive the information is.

There is frequent criticism that encryption sometimes fails, so some people question its value. Like all security countermeasures, it is not perfect. From our experience with NSA, encryption doesn't have to be perfect; it just has to be sufficient. There will never be such a thing as perfect encryption. Given enough time and resources, all encryption can be cracked. The best analogy is that encryption is like a safe; it has to be secure for as long as necessary. For example, if someone intends to rob a bank, a bank safe will never be impenetrable. It just has to keep the bad guys out long enough for the police to arrive.

Similarly, while you want to encrypt credit card numbers, several considerations are the level of effort that criminals might put into compromising the credit cards, the number of credit cards in question, how credit card data is handled during transmission, and storage that contains the data of hundreds of millions of credit cards. When the military is determining how much to spend on encryption, they consider the longevity of the information and how long the encryption will be in use. For example, a military communications satellite that might be in use for more than a decade has to have encryption that will not only repel current cryptanalytic attacks but can repel exponentially more powerful cryptanalytic attacks that be discovered in the next decade. Then they have to anticipate the possibility that the satellite might be required to be functional for perhaps another decade, if it isn't replaced as currently anticipated. That is clearly a different level of encryption required than if you wanted to make a single purchase on Amazon.com.

Nothing Is Perfect

It is inevitable that some people will take issue with some counter-measures that we include in this chapter and will complain that a countermeasure will fail. Our response is, "Yes, it will." We need to reiterate that no countermeasure is perfect, and it can and will fail for reasons that are both foreseeable and unforeseeable. The key is to implement countermeasures that provide the appropriate return on investment. It is about risk optimization.

The sciences we draw from all implement a layered approach to miti-gate loss, as they acknowledge that everything will fail. Safety programs include plans for medical response, as they acknowledge that people will eventually be injured, despite the program's best efforts. It is the same for all the technical countermeasures that you implement. The point is to ensure that you choose the countermeasures that are most likely to reduce the risk to the organization.

Putting It All Together

After the presentation of all of these countermeasures, it is easy to lose focus on the fact that the purpose of this chapter is to identify technology that implements and secures processes. Processes are both difficult and powerful. Technology can make implementing processes significantly simpler, if not enabling the otherwise impossible.

At the same time, given how important technology is to the process, a compromise in that technology can create losses at a scale that was otherwise unimaginable. So when you go to implement a process, know that the technology that can be put in place to streamline and control the process is critical, but you also need to ensure that you protect that technology.

For example, an effective technological implementation of accounting systems can ensure that there is optimized financial processing and tracking to prevent loss. It can equally enable fraud and loss at scales never seen before. The goal is, therefore, to choose the technical counter-measures to UIL, while securing those countermeasures with as much motivation as you do to secure the users.

15 Creating Effective Awareness Programs

Awareness programs are generally the bastard child of most loss prevention programs. They are frequently required by compliance efforts. In the cybersecurity field, Gartner tells customers that as of 2019, 60% of organizations just want to "check the box." In other words, they want to do whatever is minimally required to satisfy regulatory compliance requirements.

It is not a surprise that users will ultimately initiate loss. According to Verizon's Data Breach Investigations Report (DBIR), 4% of users will click a phishing message no matter what you do to increase their awareness. There are also other inevitable user failings in just about any action they might perform. Why then should organizations spend any more money than required on awareness programs?

The answer is simple: Awareness programs can save more money than you spend on them. No countermeasure is perfect. None. There will always be a failure. However, as long as you mitigate more loss than you invest in an awareness program, it is a wise investment. It is that simple.

As with all countermeasures, it is important to attribute a return on investment (ROI) to awareness efforts. Metrics are a good starting point for determining any form of ROI. It can sometimes be difficult to track the success of an awareness program, because it is hard to know every time a user performs an action correctly. This is why Chapter 10 advocates tracking behavioral statistics over time and ideally determining the value of decreasing specific incidents. These can include reduced malware incidents, reduced injuries, fewer systems outages, and whatever other incidents are relevant to your organization.

There have been many security awareness vendors that commissioned studies to specifically demonstrate the value of their solutions. The studies do seem to provide some proof that awareness efforts can decrease the number of incidents and, therefore, the loss associated with user error. These studies are specific to the use of the vendors' products, but they can be used to justify generic efforts.

To know the full success of any awareness program, you would need to be able to track and report on "near misses" as well. For example, any time a user does not click a phishing message, it is a success. Any time an engineer performs proper maintenance on equipment, it is a success. Any time someone avoids an injury because they followed procedures correctly, it is a success. Any time a user avoids unnecessarily using equipment or having a sensitive conversation in a public space, it is a success. Some near misses are easier to track than others, and you can never fully track all near misses. Even if you could, it is impossible to know how much loss was prevented. However, tracking behavioral statistics and related costs can provide some useful information along these lines.

What Is Effective Awareness?

The reality is that most awareness programs are ineffective. Most people perceive measuring the effectiveness of awareness to be difficult, so they minimize their awareness efforts. Consequently, their awareness efforts suffer. As we discuss in Chapter 5, there are fundamental problems with many, if not most, awareness programs.

So, what makes an awareness program effective? In short, effective awareness programs are those that increase the desired behaviors. Ideally, there will be a tangible value tied to the improvement of behaviors.

If an organization's goal of having an awareness program is solely to ensure some form of compliance with a regulation, then just checking the box is technically effective in proving that the awareness program exists, even if it is functionally ineffective in increasing the desired behaviors. However, if you just check the box, you cannot complain when there are no improvements in organizational behaviors or when people dislike participating in awareness efforts.

At the same time, you must consider that even if you put together an awareness program that you intend to have maximum effectiveness, it might still be effective. The false narrative of likability as a metric of awareness success permeates the industry. Although likability is not a negative for awareness efforts, likability does not mean that the programs actually change behaviors. There may be some collateral impact, such as a better impression of corporate loss mitigation efforts and a higher likelihood of reporting incidents, but it is difficult to link those results to any measurable ROI.

Awareness efforts do not have to be funny, long, short, compliant, or so on. They have to improve the desired behaviors. You do not even need a traditional awareness program. If you get people to improve their behaviors in any form, it is effective.

You must never lose sight of the overall effectiveness of the program. It's easy to focus on more easily measurable details, but the overall program is what matters. If you collect the appropriate metrics, you will likely find that some components are more effective than others. If you just have one or two components of an awareness program, such as videos, you likely will not have an effective program, as there will be no reinforcement. Effective programs take into account the concept of the forgetting curve and have frequent reinforcement through multiple means.

Governance as the Focus

Obviously, awareness programs focus on getting users to do things correctly. Unfortunately, most awareness efforts seem to focus on telling users what they should not be doing and what they should be afraid of. Chapter 5 discusses this in detail, so we will not rehash why this focus is wrong.

We agree that there is a benefit to telling people what they should avoid. Without a perceived threat, people will become complacent and not feel the need to follow various procedures. Likewise, users should be made aware of any common or imminent threat that exists.

However, this needs to be balanced with training users in how to do things right. You can't possibly explain to people all of the infinite ways they might initiate loss, but you can provide one prescribed way for them to do their jobs correctly.

A good example of this is accounts payable departments, which have to deal with frequent fraud attempts where criminals try to submit fraudulent invoices, change the payment information for legitimate accounts, manipulate invoices and payments, and so on.

And criminals are always inventing new ways to attack accounts payable departments. We work with departments that are very well aware of the fact that they can never predict all attacks, so they take the sensible approach of defining how to do each potential accounts payable function correctly. It might seem time-consuming and burdensome to their organization and their vendors, but it reduces most types of fraud.

These departments know some of the common attacks they are likely to experience and can readily determine when such an attack is taking place. This allows them to quickly take countermeasures, report the incident to management, and alert their co-workers. However, they also become complacent in the sense of security that these successes provide. They stick to their procedures, instead of going by their gut when they see something unusual. They will never fast-track something that otherwise appears to be correct.

Disciplines like accounting are infamous for the proverbial red tape, where you have to go through a set of annoying processes to accomplish certain things. While some red tape might be seemingly unnecessary and appear "stupid" in that it requires much more effort than seems justified by perceived losses, frequently these seemingly stupid processes are there for a reason.

For example, resetting account passwords can seem overbearing on many systems. However, we previously worked with online gaming companies that had problems with account takeovers. Criminals would call up the help desk, pretending to be the legitimate user, and request that the password to the account be reset. They would then sell all of the virtual goods in the account, locking out the original account holder in the process. We created what appeared to some users to be a burdensome process to reset account passwords. There, was unfortunately, a lot more at stake than typical users perceived.

Awareness programs should not be there just for compliance purposes or to provide information about common threats to the organization. They should be considered a critical piece of the overall organizational training and loss reduction programs. Again, awareness should be there to tell users how to do their job correctly, not to describe a handful of the countless ways they can do their job wrong.

For this reason, awareness programs should embody organizational governance. Governance documents should be the source for most awareness program materials.

Where Awareness Strategically Fits in the Organization

Throughout our professional careers, we have rarely seen training on how awareness fits specifically within an overall management strategy. The result is awareness programs that do not satisfy strategic business drivers.

Awareness professionals truly desire to create programs that return value. In the absence of defining value from a strategic risk perspective, awareness professionals do what seems intuitively correct, which is to empower people to make better decisions. That is an extremely noble cause, and it likewise empowers the awareness practitioner. The awareness practitioner becomes a user advocate and empathizes with the users. They tend to excuse the users for their errors and generally portray the users as paragons of virtue, who will do the right thing when they are told what the right thing is.

While there is a great deal to be said for this, the result is unfortunate. Humans are only human. They generally want to do the right thing. However, there are also the concepts of both the forgetting curve (the rate at which people forget information over time that is not reinforced or otherwise put into practice), as well as the compliance budget (users essentially budget their security efforts against competing resources such as time and other responsibilities). Also, some users are apathetic, overwhelmed, or even malicious. And, of course, people sometimes simply make mistakes.

In many ways, awareness professionals are like human resources (HR) professionals. HR professionals provide services to employees. At the same time, they protect the organization. That is their job. HR is a well-defined job responsibility that is practiced as a distinct discipline. HR professionals know what their responsibilities are. As an industry, awareness professionals are not given clearly defined practices or guidelines of their own. Awareness professionals deserve the same professional standards, methods, and respect as other professional disciplines. Awareness is a relatively young discipline, and developing such industry-wide standards will take time and effort.

An unfortunate reality is that management generally is not exactly sure what an awareness professional's job should be, as they have no idea of what the goals of an awareness program should be, except that everyone thinks it is a good idea to have one. Therefore, you need to consider what your distinct responsibilities are. They might include many things. You probably will ensure compliance, which unfortunately, is the primary responsibility of 60% of the people running awareness programs. You might put a friendly face forward to the employees on behalf of your security program. You might determine who sees what videos and when. Ideally, these are just some base functions, and your responsibilities extend far beyond this to more practical awareness matters.

Of course, your job is to deliver a clear business value. To accomplish that, your awareness program should specifically make people aware of how to do their jobs in a way that is more efficient and that mitigates losses. You should define metrics that clearly demonstrate ROI. If your job is also to ensure compliance, so be it. That, too, has a clear business value.

Awareness professionals are ideally responsible for ensuring that users are not in a position to potentially initiate a loss. That involves analyzing business processes and determining where technology can proactively stop losses from being initiated through technology and governance.

They also work with other professionals throughout the loss prevention and mitigation chain to provide guidance as to how users are actually behaving and how the other professionals can do their jobs better to make the users less likely to initiate a loss. This might be through better interface designs, better technologies, modifications to governance, better detection, and so on.

It is critical to understand that few people ever define the role of an awareness person as being part of a team and a system that intends to mitigate UIL. While you can potentially be a user advocate, remember your primary responsibility is to mitigate loss in whatever form that needs to take given your assigned position.

The Goal of Awareness Programs

The goal of an awareness program is to have people practice the desired behaviors. The desired behaviors should be defined by governance. The goal is not to show people videos, make them aware, or have them participate in games. Those are merely methods to accomplish the goal.

Getting everyone in the organization to wear a badge is a goal. Having co-workers police each other when they talk about sensitive information outside of the organization might be another goal. Getting everyone to clean and properly maintain their equipment is another possible goal. Threats, punishments, rewards, "fitting in" with the team, feeling a sense of responsibility, and so on, might be methods toward accomplishing those goals, but they are not the goals themselves.

Many awareness program managers seem to focus on the methods of their programs more than the goals. This distorts the mission to a large extent. Clearly, awareness professionals need to determine how to do their job. However, they must never lose sight of what they are attempting to achieve, while focusing on their predetermined means to achieve the goal.

In the design of a program, there is clearly a focus on the methods, and there are traditional methods for implementing awareness. These include formal training, videos, posters, newsletters, events, and so on. Each of those methods has a specific purpose and can be used in the right time and place. However, what is important is the method's ability to change behavior.

Changing Culture

An organization's culture drives its behaviors. Ideally, you want to create a culture that embeds loss reduction practices by default. Culture should be one of your most powerful awareness tools. If the existing culture does not help you achieve awareness, you want to change it to become the desired culture. You need to define practices to help people refine how they perform their jobs and also modify the organizational culture to embed better awareness throughout it.

At the same time, there are other aspects of culture that are independent of loss reduction efforts. For example, people who work in factories generally rely upon mobile devices for communication. This will not change based upon your loss reduction efforts. Even if you want to engrain in the culture that people should properly secure their mobile devices, people will still continue to use their mobile devices for communication. You need to determine whether you can change the culture in this regard and whether you should use mobile device–based communication to transmit messages to those users.

Awareness professionals are sometimes told that they need to understand their organization's culture and work within it. To an extent that is true, but they must recognize that they can't be limited to working only within existing cultural confines. Sometimes they need to be willing to change their culture, which can potentially be their strongest awareness tool.

Creating a loss reduction culture is difficult, but if you work within the general culture to accomplish it and are willing to sometimes help that culture grow, it can be doable.

Defining Subcultures

One of the primary problems we see with otherwise good awareness programs is that they treat their organization monolithically. They provide everyone in the entire organization with the same program. Everyone watches the same video. Everyone sees the same posters. Everyone receives the same newsletters. It is highly unlikely that the CEO, a delivery driver, and a cashier have the same awareness needs.

Some organizations are more homogenous than others. However, any organization of significant size, diversity, geographical dispersement, and so on, can usually be divided into many distinct subcultures. Consider Walmart, for example. Walmart is essentially a retailer, and at first glance, they would appear to be basically homogenous. However, consider the actual diversity of roles across the organization.

- The headquarters staff is a white-collar workforce concerned with accounting, sourcing, financial forecasting, communications, and dozens of other standard business functions. They use desktop computers regularly to perform their daily business functions. They work in a traditional office environment.
- The IT staff uses a variety of computer systems. Their work consists of interacting with and ensuring the proper functioning of hardware, software, networks, and related infrastructure. They have their communication preferences and business drivers that are distinct from those of the traditional headquarters staff.
- The distribution center staff works in factories and warehouses and generally uses mobile computers to ensure the packaging and distribution of products from one location to another. They have a finite usage of computers and other forms of communication. They have focused business functions that are extremely different than the headquarters and IT staffs.

- The store associates use devices to stock shelves, perform inventories, and handle customer transactions. They might have basic payment card industry (PCI) awareness needs given their access to credit card information.

Also, consider the geographic distribution of Walmart employees. For example, Zimbabwe, China, and El Salvador have three very different cultures, and their communication needs and styles will likely differ from each other. Another example is sales tax in Europe, which is incorporated into a product's price, but in the United States it is not. These differences can require different handling when it comes to increasing awareness about taxes, profit margins, and sales figures.

Whenever you create an awareness program, whether it is for security, safety, business processes, sustainability, HR compliance, or so on, you need to consider creating separate awareness programs for each distinct subculture of your organization. Admittedly, this is a daunting task for many practitioners given that they are already overworked with limited resources. Not only is it difficult to put together one program, but to do it right, you might have to create a dozen programs. You may be able to combine similar subcultures, but you need to realize that without considering the importance of separate awareness programs for subcultures, you cannot create a good awareness program.

Interdepartmental Cooperation

All awareness professionals should strive to cooperate with other departments throughout the organization. Some departments are just helpful, while others will essentially be gatekeepers whom you have to go through to get your message delivered. While you want to cooperate with everyone that you can, there are departments where you should focus your outreach efforts.

Clearly, you want cooperation from your home department. If you are a security awareness practitioner, you, of course, need the help of the Security and IT departments. Besides technical insight that you might need, they also are going to either help or hinder your efforts.

The Corporate Communications department is traditionally the gatekeeper for distributing information to the general population. You need to understand their standards, requirements, limitations, turnaround time, resources, and so on. They also might have a variety of resources available to you to assist with developing your materials.

Legal, Compliance, HR, and related departments likely have some oversight that you need to work within. On one occasion, we were working with an airline and wanted to provide security awareness training. We learned that we could not attempt to provide formal training to the flight attendants, because they had a contract that specified the time that they would be required to undergo mandatory training. If we made information security training mandatory, we then had to figure out what other training could be removed from their training requirements. Some of that training is required by law. Other training involved passenger and flight safety. Sometimes you need your training to adhere to different laws, such as the Americans with Disabilities Act, which requires accessibility for a variety of people. There are countless concerns that you should assume you are not aware of.

Physical security can frequently assist with a variety of tasks, such as distribution of materials and collecting metrics, and might have familiarity with your facilities that other departments do not. They are also responsible for a variety of awareness-related issues, and they likely have a great deal of insight into what works and what doesn't.

Safety programs have typically figured out successful methods for communicating with your organization. They have critical information to communicate, and they are typically judged by the results of their efforts, so they tend to be more successful at outreach efforts. Frequently, you can use some of their communication vehicles to share your messaging.

You should attempt to work with as many departments in your organization as possible. We cannot predict the structure of every possible organization, but we do recommend that you figure out what all other departments can potentially offer you and what you can offer them in return.

The Core of All Awareness Efforts

When we design awareness programs, we begin with a thorough assessment of the organization and its culture. Awareness programs must work within the overall culture to change the loss reduction culture. To do this, you have to understand how the organization generally behaves and how you want it to behave so you can determine what you need to improve. You also want to figure out how to change the loss reduction culture so that people behave from a security and loss reduction perspective. Your organization's security and loss reduction culture can be distinctly recognized in your people's behaviors. If you walk around without a badge, will you get stopped? If sensitive information is left unattended, will someone pick it up and secure it? If someone witnesses equipment malfunctioning, will they stop what they are doing and fix it, call someone, or just consider that to be someone else's job? All of these behaviors reflect your security and loss reduction culture.

Fundamentally, most loss reduction professionals say that you need to work within your culture. Unfortunately, "work within your culture" gives the false impression that you have to accept your existing culture just as it is. However, doing so directly conflicts with what is required to reduce your UIL, which is to actually *change* your loss reduction culture.

To change, or more specifically improve, your security and loss reduction culture, you need to essentially align the communication of your message with your overall culture. The message you are communicating is essentially your business drivers, which are the goals you are trying to accomplish in transforming your culture. Doing this effectively is also an aspect of governance. While culture, communication, and business drivers are each critical, they are meaningless without an underlying process for the program to implement. The following sections will examine the process, communication, and business drivers.

Process

Perhaps the greatest problem with most awareness programs is that they focus on developing and distributing communication without an underlying plan.

For example, in security awareness programs, there is a typical strategy of choosing one topic per month and then rolling out a video, a poster, and a newsletter related to the topic. Then there may be simulated phishing messages periodically sent out.

The result is that someone will watch a two-minute video, skim through the newsletter, and perhaps glance at the poster once or twice. Even assuming that two minutes of a video and a one-page newsletter can tell a person everything that they need to know about a security-related subject, you then have to consider that this is the last time the person will hear about the content for at least a year. The forgetting curve will quickly make the information a moot point.

The phishing simulations might decrease the overall number of incidents of users clicking on the targeted phishing messages. Although this can be a measure of improvement, by itself it is not enough.

You need to have a consistent strategy to reinforce actual behaviors. When we create awareness programs, we use a proprietary interview form that essentially collects information about an organization's industry, security incidents, structure, policies and other governance, reporting structures, contact information for people who need to be consulted and/or distribute the information, and so on. We also ask about the current state of loss reduction, other forms of behavioral modification programs that work or do not work, expected cooperation from management and other departments, any people who will have to approve our efforts, and other information that could help with our efforts. We often conduct more than a dozen interviews that reveal extremely valuable information.

Especially valuable are those conversations with the rank-and-file users. When the proper rapport is established during the interview, users will open up as to what really goes on inside the organization, why they behave the way they do, what works and what doesn't work, what has been attempted before, and frequently some of the most valuable suggestions as to what might work in the future. While you have to take what you hear with a grain of salt, talking to actual users will give you some incredible insight into the communication culture of the organization.

It is also worth highlighting that an awareness program does not usually have to rely upon its own insight. Many organizations have wellness and sustainability (recycling) programs. These are essentially behavioral modification programs. They intend to have people modify their behavior to improve their fitness-related behaviors or be more environmentally friendly. Admittedly, these programs are frequently less successful than traditional security awareness programs. However, safety programs keep very valuable statistics on what works and what doesn't work to improve behavior. Whatever the success of the programs, it is valuable to find out what seemed to work, what seemed not to work, and, most important, why.

Once you've researched the organization to identify its culture and determine what works within it, you're better positioned to communicate the business drivers to the users. What you need is a process that attempts to get the messages across on a constant basis with regular reinforcement in practice. This is where the focus on telling people how to do their job properly becomes more practical.

You need to ensure that your awareness program has forms of active communication, such as mandatory training in some form to get an initial message across. There should also be passive reminders that remind people of how to do the right thing at the right time, such as signs to remind employees to wash their hands after using the restroom. The culture should also constantly remind people how to do their job properly and how to make appropriate decisions.

Awareness professionals should be in the position to assist with enforcement of procedures, as applicable, and to ideally reward people for doing the right things. Ultimately, this should be the task of those enforcing governance.

Ideally, though, the process is just allowing people to do their work, and the environment around them subtly guides them to do things in the right way. If you can create a culture through enforcement of some form, it works best.

As you read the rest of this chapter, keep in mind that culture, communication, and business drivers are to be used as parts of a comprehensive process. After all, just as a fence and a guard are not a comprehensive physical security program, a video is not a comprehensive awareness program.

Business Drivers

Your business drivers are essentially what you are trying to accomplish. These are the underlying reasons why an awareness program has been put in place. They can include losses that you are attempting to mitigate, regulatory or compliance concerns, definition of job functions, or any number of concerns.

There are reasons that you are doing what you are doing. This is where a good governance program comes in. When you have governance, it makes the design of an awareness program that much easier.

Similar to how your culture tells you how you are going to communicate your message, your business drivers tell you the topics that will be that message. It is that simple. You need to identify distinct topics to address. They cannot be vague. You should also not endeavor to have people learn every possible aspect of a topic. The goal is measurable improvement in the business driver.

Whether the business driver in question is phishing awareness, proper maintenance of equipment, fewer workplace injuries, or better adherence to workplace standards to reduce quality issues, the topic has to be defined and then the appropriate messaging has to be placed into the communication tools.

The message has to be tailored to the communication format. A poster can only provide basic information. A newsletter can provide more information, while an in-person presentation can provide possibly all the required information.

Culture and Communication Tools

Your culture drives how you need to communicate with your user population. Do your users use mobile devices to get messages across? Are there regular staff meetings where teams meet to hear the most critical news from their organization? Do people like giveaways to keep on their desk? Are there key influencers, who always seem to be able to get others to cooperate in new efforts? The list goes on.

This is essentially the communication culture of your organization or its subcultures. You need to determine the most effective ways to reach your users. This varies from organization to organization. For example, in one large investment bank, the staff revered the CEO like a proverbial god. We found that the best way to reach the staff was to add our content to the CEO's morning newsletter. That ensured people took the security message seriously. We also learned that if we created our own newsletter, it would be deleted without being read.

In one manufacturing environment, we found that there were safety meetings held on a weekly basis that everyone had to attend. These meetings were also perceived to be valuable and people really listened to the message. We, therefore, endeavored to incorporate our messaging into those meetings. However, in other environments meetings are perceived as worthless and burdensome, and people just showed up to have their presence acknowledged and leave. Delivering messages in those environments is far less effective (and might even undermine your efforts).

Posters are generally useful as passive reminders when placed appropriately. However, when we created a security awareness program for an investment bank, we asked the CISO about the potential to use posters, and his response was extremely memorable: "We can't put up a poster next to a Picasso."

So, as you can see, newsletters, meeting, and other tools can be great in one environment but useless in another. It all depends on the culture, the perceived value, the background to the communication tools, and so on. Different tools work or don't work in different environments, under certain conditions. Either way you must consider any tool that can work within your organization.

You should never expect universal acceptance of any particular tool. Some tools will reach some people better than others. For example, some companies use Twitter to transmit information to employees, despite the fact that not all people have Twitter accounts. You might send newsletters knowing that possibly only 10% of the organization reads them. Certain forms of communication might be more useful than others, but from a cost/benefit perspective, you must consider whether the effort to implement the tool is offset by the benefits it delivers.

There are a variety of tools to consider. The following sections discuss common tools that may or may not be right for your circumstances. There are, of course, many tools beyond the ones we discuss. Any given tool might work well in an organization for one purpose but not in another. You will need to assess your organization to determine which tools are best suited to it.

Computer-Based Training

Perhaps the most widely used commodity for a communication tool is computer-based training (CBT). CBT is formal training that typically asks questions to ensure some level of comprehension of the content. CBT is delivered through a learning management system (LMS) that tracks a user's progress and provides reports to satisfy auditing expectations.

There are two common forms of CBT delivery: long form and micro-learning. Long-form training is essentially a course that is designed to fulfill the content requirements of a particular subject. It is generally done once per year or even just once per employee during a hiring and orientation process. Long-form training is often used to essentially check the box of demonstrating compliance with a regulation.

Micro-learnings involve short videos on a specific subject. These CBT modules tend to range from one to five minutes and are typically pushed out to users on a monthly basis, with a different topic covered each month.

When we are asked which format is more effective, the answer is usually "neither." With regard to all forms of training, the forgetting curve becomes relevant, even assuming that all of the content was covered and absorbed in the first place.

All of this being said, CBT is effective for compliance purposes, introducing a topic, and demonstrating that the organization believes that the subject is important enough for the organization to require everyone take the time to participate in the training.

Also, if you can find the right training, it may be more effective and have more benefits than expected. For example, we found that organizations using CBT from Mimecast, a vendor that focuses on email and web security that also produces awareness videos, found unusual engagement with their videos. They have a recurring cast of characters, and users developed a relationship with them. In at least one organization, users dressed as the characters for Halloween parties. It is safe to assume that if they engage with the characters, users engage with the content and are more likely to retain the content.

If the training is directly work related, people will perceive more value and attempt to comprehend the material more diligently. More important, the material will be applied immediately, which means that it might never have a chance to be forgotten.

Phishing Simulations

Phishing simulations are controlled exercises where an organization sends out phishing messages to their own users. They are arguably the most popular awareness tool, after CBT. The purpose is to see if a user might be susceptible to actual phishing messages and to create a teachable moment. In talking to many users, this can have an impact on raising awareness.

This is not just a cybersecurity countermeasure, but a general business loss countermeasure. If a message attempts to get a user to download malware or attempts to acquire user credentials, it is a cybersecurity issue. However, criminals frequently use phishing messages to get users to initiate criminal transactions, send out personal and sensitive information, and so on. These are business compromises that just happen to use email as a form of communication. They could also use other means of communication, like a telephone.

Although phishing simulations can be used effectively, they unfortunately are usually implemented in a way that has minimal effect. For example, there are several phishing services that include the name of the phishing service in the sender line. Users just have to read the sender line to recognize that this is not a legitimate message. When you factor in the compliance budget, they quickly disregard or report the obvious phishing message and move on to their normal tasks. They weren't effectively trained in any significant way to recognize a real phishing message, so they are more likely to initiate loss when they encounter one. Similarly, many phishing campaigns just bombard users with obvious phishing messages. When almost all users finally recognize those phishing messages, an organization declares success. Unfortunately, this is very ineffective.

Using the example of scuba diving, when an instructor puts his students in a pool to practice basic scuba skills, after a while, everyone can demonstrate a passable knowledge of those skills. However, if students are only put in the shallow end of the pool and keep being tested on the same basic skills, they will quickly lose interest. At the same time, in no way does constantly demonstrating basic skills alone qualify the students to be in open water. The water is not perfectly clear, as it is in a pool. There, water is not still, as it is in a pool. The water is not shallow, as it is in a pool. The list goes on. Most phishing simulations are akin to scuba diving in a pool.

This is why we advocate continually increasing the sophistication of phishing campaigns and simultaneously running multiple phishing campaigns of multiple sophistications to ensure there is constant learning. This ensures that your users are constantly improving their skills and lowering the organization's susceptibility to loss. When we work with companies to run their simulated phishing campaigns, we frequently use actual phishing messages sent to the company. We pull out the damaging components of the original messages, send the now-safe messages out to the users, and examine who falls for the messages, while also ensuring that they are trained to detect such messages. Additionally, there are some phishing simulation services that offer this functionality as a part of their service.

We don't expect to completely eliminate users falling prey to phishing, but you should see a measurable decrease in clicks to actual phishing messages, beyond those attributed to better technical countermeasures.

Newsletters

Newsletters are a form of information delivery. Even though you are pushing the information to the users, we generally consider it a form of passive communication, as it is delivered in a way that allows the user to ignore it. The information might be on a specific subject or multiple subjects. Newsletters are generally limited in length so that they do not take a significant amount of time to read.

Newsletters vary in quality, as well as usefulness. The more professionally prepared they are, the better. They must also be written in a style appropriate for the audience. A newsletter appropriate for executives will likely not be appropriate for a factory floor. There is different terminology used in those environments. Again, the newsletter must adhere to the culture.

Minimally, you need to determine who is reading the newsletter and what you expect them to obtain from it. Also consider taking your content and adding it to an already successful newsletter.

Knowledge Base

A knowledge base is an information store where people go to look for information on a given subject. Many organizations use SharePoint, intranets, or similar information storage tools to provide this resource. Whatever your awareness subject (security, safety, fitness, mechanical, etc.), it is extremely helpful to create short files where any person who seeks out information relevant to their concerns can find it.

As opposed to posters, newsletters, and other forms of information that is pushed to the users, the knowledge base sits readily available and contains as much information relevant to a subject as possible. While posters, newsletters, etc., contain a finite amount of information, you can provide limitless information to anyone who chooses to search for it.

As important, a knowledge base has the ability to provide information on an unlimited number of subjects. If your organization provides information about how to protect your home or children, it can provide goodwill and likely encourage further browsing of the knowledge base and engagement with the security program.

A knowledge base can be used to enhance other awareness materials. For example, newsletters can link to an extended article on the knowledge base for people who want more information. Posters can have a QR code or provide a URL to specific documents in the knowledge base. It is, of course, burdensome to both create the content and keep it up-to-date, but it is worth it.

The one potential downside is that the material has to be maintained and kept up-to-date. For example, if you have an article on how to secure a personal iPhone, when Apple updates the iOS operating system, you might have to update the relevant articles. This can become burdensome. Secure Mentem, Ira's company, provides a subscription knowledge base that is properly maintained.

Posters

Everyone is familiar with the concept of a poster, which is a one-page paper that provides some content. The amount of information is limited, but if well-placed and timed, it can serve as a valuable reminder of some piece of information. It is good for reinforcing information and interrupting the forgetting curve.

At the same time, posters can become background noise when they are not distinct, well-placed, or frequently changed. With the proper placement, good design, and a focused message, even a simple "Employees must wash hands" poster can serve as an excellent passive reminder.

Monitor Displays and Screensavers

Many organizations have monitors throughout their facilities. These monitors display information of general and organizational interest, usually in loops. Unlike static posters, the screens can change to display a variety of different subjects. Awareness teams should find out the procedures for adding content into the loop of the display and work to create that content. Typically it involves modifying poster content for a 16:9 display ratio.

When computers go to sleep or when they are turned on, you can put a graphic up on the screen that can provide awareness messaging. They can be used for security tips, or they can be used to provide specific reminders relevant to the person's task.

Mouse Pads, Coffee Cups, and More

There are a variety of passive communication tools that you should consider utilizing. While you don't want your awareness program to seem juvenile, you do want to get your messaging out in ways that are "sticky."

These methods include the typical giveaways that most organizations have. In some more formal environments, you can create high-quality coffee mugs. We previously worked with organizations that provide yogurt machines for their employees, so we developed cups with messaging that people used to dispense the yogurt. We rotated messaging so that people compared the tips on the cups.

You can use whatever you think will work. We regularly provide mouse pads with messaging, squishy toys, pens, sticky pads, and other desk supplies branded with security messaging. The goal of these giveaways is not to create massive security change but as a passive reminder that keeps the thought fresh.

Special Events

Events are a good way to get people better engaged with the awareness effort. The form of events is limited only by your creativity. It is easier to start out by participating in events held by other programs. Having a booth of some form at a wellness festival is a good way to get out your messaging. Ideally, you relate your messaging to the theme of the event.

Events of your own might include bringing in a speaker, holding contests, sponsoring a party or some type of get together, and setting up an information booth in a public area. Again, you need to figure out what is most appropriate for your circumstances and available resources.

Meetings

Many groups within a given organization hold regular meetings. It is probably most practical to join already scheduled meetings and add your content. However, you can potentially schedule your own meetings. These meetings may be scheduled for the entire organization, or you might choose to hold meetings targeting different departments and tailor your content to them.

Ambassadors

It is likely that you do not have the resources to engage your entire organization. For that reason, you may consider identifying and recruiting people throughout your organization to help spread the awareness message. These ambassadors, sometimes called *champions*, are trained sufficiently to share your message, answer basic questions, and reach out to others with more challenging questions or situations.

Having these ambassadors allows you to engage with more people in a personal way. It is definitely more effective to put a personal face to your awareness effort than to just push out posters and videos. Knowing that there are co-workers behind the efforts increases people's enthusiasm for following the advice.

Putting It Together

Many organizations define their awareness program for an entire year at the beginning of the year. Each month then focuses on a single topic, where all the communication tools reinforce that one topic. In theory, you might expect that to create maximum absorption of the topic.

In reality, we believe that creates problems. Consider that when you use that structure, your users might not hear any more information about that subject for another year, at best. There is no interruption of the forgetting curve. Also, if some incident or outside concern arises, you don't necessarily have sufficient flexibility in your yearly structure.

A better approach is to use a quarterly structure, where you have three topics that you promote simultaneously. This allows for at least three months for reinforcement of the information. Table 15.1 demonstrates how this may be implemented.

Table 15.1 Quarterly Plan

Component	Month 1	Month 2	Month 3
Poster	Travel security	USB security	Social engineering
Article	USB security	Social engineering	Travel security
Newsletter	Social engineering	Travel security	USB security
Lunch and learn	Travel security	USB security	Social engineering
Event roadshow	Kick-off booth (Human Resources)	Security cube (information technology)	Speaker (marketing)
Table tents	USB security	Social engineering	Travel security

In the awareness plan depicted by Table 15.1, the chosen topics are travel security, USB security, and social engineering. The topics are rotated across the different communication tools to constantly reinforce the messaging for all topics. There is a frequent reminder for all topics.

The plan also shows how different events, which might not be tied directly to the topics, are included. Similarly, there is outreach to different departments via the roadshows. Additionally, it also allows for flexibility in case of any incidents or changes that are otherwise required.

Metrics

Metrics should be embedded throughout your program. There are many types of metrics, such as likability, usage, behavioral, and return on investment. As your awareness program proceeds, your ideal metric is ROI. This shows that you are satisfying a business function.

In the absence of ROI calculations, improvements in behavioral metrics is the next best result. It shows that you are achieving the stated goals of the awareness program, even though you cannot provide a precise, quantifiable financial result.

Usage statistics tells you which of your efforts appears to be the best received by the users. This tells you where to better allocate your efforts. Likability is always nice to have, but there is no clear benefit to it, beyond just good promotion. Likability should theoretically impact effectiveness, but there is no specific cause-and-effect relationship between likability and results.

Chapter 10 discusses metrics in more detail.

Gamification

A lot of people mistakenly believe that gamification means playing games. That is a common misconception. In reality, gamification is a system that applies principles to business problems to change people's behavior.

The rewards systems for salespeople is an example of gamification. Salespeople are rewarded for their success in sales, with some incorporation of specific types of sales as appropriate. The business driver is increased sales.

Frequent flier programs are another great example of gamification. To encourage people to fly a specific airline and participate in partner programs, such as a branded credit card, people are rewarded for flying more frequently with that airline. The more you fly, the more likely you are to earn upgrades. If you use the branded credit card, you earn miles, and, therefore, free flights, more quickly. Benefits like this are the primary driver for brand loyalty.

When implemented properly, gamification can be one of the most valuable tools in the awareness arsenal. It is admittedly difficult to implement, and it is appropriate only for certain cultures, but it can achieve some of the best behavioral modifications.

Gamification Criteria

The truth is that many awareness professionals do not understand exactly what gamification is. They believe if they create a game, they have created gamification. Consider the ABCs of applied behavioral science that were discussed in Chapter 8. Antecedents create behaviors. Behaviors create consequences. Consequences then drive awareness, while further influencing behaviors.

Using consequences to drive behavior is one of the key differences between games and gamification. A game essentially is a creative awareness tool that does not reward people for behaviors but is solely a form of information. By contrast, gamification ideally creates positive consequences for actual, not simulated, behaviors. If you want true gamification, you need to ensure you are capturing behaviors in practice and reinforcing them appropriately.

In her iconic book *Reality Is Broken*, Jane McGonigal defines four traits of a game. Those traits are goals, rules, a feedback system, and voluntary participation. Those are fantastic traits for designing a game.

First, achieving goals provides for rewards. The criteria for achieving the goals and receiving the reward are the rules. The rules have to be properly defined. In other words, people know what they have to do to be rewarded. The feedback, or tracking system, has to allow for users to know where they stand in relation to accomplishing the goal. Voluntary participation essentially means that you are not forcing people to be part of the gamification.

The rewards have to be desirable. Creating a contest that nobody cares about winning is definitely not going to be useful. For example, if you want to reward frequent fliers, most fliers will not remain loyal if their only benefit is a free drink. The goals have to be achievable. For example, if frequent fliers have to fly 100,000 miles to achieve basic levels of rewards, few people will participate.

Structuring Gamification

To create a gamification program, you essentially start with the same fundamental aspects of an awareness program. In short, culture tells you what good rewards are for your chosen goal. Business drivers tell you what to reward. It is that simple.

For example, in one investment bank, we wanted to get the traders to implement multifactor authentication. They made too much money for the company to force them to do almost anything. Even though their behaviors theoretically caused millions of dollars in losses, they were credited with making the bank hundreds of millions of dollars.

The business driver was to get them to implement MFA, which was anticipated to save the company millions of dollars. However, we had to make it voluntary. From a cultural perspective, the one thing they prized most was time with the CEO, whom they revered. We had the CEO agree to participate in the program, and we established that if people implemented MFA, they would be entered into a drawing that would provide for three people to play a round of golf with the CEO. There was 100% participation. Over time, more security-related behaviors were added to criteria for entering a drawing, as the CEO agreed to monthly rounds of golf to support the security program.

This is a very tactical use of gamification. However, you can implement strategic programs, similar to frequent flier programs, where you track ongoing behaviors and provide incremental rewards. You track behaviors that are measurable and then add points every time a user does something related to a business goal. For example, in the cybersecurity field, you might award points every time a user reports a phishing message.

Gamification Is Not for Everyone

Participation in gamification efforts must be voluntary. You cannot expect 100% participation. Some people might not care or want to expend any effort. That is okay. Again, all security efforts are about risk reduction, not perfection.

At the same time, some parts of an organization may not be appropriate for gamification efforts. For example, if you have a cybersecurity gamification program and many of your employees are stock clerks, they are likely not using a computer regularly enough to participate in the program. You need to know your user populations and know where and when to apply gamification.

Getting Management's Support

Probably the most critical factor for success for any awareness program is management's support. Without management's support, you will not get the budget, departmental support, visibility, and other resources that you need.

For many organizations, awareness is a "check the box" type of activity. They will support what is minimally required by regulations, and no more. In other cases, management enthusiastically champions awareness efforts. It all depends upon management's perception of the value of awareness.

In many cases, perceptions reflect past experiences with awareness programs. If past awareness efforts resulted in little value, you will need to improve the perceived value of awareness programs in general. In other cases, you might need to attempt to portray the increased value that your program will bring. There are many potential methods for doing this that vary based on your culture and the people involved. However, there are two general methods to improve support: create a program specific to management and demonstrate the business case.

Awareness Programs for Management

If your management is hesitant to support your efforts, you should consider creating an awareness program that provides value for the decision-makers. This isn't limited to just their professional needs. Research the decision-makers and see whether they have any personal interests where your awareness efforts might be meaningful for them.

For example, if they have teenagers, and you are trying to get support for security awareness efforts, you might consider a social media awareness presentation that is designed for parents with the intent of making them aware of what they should be concerned about regarding their children's social media usage. If they had previously asked for special technologies in their home, you might want to provide information on how to protect their computing environment. You are only limited by your creativity and available resources in creating these awareness programs.

Once you demonstrate the personal value to them, you can then lobby management to provide similar benefits to the rest of the organization.

Demonstrate Clear Business Value

If management does not believe there is a value to awareness training, you need to demonstrate the value in very clear and ideally quantifiable terms. You need to highlight how the results of the awareness program generate a return on the investment. You need to consider the reduction in risk. You need to determine the appropriate metrics that you intend to focus on and then give some expectation of the improvements in those metrics.

You need to show management that you deserve more. This can mean more time, money, or other resources as the case may be. If you cannot come up with a business case as to why you deserve more, you need to stop and consider what your mission is and if management is wrong in their perceptions of their efforts.

Enforcement

The goal for awareness is to influence behaviors. Behaviors generate a consequence. Consequences can either support your efforts to improve behaviors or doom your efforts. Without enforcement, you are likely dooming your efforts.

In short, you need to attempt to create some form of enforcement that discourages people from the undesired behaviors. We realize that this is generally outside of the traditional purview of awareness programs. However, assuming there is some form of governance that the awareness program embodies, the enforcement is not necessarily the responsibility of the awareness program, but of the organization as a whole. This is where the concept of a "just culture" comes into play. Users should be provided with the knowledge, skills, and resources to do their jobs as defined. If these conditions are met and users do not follow the guidance and cause loss, there should be some form of consequence that attempts to drive the desired behaviors.

When it is easier not to adhere to the guidance provided by the awareness program, people will simply choose not to follow the guidance. Because of the compliance budget, even well-intentioned users won't allocate their time and energy to follow the program. You need to consider that the enforcement itself is an awareness effort, and without it, you not only miss a critical awareness resource, you are rendering the tools you put in place moot.

Experiment

We lay out broad guidance as to how to implement an awareness program. Not all guidance is appropriate for all organizations. Likewise, there is no one right way to implement an awareness program. You need to examine our recommendations, as well as those from other sources, to determine what is the most appropriate for you.

It is also very likely that you will not get it right the first time, which is just one of the reasons that three-month awareness programs can be beneficial. They allow you to see what is succeeding and what isn't.

Many awareness professionals will not advocate several of the things that we do. We do look at awareness as a business function and not necessarily that of advocacy for the user. The culture should be a "just culture," where users are provided with all of the necessary resources to do their job properly. This also means that UIL mitigation practices are to be not only encouraged, but in fact required, just as other business functions are. Awareness efforts exist both to recommend good practices and to assist all users in doing their jobs properly. This is a critical distinction.

We can also not stress enough the importance of proactively collecting metrics. Some awareness efforts might initially seem unproductive, but metrics might definitively reveal that the efforts are more productive than expected. Also, when you find that some of your efforts are extremely productive, you will want to continue using them.

At the same time, you will probably find that some tools are either generally less effective or lose their usefulness over time. That is okay. In fact, it is an inevitable part of the process. You need to continually evolve your awareness program to accommodate new concepts, ideas, business drivers, tools, technologies, and so on. Not only does this keep your program state of the art, it constantly engages your users.

IV Applying Boom

We have to admit that it surprises us how, for the most part, there is a lack of coordination in developing a comprehensive end-to-end plan with regard to loss prevention and mitigation programs. Yes, there are countermeasures put in place, but there is a major difference between implementing a set of tactics and implementing a strategy.

Tactics can provide some return on investment, but implementing tactics alone isn't as effective as implementing them as part of a comprehensive strategy. For example, sending police officers to patrol random streets at random times is not as effective as studying crime trends, attempting to determine the root cause of crimes, researching successful crime reduction strategies, considering multiple tactics to reduce crime, and then determining the optimal combination of tactics as part of a strategy.

Firefighters just don't run into a burning building to spray water on the fire. They have to first plan for the possibilities of fire. Where are the optimal places to have fire stations? Where are roads and population clusters? What type of equipment is needed at each station given the likely fires in the area? When you get to a fire, how do you enter the building? Are there hazardous materials? Consider the 2020 Australian wildfires. They didn't just send in random fire crews and tell airplanes to find the fire and drop fire retardant on it.

Unfortunately, risk reduction practitioners across industries are rarely trained to consider a comprehensive strategy. They spend their time figuratively putting out fires without a strategy.

In looking at different methodologies for developing a strategy, the simplest framework we have found is applied in counterterrorism. The framework is named Boom. The name Boom marks the actual terrorist attack. Looking at it on a traditional timeline, to the left of Boom are the events that led up to the attack. To the right of Boom are those events that take place after the attack.

While it is intuitive that you want to prevent an attack proactively and you want to stop an attack in progress, what you do after an attack is as important, if not more important, than preventing the attack. For example, you need to expect and prepare for secondary attacks. You need to ensure that there are enough medical facilities in place. You need to ensure first responders are properly trained. You need to study the attack and determine how to prevent future attacks, catch accomplices, and so on.

While your potential losses are ideally not as dire as a terrorist attack, the same methodology can be used for most types of loss mitigation. Part IV walks you through the process of creating your own strategy for mitigating risk.

16 Start with Boom

Boom is a concept that has been used in the counterterrorism field. Essentially, Boom deals with when an attack or disastrous event takes place, and it is divided into three phases: Left of Boom, Boom, and Right of Boom. Left of Boom is before the moment of attack/disaster, Boom is the moment the attack/disaster takes place, and Right of Boom is what happens afterward.

Recognizing the phases of Boom is useful far beyond their military application. These concepts can be useful in addressing user-initiated loss (UIL) as well. For example, here are the concepts of Boom in the context of phishing:

- **Left of Boom:** Bad people send a phishing email to the user.
- **Boom:** The user clicks the link in the phishing email.
- **Right of Boom:** Bad things happen as a result of the user clicking the link.

You need to plan ahead to try to mitigate all three of these things. For example, here are steps you might take in advance to mitigate phishing each stage of the Boom cycle:

- **Left of Boom:** You put measures in place to try to prevent phishing emails from ever reaching a user, you educate the user to not click such links, you can prevent them from using personal email on company machines, and you can keep the user from having access to more sensitive parts of your system (so that clicking the link will not result in as much damage).
- **Boom:** This is also the actual moment where a user is faced with the potential to initiate loss. Even in the moment of the user clicking the link, you can have mitigating measures. Any systems you

have in place can actively mitigate the amount of damage. You might be able to detect the Boom as it occurs, so you can immediately take action. Even the user who clicks the link might recognize their error in the moment, and such awareness allows them to leap into mitigating action and immediately alert the appropriate people. Ideally, the user recognizes the attack before clicking and then alerts the appropriate people to take action and quarantine this message and others, in case other users are not as aware.

■ **Right of Boom:** You react to what has happened, attempting to reduce the potential damage. You can also analyze what happened, which will help you improve your next Left of Boom phase.

Keep in mind that you take actions to mitigate all of three phases of Boom in advance. You can prepare for the moment of Boom as much as possible, but when the user actually clicks the phishing link, your attempts to prevent it have failed, and your plans to mitigate the loss kick in.

You need to look at preventing UIL from a systems perspective and effectively address Left of Boom, Boom, and Right of Boom. Although you can think of them linearly in time, in reality they are cyclical. No matter what you do to mitigate Left of Boom, Boom, and Right of Boom, UIL will inevitably take place at some point in time. Regardless, you need to both plan to prevent it and learn valuable lessons from the moment when it occurs. Depending on your needs, you can begin by focusing on any part of the Boom cycle.

Most organizations' risk mitigation strategy is linear in nature. They start with prevention and then ideally build in detection and reaction. While some organizations decide only to implement detection because it is somehow impractical for them to perform prevention, that decision is still predicated on examining the potential prevention.

In conducting workshops on applying this concept, we made the mistake of defining risk mitigation as a linear strategy. We walked attendees through the process of naming a potential attack, figuring out how an attack can come to being, and then moving forward. This was confusing in that it was difficult to figure out where to start, as there are a seemingly infinite number of possibilities. Essentially, our mistake was starting the conversation by beginning with Left of Boom. Ultimately, we determined that it is better to begin with Boom.

We found that when we allowed attendees to first discuss real, existing attacks in detail (the steps taken during the attack, where it succeeded, etc.), they were then able to go back and better define the enablement of the losses. For this reason, we strongly recommend that you start by first analyzing how, at the point of Boom, users should respond to the potential loss, the recommended processes, whether you can prevent the losses, how technology can help, etc. You can then move into Right of Boom, as you can think about how you might mitigate the UIL that has been initiated. Then you can proceed to Left of Boom, being thoroughly familiar with the UIL and its aftereffects and now anticipating how the user can be put into the position of initiating a loss.

To that end, we found that the following process is the most systematic in identifying and mitigating Boom at the actual root of UIL, which is the user. Again, our goal at Boom is that the user will not initiate loss. We, therefore, need to define how and where UIL can be prevented at the source. Our goal is not to create healthier canaries that don't die in a coal mine, but we do have to acknowledge and account for the fact that the analogy only goes so far, and that the canary, in this case, is more than a detection mechanism, but an actual threat.

What Are the Actions That Initiate UIL?

While it sounds simple, it is difficult to anticipate every possible way a user can initiate loss. There are countless forms of loss, with an equally incalculable number of ways each form of loss can be initiated. The insurance and finance fields each address loss in their own unique ways, but many other organizations struggle with understanding UIL. The curse of technology loss mitigation programs is that professionals often consider this to be too hard to do properly and, therefore, ignore it or do it in ways that don't adequately identify and mitigate risk.

A great way to start addressing loss is to recognize where existing UIL is taking place in your organization and identifying and prioritizing where the Boom actually is.

Start with a List

The first step is to identify the most significant UIL that your organization experiences. Some of these types of UIL are obvious and common.

Phishing attacks come immediately to mind. Others depend on your industry and circumstances. For example, with accounting, there might be data entry errors. In manufacturing environments, there might be poor maintenance or careless practices.

Also, while some losses are not common, they can be extremely costly. These costs can be monetary, operational, and/or reputational. For example, if personally identifiable information (PII) is released, it could be embarrassing to the organization. There can also be heavy fines for the organization. Preventing incidents that trigger investigations and regulatory actions are also high on the list of potential UIL that you need to mitigate.

From that point, you begin to add every conceivable user action to the list. The list will definitely grow long, and if nothing else, it is a good exercise. You are looking for classes of UIL. For example, falling victim to a phishing message can involve the potential for downloading malware, compromising user credentials, sending out sensitive information, and visiting malicious websites, among other email-based attacks. Essentially, you are looking for a specific situation where a user can initiate a loss, no matter how many different types of losses may occur.

Order the List

The UIL actions you listed first are the ones that will most likely be the ones you want to start with. Even in the best circumstances, it is unlikely that you will have the time and resources to address each and every UIL on the list. For this reason, you want to pick the top three to five to consider, at least at first.

Some industries, such as accounting, already embed this strategy into everything that they do. However, if you are in cybersecurity or other fields where UIL is not considered as part of a comprehensive risk reduction process by default, you (and your organization) are going to have to get used to this strategy.

There are a variety of factors to consider in ordering your list. Clearly, the value of the potential loss would be a top concern. There are, however, a few other issues to consider. For example, if mitigating one type of UIL would likewise have a great deal of overlap for mitigating other types of UIL, that would make mitigating that UIL a higher priority. For example, if you determine that users can be manipulated in accounts payable, which has historically created massive losses across all industries, would the processes, technology, and awareness help to mitigate other losses attributed to social engineering types of attacks? If so, and if you can quickly adapt the techniques to other types of losses, then you should raise the UIL for accounts payable to a much higher priority.

At the same time, you need to consider whether there are some types of UIL that are easy to mitigate at Boom. While the losses might not be high, the fact that you can have a quick win has some immense intangible returns. For example, a fast success can be used to gain support for future efforts. Don't underestimate the concerns of stakeholders that you are attempting to change a proven process that might otherwise appear to be reasonably functional. While the stakeholders might think that you have some potential to provide value, they are usually perfectly happy to not introduce risk and maintain the status quo. A couple of quick wins will help to overcome their concerns.

Once you think you have a prioritized list, you can then start with one or more specific efforts to mitigate UIL. This is where you now need to work one potential UIL loss at a time and begin your mitigation efforts.

Metrics

Once you've identified a specific type of UIL that you want to address, you need to start by collecting metrics. While Chapter 10 discusses the different types of metrics in detail, at this point you need to determine the metrics that are most applicable for the UIL you are attempting to address. Those metrics should ideally be value metrics, such as productivity, fewer losses, fewer incidents, etc. so that you can truly prove the return on investment that you are providing.

In the absence of value metrics, you should find metrics that are perceived to be meaningful in some other way for your organization. These are again specific to your organization.

At the same time, you might not have to rely upon metrics unique to your specific concerns. It is possible that some other parts of your organization might already collect relevant metrics. These metrics would also have the added benefit of being already identified as important to your organization. For example, the CFO might already have processes in place to collect metrics. There might be Six Sigma and other quality control metrics being collected to streamline operations. If your efforts can measurably improve those metrics, this significantly helps your future efforts.

Whichever type of metrics you choose, you need to ensure that you collect the existing baseline metrics before you start implementing anything. At first, you can use the scope of the losses to gain support for your efforts. For example, if you want to better mitigate the UIL associated with phishing, having tangible metrics allows you to make a strong argument for any of your efforts.

Obviously, when you take further metrics after your efforts have been implemented, you can prove the value of your efforts and use those metrics to get other business units to cooperate with you. At the same time, if the metrics either are not moving or are moving in the wrong direction, it can be valuable feedback that helps you to understand how and why your efforts are not performing as hoped.

Being able to compare the metrics of how, why, where, and the amount of UIL when Boom occurs enables you to better understand each instance of Boom and how it relates to ongoing mitigation efforts. Ultimately, metrics will help you know exactly how your efforts perform for a wide variety of reasons, ranging from political to actually useful in making improvements.

Governance

When you begin to address UIL at Boom, you begin with the fact that the user is now directly faced with a situation where they can initiate a loss. We assume that, at this point, your Left of Boom efforts have failed. The user for all practical purposes is holding a loaded gun to your crown jewels. What do you want and expect them to do at the moment of Boom?

This sounds intuitive, and most practitioners, and especially awareness practitioners will say that this is what they are already doing. Unfortunately, many of them at best give vague descriptions of what users should be afraid of, and not exactly what they should do. For this reason, you need to have a clear understanding of exactly what you want the users to do, step-by-step. Ultimately, this means ensuring your governance efforts are what you want them to be at the moment of Boom, because they directly affect UIL at that moment.

For example, if you want a user to not click links in phishing messages, they have to know what specific steps to take to determine whether a message is a phishing message. You also likely want your users to delete and/or report the message. Therefore, the question is whether you have laid out step-by-step instructions for every step of the process from start to finish. Chances are good that you've only shown a vague awareness video that depicts the entire process in a two-minute video. This is clearly not anywhere close to a definition of a guideline or procedure. Might such a definition sound tedious? Possibly, but without such a definition, you do not have a clear process that you can expect your users to follow. You might also contend that determining if an email is a phishing message is common sense, but there is no common sense without a clear definition of common knowledge. You need to establish that common knowledge for your users.

You need to put yourself in the users' position and consider the specific steps the users must follow to not initiate a loss. This includes identifying users do their jobs right . . . from start to finish. While you might incorporate standard mental models and perceptions of common sense into how you define a user process, you need to actually define the process in detail.

The detail as to where you end the governance for Boom depends on where you define Boom. We recommend that you consider creating detailed guidelines and procedures until the point that the user is no longer involved. For phishing messages, for example, if after a user has downloaded malware, if there is some indication that there is malware, you should define how the user is to respond to that indication. If not, the process has moved to Right of Boom. If a user is supposed to maintain equipment, you should clearly detail when and how to maintain equipment properly. There should likely be a step to ensure that the maintenance work was completed properly. However, after the user has supposedly finished maintenance, that is where Right of Boom begins.

User Experience

In many circumstances, the user does not operate in a vacuum. You are likely providing them with computers and equipment on which they are supposed to perform their jobs and tasks. The question then becomes whether the user experience, frequently referred to as *user experience* (UX), facilitates or prevents UIL. For example, if you have a system that uses small fonts, many people might not be able to properly read the output, which can lead to error and create loss. Sometimes the interface is overwhelming, is confusing, and operates differently than other interfaces, which is what happened in the case of the Boeing 737 MAX crashes discussed earlier in the book.

In most cases, UX drives user actions. It biases people toward certain actions, while discouraging others. If a UX is well-created, it will drive people to make the right decision. It will warn them of potentially harmful actions. As you examine UIL, you need to examine how your UX facilitates governance.

When you put your efforts into studying and mitigating a user action at Boom, it becomes too simple to focus on telling users how they should behave. You need to examine the UX in detail and determine how you can better lead users in the right direction. When we previously discussed safety science and how 90% of injuries can be attributed to the environment, the UX is essentially that environment. Therefore, you need to put a proportionate amount of effort into examining the UX, compared to awareness and similar efforts. This cannot be overstated.

Prevention and Detection

A well-designed UX builds in both prevention and detection. UX should limit user actions. In this way, you lead users through a prescribed set of actions that proactively mitigate UIL.

Governance, in other words, process, should drive the design of the UX, which technologically implements the governance. As governance is designed to proactively implement protection, the chain of events would likewise lead to the UX implementing protection. Users should only have the capabilities that they need to do their jobs. The UX leads people through the process defined by the governance.

Some people criticize a limiting UX as potentially stifling innovation and limiting the capabilities of users. Some people want users to be empowered as much as possible. While there is some validity to that perspective, a good UX will empower users as much as they need to be empowered. There are no users who need unfettered access to everything, and in fact, it might actually be illegal to give unlimited ability to users. Ultimately, you can minimize the chance for the user to initiate loss at Boom, and if they do initiate it, mitigate the potential effects in the moment.

Similarly, a well-designed UX builds detection into the system. It detects when there are actions that might cause harm. They tell people when their actions might be questionable. For example, many email systems check links before forwarding people to a website. Sometimes providing users with a warning message helps them avoid the Boom of initiating the loss. What's more, even if the user is in a hurry and initiates the loss, the notification in that moment can serve as a reminder for them to leap into mitigation action. Similarly, certain use actions might result in a notification automatically being sent to an appropriate team for review at the moment of Boom.

Awareness

Basically, the purpose of awareness is to promote and implement governance. In other words, you expect governance to detail the proper ways to perform a job function, and awareness should focus on making people aware of the proper way to do their job. While instructional materials are useful and the UX can potentially lead people in the right direction, there should be as many constant reminders as possible about the correct process. We encourage you to review Chapter 15, "Creating Effective Awareness Programs," for information on how to implement an appropriate program.

Feeding the Cycle

One critical element of the entire user experience is that some users will initiate loss through new and different means. Therefore, it is critical that your UIL mitigation program is dynamic and responds to shortcomings in the initial design. We are admittedly hesitant to use the word *shortcomings* as it is expected that just like all countermeasures, your program will not be perfect.

Whenever you detect a UIL incident at Boom, it should not be looked at as a failing, but an opportunity for refinement. It is impossible to foresee all potential forms of loss initiation.

Likewise, you may even choose not to mitigate something, as it initially seems like a poor choice from a risk perspective. However, after the program is put into practice, you determine from what happens at Boom that you did not judge the risk accurately.

Your governance should be a living entity. You need to ensure that your UX can be readily modified. Similarly, your awareness program should not be set in stone and planned a year in advance. Each and every aspect of your UIL mitigation program must be modifiable based on ongoing feedback. As Boom and UIL occur, you need to recognize them as opportunities for identifying where your program can be strengthened.

Feedback loops are critical to constant improvement in mitigating UIL. Much like safety programs look at a user failing of a symptom of system failure, whenever a user fails at the point of Boom, it represents an opportunity to improve your efforts.

Stopping Boom

The steps defined in this chapter approach a single UIL type at a time. Ideally, you will see that the countermeasures that you implement will mitigate many forms of UIL. While you may target a specific form of UIL, there should be collateral benefits.

At the same time, we also expect you to attempt to mitigate up to three forms of UIL at a time. You may choose several forms of UIL independently, or you may choose UIL types that are synergistic, with many overlapping countermeasures.

While this chapter is admittedly short, it is one of the most critical chapters in the book. We need to identify how users initiate loss at Boom, defining how they should behave so as not to initiate that loss, provide them an experience that leads the users to the appropriate actions and behaviors, and then ensure that users are aware of the governance and the system in place.

If we can stop a loss before it is initiated, there is obviously no loss. We don't have to worry about the loss itself. We created a "bad story" to tell at parties, where there is nothing interesting to investigate, and where we do not have to pull resources away from other issues.

Clearly, though, this will not always be the case. Therefore, we must ensure that there is a comprehensive program in place, which is the purpose of the next chapter.

17 Right of Boom

Despite your best efforts, and those of every person in your organization, a user will initiate a loss. You will either have put a user in a position to initiate a loss, failed to train them properly, or failed to filter out a potential attack using your users as an attack vector. The user will then take an action that will initiate the loss.

The moment the user initiated the loss is the Boom. It doesn't matter if the loss was initiated because the user made a mistake, was manipulated into taking an action they would otherwise never have taken, or was reckless or malicious. The only thing that matters is that a loss was initiated.

Of course, the motivation of the loss initiated will matter when you investigate the incident during Right of Boom. Knowing the motivation may help identify other actions that a malicious party has taken. For example, if there is a nation-state attack and a user initiated a loss by clicking a phishing message, you need to look for certain types of malware and persistence on a network. If an audit finds that someone might have embezzled money, you should determine what else they might have done and the extent of the crime.

This, however, leads to the dichotomy that when a user initiates a loss, it is your job to determine the scope of the loss and mitigate it as much as possible. People like to put the focus on Left of Boom, with the system detecting and stopping the UIL before the loss is realized. However, there is more to address with regard to why it is occurring, and there are potentially serious implications to be considered, both of which are examined at Right of Boom.

Repeat as Necessary

Traditionally, a heading titled "Repeat as Necessary" would belong at the end of a chapter. However, we first need to acknowledge the fact that the guidance in this chapter must pick up where the previous chapter left off, which was with Boom. During Boom, there is an event or attack of some form. The event can initiate many losses, intended and unintended.

For example, consider the case of COVID-19 as it spread around the world. There were countless potential losses that needed to be addressed. Clearly, there was the need to mitigate potential death. There was the need to ensure that hospitals could treat the increase in patients. There was the need to ensure treatment for people with other injuries and illnesses independent of COVID-19. Then there was the need to mitigate the financial losses. This is only touching upon a few of the obvious potential losses. Mitigating such concerns requires generally independent tracks, which can be considered both simultaneously and sequentially. While there might be some overlap between the different tracks, each potential loss must be considered for mitigation.

In a less complicated but much more common example, clicking links in phishing messages can initiate a variety of losses. A phishing message can install ransomware that destroys a system. It can install spyware that surreptitiously takes control of the system or spies on the users or network. It can send someone to a website to get them to divulge credentials. It might just serve annoying adware.

In the case of phishing messages, Left of Boom involves you trying to prevent the phishing message from getting to the user and providing the user with awareness of what to do if it does reach them. Boom has you attempting to stop the user from clicking links in the phishing message in a variety of ways. In Right of Boom, the phishing message's link has been clicked, and you are trying to proactively mitigate the resulting potential loss. If all else fails, you contain the damage.

For Right of Boom, you must try to consider and evaluate all of the potential UILs that result from a particular Boom. Accounting for and mitigating more than 90% of UIL is definitely not a simple job. Having a process, however, to step through all of the potential UILs at least provides a focus.

What Does Loss Initiation Look Like?

To mitigate losses in Right of Boom, you need to be able to identify them. This isn't frequently obvious. A worker taking a computer from one facility to another might be a normal job function. However, if the employee chooses to go home for the day or even stops for gas, the computer may be stolen from the car. For example, in a 2018 case reported on by the BBC (www.bbc.com/news/uk-england-43047224), a senior counter terrorism police officer had highly classified materials stolen from his car. Cases like this are not isolated. Thefts from cars can be either highly targeted or, more commonly, opportunistic by random criminals looking to make a quick score. Fundamentally, a regular behavior can easily become a UIL.

For this reason, it becomes impossible to completely identify all potential UIL during Left of Boom, before loss is initiated. Therefore, you must assume normal, or, possibly better phrased, allowed behaviors can potentially initiate loss. However, in the case of the police officer, the behaviors were not allowed and included first removing the highly classified materials from police premises and then leaving them in the trunk of his car for several days. He wasn't even sure when they were stolen. That type of gap between recognizing when and how the Boom took place and when Right of Boom mitigation efforts could begin is obviously important.

Both authors have worked in classified environments and have been entrusted to properly handle sensitive information. There can be a fine line where a potential loss (Left of Boom) is initiated (Boom) and proceeds to become actual loss (Right of Boom). Obviously, you can look to past experiences and violations of governance as a great source for identifying UIL and determining what measures you can have ready for mitigating loss in Right of Boom.

Although governance is all-encompassing, it is rarely 100% effective at producing absolute compliance. Likewise, there will inevitably be losses that were never previously experienced. Additionally, some losses are ignored or risks miscalculated. So, as you consider preparations for addressing UIL at Right of Boom, focus on the clear concerns and prioritize the identification of losses from past experiences, but be open-minded and flexible about which initiations to prioritize.

What Are the Potential Losses?

A given Boom, or action by a user, can create a multitude of potential losses. For example, clicking a link in a phishing message can lead to ransomware locking systems, credential theft, and adware, among many other potential attacks. A single user act can create multiple types of UIL, all of which need to be prevented, detected, and mitigated. Again, this is why it is critical to stop the initiation of a loss as early in the process as possible. Clearly, you try to do this at Left of Boom and Boom, but when these efforts fail, you need a plan for how you handle them at Right of Boom.

At this point in planning for Right of Boom mitigation, we recommend you make lists for each potential user action (Boom) that can initiate loss and all of the potential losses that can result. These losses will generally be specific to your organization and industry.

Different methods work for different people. Some people create mind maps, and if you are familiar with mind mapping software or tools, they can be an effective method to accomplish what we describe in this section. You then have to transfer the results to a usable format.

Before we get too far, let's touch on mind maps. The human brain processes a great deal of data in a short amount of time and can often be disorganized, making it challenging to retain and recall information. Enter the mind map, created by author and consultant Tony Buzan. A mind map is a diagram used to visually represent and organize information, ideas, and the relationships between points, and follows the essentials of divergent thinking. Unlike convergent thinking, a logical process for deriving a solution, divergent thinking is nonlinear, encourages creativity, and stresses exploring multiple concepts.

This technique is often used during brainstorming sessions and is designed to facilitate cooperation, imagination, and free-flow thoughts. Mind maps can transform lackluster lists or complex information into fun, graphic representations that stimulate creativity and productivity. Some scenarios for use of mind maps include the following:

- Brainstorming
- Business planning
- Curriculum development
- Strategy development

- Consolidating information
- Summarizing information

The simplest analogy for thinking of a mind map is a tree. Think of the main topic as the trunk of a tree with subtopics as branches, and extended tasks or ideas like twigs and leaves.

Mind maps have a few things in common. They are meant to stimulate the creative side of the brain and help organize ideas. Additionally, they are comprised of lines, words, shapes, symbols, or images. The mind map will begin with a single main topic that branches into subtopics that can go multiple levels deep. See Figure 17.1.

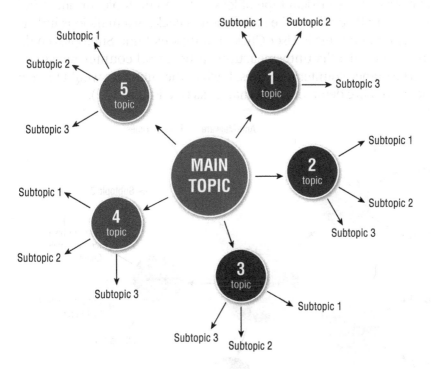

Figure 17.1: A mind map

The following are the basic steps for creating a mind map:

1. Write the most important idea in the center. This is your primary topic. Use colored pens, sticky notes, or other materials to help create the map.

2. Draw lines out from the main circle to subheadings or secondary topics or ideas.
3. Expand on the subtopics with additional tasks or ideas as you think of them.
4. Continue to dive deep into the next level of tasks, ideas, facts, or considerations. Draw lines from the appropriate heading to help organize.
5. Change the drawing around, or move sticky notes, to help organize as needed.

When using this method to expand solutions for Right of Boom, you could consider one critical type of loss as the main topic for one mind map. Let's briefly envision the user action of clicking a malicious link as Boom. The main topic is User Clicked Malicious Link. Subtopics could comprise technical countermeasures, procedural countermeasures, and performance countermeasures. Each of the subtopics would branch further into more detail or additional ideas (see Figure 17.2).

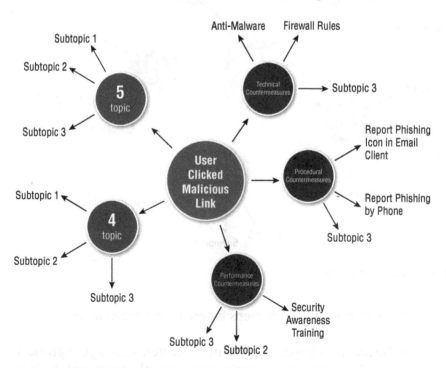

Figure 17.2: A mind map for User Clicked Malicious Link

While mind maps are creative, others may prefer to create lists of lists. You create one list of the potential losses that can arise from a user action. Each list item then becomes a list itself as to what losses can be initiated. Remember, each of these techniques should be collaborative to ensure that multiple perspectives are taken into consideration to create enough solutions or ideas to the point of saturation. In other words, experienced team members will have different points of view and ideas to contribute. The team may not think of everything, but they will get to a point of saturation and can't think of anything else. Also, people have different ways of collaborating, learning, and brainstorming. While the techniques provided here are certainly helpful, consider asking those working on this effort, which is their preferred method. Whatever method you choose to use, as long as you can document it and then present it in a form that your organization can use, it is acceptable.

We will come back to the lists or mind maps later, as there will be overlap between the countermeasures that you implement. You will find that prevention, detection, and mitigating one potential loss usually overlaps with prevention, detection, or mitigation with another potential loss. You will need to be able to track the potential overlap.

Throughout this chapter, we specifically use the word *mitigation* instead of *reaction*. The reason is that *reaction* implies that there is a specific response to an initiated loss. It is, however, possible that there are proactive measures in place to counter a loss. Proactive mitigation may include not allowing administrative privileges on computers, which stops most malware from being installed on the system. As you see, there was technically no response, as the computer configuration stopped any loss without further actions.

Perhaps the greatest benefit of our methodology is that we advocate a proactive system for mitigating loss. If proactive measures do not mitigate the potential loss, reactive responses should be planned in anticipation of the need for the response. Either way, mitigation is thought through and anticipated.

Preventing the Loss

The ideal situation is to prevent a loss during the Left of Boom. As you move from Left of Boom to Boom to Right of Boom, the possibility of the loss being realized increases. Once Boom has occurred, the ideal situation is to immediately prevent the loss from being realized.

As we discuss later, you might choose not to immediately prevent a potential loss for a variety of reasons (and in some instances, you might not even be able to prevent loss at all). However, to know what those reasons may be, you need to consider potential methods for proactively preventing the initiated loss.

So, for every potential loss on your list, next to it list the potential methods for preventing a loss. This requires knowledge and experience in the specific domain in question, such as technology, accounting, operational environment, and so on. If you don't possess sufficient experience in a given domain, you might need to go to other experts who better know all the possible methods for preventing the loss. This is true for each phase described in this chapter. Consulting with experts can also be especially helpful if you are an awareness person who is trying to expand your responsibility or an operations person attempting to mitigate UIL in a highly complex environment with many technologies.

One common example of potential UIL is ransomware. When you consider a ransomware attack, the attack is initiated when a user clicks a link in a phishing message, downloads a file from an infected website, installs a malicious USB drive, or does something similar. Each one of these actions would be a different potential loss-initiating action to mitigate. Regardless, when the user initiates the attack, Boom occurs, and then you are in Right of Boom and need to prevent loss.

One step you can take to prevent ransomware from resulting in loss is to limit the ability for a user to install software on a computer. When no permission is given to install software, the user's click does not result in ransomware being installed. Additionally, you can have traditional, signature-based anti-malware, which will prevent known ransomware from being loaded. You can also install behavioral-based anti-malware, which looks for potentially harmful activity in software and prevents it from running. You can also limit user access so that if a user activates ransomware, the damage would be minimal. There are other alternatives that include running all software on test systems before installing it. All of these measures might have been put in place at Left of Boom, but they go into effect and prevent loss at Right of Boom.

It is also important to consider whether a process can lead to protection. While a user might take an action, such as leaving materials and information in unsecured places, regular patrols can find the vulnerable materials and pick them up. For example, at one point in his career, author Ira Winkler worked in a sensitive compartmented information facility (SCIF). The first week in the facility, he did not lock up his burn bag, a paper bag for all classified material meant for disposal at the end of the day. However, the facility had guards perform rounds and proactively collect any burn bags left vulnerable. Ira did not even realize he left the burn bag out until the next morning when he received a call from the head of security to retrieve his burn bag. Not only was that good, proactive security, it served as a valuable awareness lesson, which is a great example of how the Right of Boom collection of the burn bag and the Left of Boom awareness lesson can sometimes overlap.

Compiling Protective Countermeasures

At this point, you need to repeat this process of identifying countermeasures for every UIL that you have identified from the Boom analysis. You will likely come up with many countermeasures for each loss, and many of those countermeasures might be common to multiple types of loss.

Consider the example of ransomware. Disabling USB drives will prevent ransomware from malicious USB drives. Limiting user access, anti-malware, and behavioral analysis software will be common to preventing many forms of ransomware and possibly addressing other types of UIL as well, such as user theft, viruses, hacker attacks, and so on. As you go through all of the losses, you need to compile the list of preventative countermeasures and analyze the more useful ones.

Clearly, there are going to be many countermeasures that just address one form of loss. They might, however, be able to effectively prevent a large amount of loss and the justification is obvious. There are also many countermeasures whose value is not due to mitigating a single loss, but the combined value of many small losses.

This can create a misprioritization of certain countermeasures. Salespeople are widely trained to sell to "the pain." It is only right that organizations prioritize countermeasures that prevent the largest losses.

However, they should also consider overall return on investment and the prevention of multiple points of pain.

Detecting the Loss

It is sometimes possible to mitigate potential loss without any indication that it was initiated. However, as we state time and time again, no protection is perfect, and your loss mitigation program must anticipate and prepare for the failure of protection measures.

For this reason, detection in Right of Boom is critical. The process of considering your detection capabilities is essentially the same as it was for protection. In this process, however, you ask what the potential signs of an initiated loss are.

You want to detect the initiation of a loss as early in Right of Boom as possible. For each loss, it again is helpful to create a mind map, list, or whatever is appropriate. If there was protection in place that should have mitigated the loss, such as the case of malware being prevented through a variety of means, it is important that you consider that the protection has failed and determine what detection could pick up on such a failure.

Using malware delivered through phishing attacks as a continued example, attackers might use malware that is highly advanced and attempts to avoid known anti-malware countermeasures. However, organizations know to look for advanced malware by looking for surreptitious communications between computers.

Again, it helps to bring a team of people together, with a variety of skill sets, to analyze the initiation of a loss. In the ideal situation, you identify multiple potential UILs and then bring together an interdisciplinary team to walk through how the detection of the initiation of the losses can be achieved. Then you want to figure out where else detection can be implemented further down the kill chain, if the loss is not detected at initiation.

As with protection, it is possible that detection mechanisms can overlap among multiple types of losses. It is likewise critical to understand that process has a critical impact. Accounting provides great examples of using process as detection for fraud and other forms of financial and other loss. Clearly, accounting has regular audits, and in many cases, those audits occur daily. While audits can detect financial malfeasance, audits that include inventory and overall input and output (in whatever form) can detect inefficiencies, as well as outright fraud and theft.

Again, your detection is specific to your environment, industry, and domain. It is impossible for us to anticipate all losses and provide examples specific to every reader; however, the process is generally straightforward. It is also simple and obvious. The reality, though, is that the process we describe is not formalized.

Before, During, and After

It is important that you determine detection mechanisms that look for signs of a UIL everywhere at Right of Boom. This means that you want to attempt to identify detection capabilities that find loss initiation before a loss is being realized, while a loss is being realized, and even after a loss is realized. It is possible that your detection might miss signs along the way. However, as we discussed, there is value to at least knowing that a loss occurred for a wide variety of reasons, minimally to know how to improve the system to prevent future losses, or to at least know the scope of the loss.

Clearly, if you detect the signs that a loss can be initiated, you can mitigate it, or at least better plan for the loss. If you can detect the loss as it is being initiated, you can potentially stop it in its tracks or reduce the realized loss.

Again, phishing provides a simple example. For example, when a user clicks a link in a phishing message that intends to send them to a website and get them to give up their user credentials, that is the Boom. Ideally, when the user is sent that malicious web page, your system detects the web page is malicious and can then initiate reaction, which is Right of the Boom. If that fails and the user enters their credentials on the malicious site (a new Boom), when an attacker attempts to exploit the credentials (when a loss will actually occur), the system detects an unusual login attempt from an unknown system and can then prevent the login (again at Right of Boom). However, should that then fail, the system should detect the unusual activity on the system, and then forensics can be performed to examine the nature and extent of the compromise (which is further at Right of Boom).

Mitigating the Loss

In the previous example, mitigation follows detection, which is how it traditionally works. The potential loss is in the process of being realized, or has been realized, and you need to take active measures to stop the loss, reduce the potential damage, or figure out the best course of action after the loss is brought completely to fruition.

In a manufacturing environment, you might see someone fail to perform proper, scheduled maintenance. That failure can lead to mechanical damage. If there is a process that examines maintenance logs proactively and detects that maintenance has not been performed, the maintenance can be performed. If there is an operational indication that systems are not running optimally, you can then perform the maintenance. If the system breaks down, you clearly then have to fix it. As important, though, is that you need to find out what led to the breakdown and implement whatever processes, technologies, and/or awareness you need to ensure it never happens again, at least to any reasonable extent.

Also consider that mitigation may be embedded proactively within the process and may appear to be prevention. For example, in many cars, there is a maintenance light that indicates that something is wrong and maintenance needs to be performed. Process can also force preventative maintenance in these examples.

Mitigation typically follows from detection. It is the expansion of the mind maps and lists that you created during your examination of protection and detection. You need to consider the potential mitigation mechanisms for each detection event. Again, it is possible to mitigate directly as a form of protection. Your goal is to continue to hypothesize through all potential options.

The options are not all going to be chosen, but the more options you identify, the more likely you are to find the better solutions. As with our discussion of protection and detection, it is likely that many mitigation options will address many different UILs. You now need to determine the risk mitigated by a given countermeasure.

Determining Where to Mitigate

Although it is best to mitigate damage as early as possible in Right of Boom, the reality is that it is not always plausible to do so. There can be a variety of cost or logistical issues that lead you to let a potential loss go unmitigated.

For example, alcohol is expensive and is a high-profit item. Alcohol is traditionally served in shots, which is a relatively small size. It is easy to over-pour a shot, with over-pouring potentially 25% to 100% more alcohol than purchased. Bartenders also have an incentive to curry favor from patrons by over-pouring. This can cost an establishment hundreds to thousands of dollars of revenue a day. This doesn't even account for the possibility of bartenders giving away free drinks.

To stop this problem, you can monitor each and every bartender at every serving. This isn't practical. Most organizations resort to point-of-sales systems that track sales for each bartender and then perform accounting to see how much alcohol was used in a day and match that usage to recorded sales. In this case, you haven't mitigated the loss before it occurs. You haven't mitigated the loss while it was occurring. You mitigated the loss afterward by first determining which bartenders are responsible for the most over-pouring and then either providing better training or terminating the bartenders as appropriate.

An alternative is to buy new systems that automatically portion the alcohol; this provides some benefit, but also ruins the personal touch of the bartenders, which many people appreciate.

During the COVID-19 pandemic, some companies were concerned about lost productivity from employees working at home and installed spyware to monitor employees. Clearly, this can monitor lost productivity in real time. However, this has a variety of impacts that include lost morale, public scorn, etc.

For this reason, as you go through your mind maps, lists, etc., you need to consider, for each potential UIL, at which phase of Right of Boom is the most practical to implement the identified countermeasures. Again, even though you implement a countermeasure intended to mitigate a loss before it is realized, the countermeasure can fail. So, you want to implement all countermeasures that are practical.

Avoiding Analysis Paralysis

At one level, we advocate analyzing as many paths for loss as possible. At the same time, we acknowledge that you can overanalyze the situation and create too many paths, many of which are frequently not common or deserving of mitigation. There is no single right answer as to when to stop your analysis.

We do, however, recommend that when you believe that you have addressed the most common UIL threads, you further consider the UIL paths that would lead to large losses. If you underestimated the risk, you can go back again and examine that thread. As we highlight time and time again throughout this book, your efforts should be ongoing, and you are never expected to stop all loss.

Your Last Line of Defense

There are many critical flaws with this mantra used by many awareness professionals: "The users are your last line of defense." Again, you need to expect that every countermeasure will fail, and users will statistically fail at a significantly higher rate than technology. That doesn't even include the guaranteed reality of malicious users deliberately initiating loss. Your loss prevention program must have an entire process for creating your last line of defense. Your user is not your last line of defense. Your last line of defense from UIL involves those countermeasures implemented for the expectation that your users will fail.

Systematically approaching Right of Boom allows you to proactively plan for the likely losses that you will experience from UIL. By defining the forms of UIL that you can experience, it allows you to step through the enabling factors and the potential countermeasures. You then determine which of the countermeasures are most practical to implement. Again, as we sit here and consider this, we think this should be common knowledge and, therefore, common sense. The unfortunate reality is that industry tends to look at user mistakes, and the solution is to simply make a smarter user to be your last line of defense. You need to consider that the user is just part of your system, and you need to adapt the system to the failures expected from the system.

18 Preventing Boom

It might seem natural to put this chapter ahead of the previous two, given that it makes sense to mitigate an attack from start to finish. After all, if you can prevent the attack from ever happening in the first place, the rest of the effort is moot.

However, in many cases, there are completely different people working on different phases of the problem. There are various aspects of the problem, each requiring specific skill sets to address the relevant vulnerabilities that can be compromised at each phase.

For example, if you think about a potential terrorist attack, preparing for Left of Boom involves tracking potential terrorists, identifying planning the attack, and so on. The skill sets relevant to preparing for Boom might involve hardening potential targets, setting up surveillance systems, and so on. Preparing for Right of Boom would involve ensuring there are enough hospital beds, setting up potential choke points to prevent assailants from escaping, training responders, and so on.

Clearly, there will be some interaction between the involved parties. The surveillance systems that were used to monitor activities during the Boston Marathon bombings were used to investigate the bombing and identify the terrorists. People tracking terrorists and attempting to prevent the attacks have to prepare the responders for potential attacks they think might be in the planning stages. However, the general job tasks are very different.

While we hope that many readers of this book will be in the safety, accounting, and other professions that have long learned to deal with user-initiated loss (UIL), readers from other disciplines are likely not familiar with approaching UIL from a systems perspective. It is also likely that the readers of this book will be responsible for the prevention and mitigation of UIL in its entirety. They are responsible for all phases of Boom. If you are one of them, you will need to think things through from start to finish. That being said, we found that it is not as easy to start at the beginning.

We ran multiple workshops that dealt with all the phases of Boom, and we found that the natural inclination of participants is to start at Left of Boom and work their way chronologically through the attack. However, when participants tried to identify future probable attacks or losses in general, it proved to be too difficult for them, due to the infinite possibilities and their abstractness. In later workshops, we decided to start the participants at Boom, where a user was at the point of potentially initiating a loss. It is easier for people to begin thinking from a very focused point, where options and variability are typically finite.

After workshop participants worked from Boom through Right of Boom, they had a solid base to more easily conceive of the ways a potential opportunity for loss (i.e., Left of Boom) develops and comes to fruition. As important, we found the best way to address Left of Boom is to backtrack from Boom itself.

It is, for example, easier to ask, "How did this phishing message get into my inbox?" than it is to consider the answer to "How will bad people target my users?" Clearly, the latter is a much larger problem to address, as opposed to the former, which asks a very specific question. More important, you will eventually get to the same answers if everything works out perfectly, but it takes longer to start from the beginning. Essentially, by starting from Boom and working backward, you are proceeding with hindsight.

So, as we define how to execute Left of Boon, we do so in reverse chronology. This does not preclude performing some analysis starting at the beginning, and we will encourage that as a form of error checking. We recommend you proceed in the way that you, and ideally your team, finds to work best for your circumstances.

Why Are We Here?

Why are we here is a simple question, but it is the root of this chapter. In other words, what enabled the user being put in a position where they can initiate a loss?

In the ideal circumstance, the user is just doing their job, which entails the user potentially making the wrong decision. If the user does something to initiate loss, you rely on the controls you put in place for

Boom and Right of Boom to mitigate the potential loss. This circumstance, however, assumes that the governance was designed and implemented perfectly and that the technology accounted for all issues that can initiate a loss. Clearly, this rarely happens, if at all.

We therefore, have to consider how the user came to be in a position to initiate a loss, which puts us at Left of Boom. For example, if a user is looking at a phishing message, it is because your system failed to filter that message and delivered it to the user's inbox. You then have to consider how that happened.

One approach would be to start at the beginning, which would have you consider why the phishing message came into being. You would need to first conceive of all the potential attackers out there and what their motives may be. You would have to understand that some criminals want to launder money. Some criminals specialize in malware and ransomware and make money from collecting bitcoins. Some criminals want to collect credentials so that they can log into accounts and steal proprietary information. As you can see, this can be overwhelming, and you might still never get all possible circumstances.

Instead, you could focus on the specific consideration of how a phishing message got into the inbox, which is a finite question to ask and answer. The answer may not always be obvious, but it is a generally bound question. While it helps to have a high-level understanding of the overall nature of the problem and to have an idea of the entire path to the creation of Boom, it is not required if you can think methodically and are able to reverse engineer things from the Boom.

Reverse Engineering

As described, you need to look at the decision point where a user was in the position to initiate a loss, and then determine what immediately led to that point. We laid the groundwork for beginning this process in the previous two chapters, where you examined Boom and Right of Boom and listed UIL instances and potential mitigations. This chapter will build on that foundation and explore various aspects of this in Left of Boom. The ways you achieve this are not always as obvious as you might initially expect.

For example, consider the simple act of tailgating, where an infiltrator attempts to enter a facility by coming immediately behind a legitimately credentialed person. In this instance, Boom is essentially the point whether or not a legitimate user will either let in a person trying to follow them through the door. Then the question is how the would-be intruder got to the door (which is basically the Left of Boom phase). You have to consider a variety of options. Is the door on a public street? Is this door at a private, enclosed courtyard? Is the door connected to a parking structure of some form? There might be multiple doors with multiple circumstances.

With phishing messages as an example, you might determine that the message came in through an email message, so it is the email that is at fault. Many people might say that the email server might be the issue. As a finer point, the average user looks at emails through some sort of email client, such as Outlook. Then there is also the consideration that the user might have the email in their traditional inbox or in their spam filter, but still available for review. So the first place to consider is the email client. The email client in turn received the email from the server. The server received the message after the sending system was allowed to connect to your network.

Keep in mind that every step along the way represents a potential point of protection, detection, and reaction. Again with email, you can add software protection to the clients. The email servers can have a variety of protections added to them. There are also industry collaboratives that track malicious email senders and then send out information to organizations so that they can block emails coming from those servers across the Internet.

As you can see, we reverse engineer a kill chain for each Boom. This should be a methodical process to consider the proverbial who, what, when, where, why, and how each phase came into being.

If you miss a step, you are missing an opportunity to mitigate the loss proactively. The lost opportunity might be the most effective time to mitigate the attack. It could also be inconsequential. The ideal situation is to provide you and your organization with as many opportunities as possible to consider mitigating the loss.

The important word in the previous sentence is *consider*. It is unlikely that you will mitigate the loss at every opportunity. Doing so may not be practical. It will likely not be cost- or resource-effective. In some places, it might be redundant.

It is also critical when you consider a point of loss facilitation that you look at the facilitation occurring through technology, process, and/or awareness. So when you look at a potential loss at the point of Boom, you need to consider all aspects of how that loss came to being. If it is a technical risk, it is obvious to look at the technology. However, it is also critical to look at why the technology put the user in the position.

You also need to consider governance, awareness, and technology for each point that you identify in Left of Boom. The following sections will explore those topics.

Governance

A call center operator might receive a call from a criminal attempting to trick (social engineer) the operator into divulging a credit card number of a third party. At first glance, you think this is an aspect of social engineering prevention, and there should be training so that the operator knows how to respond properly. You might also try to add technology, such as dial number recognition, to confirm the telephone number of the caller matching that of the third party. However, you must also consider a less obvious aspect of Left of Boom; why does the operator have access to the credit card number in the first place?

There are many people with access to information, facilities, equipment, and so on, who don't need that access to perform their jobs. It is critical to address the governance aspect that asks very basic questions, especially and including, "Is it really necessary for a user to be in the position of Boom?"

So the questions can include the following:

- What process has put the user in this position?
- Why should the user be in this position?
- Is the user necessary for this process?
- Does the user have all of the information that they need?
- Does the user have access to too much information or resources?
- Is there an option for the user to be in this position?

There are clearly other questions that are relevant for your organization and environment. They all involve questioning the user being in the position, the user's accesses, and alternatives for the user to reduce the overall risk.

While the goal is not yet to mitigate the problem, as you see, many of the questions can imply a solution to the problem. It will be the same for awareness and technology.

Awareness

At every step, you have to ask if there was some form of awareness failing. Do we arrive at Boom because there was some form of awareness failing during Left of Boom? For example, consider that terrorist attacks have been successful when people have missed or failed to report questionable activities. There have also been terrorist attacks that were prevented because of "user" awareness. In 2010, a terrorist attack in Times Square was stopped because a T-shirt vendor noticed something unusual and reported it to the police.

As you examine a given point in Left of Boom, you need to consider whether there is a potential moment where awareness, such as a need to follow governance or detect something, is an enabler of a step or will potentially stop or further an attack in the current step.

Relevant questions to ask regarding awareness-related tasks could include the following:

- Is there governance that needs to be followed?
- Can a user take an action that can mitigate a loss? Or enable a loss?

Users are part of the system, and as such, if each user who is required to act in a consistent way either does so or fails to do so, you need to analyze that as a critical step similar to how you would consider a technological failing.

Consider the Compliance Budget

Even aware users may not behave properly for a variety of reasons. To the extent possible, you need to consider what factors can influence the compliance budget. For example, if you need users to perform preventative maintenance, you need to explore what other pressures might impede their ability and willingness to perform the maintenance. There may not be sufficient time in the day to perform the work. There might be production standards that discourage stopping production to perform maintenance.

Again, there are a variety of factors that can prevent even the most well-intentioned users from doing what they need to do. To the extent possible, you need to mitigate any impediment to preventing loss.

Technology

The role of technology varies by your industry, environment, and the individual type of loss. Likewise, even for a given type of loss, technology applicability will vary from step to step. Some technology-related losses rely on poor governance. For example, a failure to create and implement proper secure system configurations is a process failure, even though it relates directly to technology.

However, while technology implementation may be an operational or governance issue, the choice and potential failure or success of a technology are technological issues. To that end, at each phase you need to look at each step and ask which technology can be of use at this phase.

As important, you need to determine what technology in Left of Boom got you to Boom. This is not necessarily bad. Again, in any form of operation, you place yourself at risk. However, it is reasonable to ask if the technology functioned properly to that point. It is then reasonable to consider if there might be a way to get to that point with lower risk.

It is at this point you need to thoroughly understand the involved and potential technologies. This includes both the capabilities that your organization currently has and the ones it doesn't. You need to determine if there are new capabilities since the products were conceived.

During the 2020 COVID-19 outbreak, schools used the Zoom video conferencing application to conduct online classes. At the time, Zoom used 10-digit numbers to identify individual virtual meetings. Tools were then created to brute-force-guess meeting numbers. Attackers were then able to randomly enter the meetings. The crime became known as *Zoom-bombing*. A criminal entered a school classroom meeting and exposed himself to all in the meeting.

While in the case of Zoom, you could consider the fact always using a 10-digit number to identify a meeting is what opened the meetings up to attack, as well as the fact that it simplifies the ability of users to join the meetings. At the same time, there was a fundamental governance problem in that the meeting organizers did not implement passwords or specifically configure the system to create waiting rooms that allowed organizers to filter people entering the meetings. Implementing the passwords alone would have kept the criminal out of the class meeting.

It can be argued that there was a rush to implement remote classes and that these early Zoom-bombings were a result of rolling out the tool prior to performing a thorough risk assessment. At the same time, it is an example of the need to integrate Right of Boom into your Left of Boom analyses.

So at one level, Left of Boom involved the technology having a technical vulnerability in the limited numbering of the meetings, allowing attackers to potentially "find" meetings. At the same time, the operational use of the Zoom service—the governance that did not require teachers to assign a password to the meeting—was also a vulnerability. So, these subtleties provide steps to consider as you analyze Left of Boom and work to reverse engineer Boom from a technology perspective.

This example demonstrates why it is important to understand the capabilities of the technologies and its strengths, weaknesses, etc. If you individually are not familiar with the technology and systems, you should involve others or perform the appropriate research. The teacher involved in the Orlando incident was likely not aware of the ability to add a password or otherwise technologically limit access to the virtual class. We don't necessarily blame the teacher as much as the school and school administration that provided the capability without providing proper guidance on how to use the technology.

Likewise, you need to consider technologies that are not obvious. As necessary and feasible, you need to seek out technical guidance. Are you familiar with technologies that you are not using but could be helpful? Are you familiar with technologies that are common in your industry that you may or may not be using? Are you considering whether something would be useful that you are not sure exists?

Again, as you look at each step in Left of Boom, you need to ask the following:

- Why are you at that step?
- What technological issue has you there? Remember, this is a neutral question, as you may be there just because it is part of a normal business operation.
- What technologies at this step can get you to the next step more securely?
- What technologies can remove risk at the current step?
- Can the technology be redesigned or reconfigured to be more secure?

- Can more functionality be added to the technology?
- Even if the step does not apparently involve technology, can it be introduced to reduce risk?
- What technologies led to the current step?
- What governance is relevant to the technology?
- Are there awareness-related issues that impact the technology?

Perhaps the most interesting question to consider is the one regarding when technology is not obviously involved. For example, you might consider the concept of someone tailgating a person into a building. There is the potential to add a turnstile. You might also consider placing cameras and surveillance systems to watch for tailgaters. Seeking out physical security experts who have broad experience can help increase the possibilities for identifying new technologies.

Step-by-Step

As we previously mentioned, you need to look at Boom and then figure out how you got there. You then need to step back and determine how you might have got to that point and continue to do so until you believe you are at a point that is completely out of your control.

In the same way you used mental maps, lists, or whatever format you used to step through the Boom and Right of Boom phases, you need to reverse engineer from Boom, step-by-step. Much like there may be several possible branches coming off every action and Boom, afterward, there might be several branches leading to Boom. You have to find those branches to determine how to best mitigate potential UIL.

The goal is as always to understand how you are in a position that is enabling Boom. At the same time, you simultaneously determine how to reduce the likelihood of a user being put into a position of initiating loss.

As you complete the process to the best of your ability, you then have to compile a list of potential countermeasures. As with other phases of the Boom lifecycle, when you have your list of countermeasures, you then need to create a prioritized list of those countermeasures as you did for Boom and Right of Boom.

19 Determining the Most Effective Countermeasures

After going through all phases of Boom for all potential Booms, it is easy to be overwhelmed by all the data, countermeasures identified, and all the options. In theory, with unlimited resources, you can implement all potential countermeasures at all phases of Boom and attempt to stop all losses. Clearly, this is not realistic in even the best of cases.

A comprehensive approach to UIL would seem to be obvious. Clearly, it is best to look at all potential UILs and then figure out which losses to mitigate. That decision would be based upon the expected values of the losses and then make a risk-based decision across all potential UILs as to which countermeasures you put your efforts into.

Unfortunately, that is not the way it is typically done. People look at a given problem and attempt to find a solution to the problem. There are many qualified, intelligent people out there who are in positions of responsibility. Unfortunately, many people in positions of responsibility are not as skilled as they probably should be before being put in such a position. Likewise, even some of the most astute people can't act as strategically as they would prefer given pressing issues, crises, budgetary limitations, etc.

As you go through this chapter, understand that we present a strategy that is theoretically free of outside burdens and locked in business processes. We realize that this is rarely going to be the case. However, also understand that compared to the typical method of looking at a problem one at a time, it provides for a much more rational decision-making process that balances concerns.

However, even if you just look at one UIL at a time, you at least get to look at it from all potential angles, Left of Boom, Boom, and Right of Boom. You can analyze which countermeasures are most effective at stopping the loss, whether it is more practical to let the loss initiate and mitigate it after Boom, whether to let some loss be realized and partially mitigate it, etc.

Using phishing as an example, you may put a basic email gateway in place, ignore awareness efforts, and implement multiple layers of anti-malware. We are not recommending this tactic, but just using this as an example of making a decision based on analyzing the complete lifecycle of an UIL.

As you read this chapter, the ideal situation is to study all of the individual UILs, determine the potential countermeasures for each of them, consolidate the countermeasure, see which countermeasures have the greatest overlap and the highest return on investment, and then choose the most effective countermeasures based upon available budget. However, that is not the case. We therefore propose an alternative that seems to be reasonably effective.

We intend and expect that readers will consider our advice and implement a strategy that works best for your circumstances. There is no right or wrong way to do it as long as your strategy accounts for risk and makes progress toward reducing your risk. Whatever strategy you use can be modified over time.

Early Prevention vs. Response

There is a general fact that the earlier you detect and prevent an incident, the less loss you incur. In the infamous 2013 Target data breach, a criminal broke into the Target network and was able to eventually steal the credit card numbers and other information of 110,000,000 customers. Target claimed the incident cost the company $292 million.

The incident reportedly began with a compromise of a Target vendor whose employees divulged login credentials after falling prey to phishing messages. The stolen credentials then allowed the criminal to log into a network with access into the Target operational network. If the phishing attack was stopped at that time, there might have been no noticeable loss. Perhaps, if there was multifactor authentication required for vendors to access the network, even after the employees fell for the phishing messages, the attack would have been stopped, and the cost to the company would have been password resets and a minor operational inconvenience.

Even if the attackers were able to log into the systems initially, if unusual activity was detected, the accounts could have been locked. The cost of a potential breach investigation could have been incurred, but it would have been relatively minor. There are many steps along the way, but consider that even if the criminals had been detected at the point prior to the actual exfiltration of information, the cost of the incident would have still been significant, but likely one-tenth of the final cost of the incident. There would have had to be a thorough analysis of the breach, and a great deal of technological cleanup would have had to be performed. However, the Target incident would have never had to incur the costs of the data breach, fines, lawsuits, etc., that resulted in the bulk of financial losses.

In the software development field, there is the traditional software development lifecycle with four phases: analysis, design, implementation, and maintenance. The generally accepted rule of thumb is that the earlier you find a software bug, the cheaper it is to fix, supposedly by a factor of 10. So if you find a problem in the analysis phase, you can just correct a line in a document. However, if the bug is not found until after it is implemented, it will cost 1,000 times more to correct, and likely much more, given that you have to rewrite the software, test it, and then roll it out to potentially millions of computers around the world. Even if you implement an agile development strategy, it is still true that the earlier you catch an error, the less it costs to remediate it.

In a non-computer-related example, consider how poor maintenance can lead to critical equipment failures. There is the old adage, "A stitch in time saves nine." The implication is that if there is a small tear, it will eventually get significantly larger if you don't properly fix it early. The same is true for all equipment with regard to preventative maintenance.

Consider the same problem in the attack kill chain. It is hard to come up with a multiplication factor, but similarly, the further the attack is allowed to progress, the greater the loss and the greater the mitigation costs. So clearly, there should be a concern to stop attacks as soon in the kill chain as possible. The implication might therefore be to put as much budget as possible into protection.

At the same time, we have to consider that it is impossible to provide perfect prevention. Likewise, a motivated attacker will inevitably find a way to get in. For example, even if the Target hacker did not get in through the phishing message, they likely would have kept trying until they did get into the Target business network. It is also possible that criminals tried many other attack paths to get into the network, until they were successful through the HVAC vendor.

It is therefore important to consider that when you are choosing your countermeasures that you are balancing a wide variety of concerns. Probably your most pressing concern is a limited budget. From that point, you are then considering the countermeasures that should have the highest return on investment, as well as those that most effectively detect and react to the user failures.

Start with Governance

Governance is cheap in theory, at least at the start. You can conceive, in some form, how a process should be implemented in a way to most effectively mitigate UIL at each phase of Boom. All it takes is an analysis of what has occurred and what should occur. You can identify the ideal scenario and determine what it takes to implement it from a technological perspective.

For this reason, we recommend that for each and every UIL you have identified to this point, you consider step-by-step how that process should proceed in the ideal world. Again, consider the finite phases of Left of Boom, Boom, and Right of Boom. Knowing the losses that previously occurred provides practical guidance for how to avoid loss.

Consider accounting procedures. Left of Boom involves establishing procedures that limit the ability for users to be in the position to cause loss. Planning for Boom involves users only being in a position to initiate limited transactions, training on how to do it right, and creating a user experience that facilitates the proper entry of information with the appropriate verifications. Right of Boom involves auditing the transactions and ensuring that processes were followed.

In the handling of personally identifiable information (PII), there should be established procedures created for the release of PII. For example, there is a common tax season scam where criminals send phishing messages to the HR department and claim to be the CEO and want the HR employee to send tax information to "the new accounting firm." When an HR employee receives the message, they should follow the established procedures, which would be along the lines that all requests for PII should be sent to the head of HR, who needs the approval of the general counsel to release the information. So whatever pretext is used, even if it is an actual request from the CEO, the low-level HR person is not in a position to send the information outside of the company.

In the ideal world, you account for all potential issues from the start. The reality is that this is unlikely. It is impossible to account for every possible issue in advance, as it is impossible to foresee all issues, and adjustments have to be made.

From our personal experiences, we learned that many supposedly heinous processes have a purpose. For example, when author Ira Winkler started his first consulting business, he believed that it would be a great travel policy to provide all consultants with a credit card that the company paid directly so employees did not incur excessive debt from the combination of airfare, hotels, meals, etc. However, Ira soon learned that to recover the travel costs from clients in a timely manner, he needed the consultants to provide expense reports in a timely manner. Unfortunately, while some employees would be diligent about providing the expense reports with the required receipts, more than a few were not. Compounding the problem, Ira only had the total amount charged and not the detailed receipts that his clients required to create the expense reports himself.

For this reason, he had to change the travel expense policy for consultants to pay all their expenses and then put in the required expense forms for reimbursement. Despite this, several consultants were still slow in providing the forms, even after multiple requests. Another policy had to be created requiring consultants to submit expense reports within one month or they might not be reimbursed, as clients required invoices in a timely manner after the contract was completed and closed.

As you can see, governance will evolve over time for a wide variety of reasons. Again, though, you need to attempt to anticipate the process to the best of your ability.

After walking through the previous three chapters for each UIL of concern, you likely have a good idea of the process that you want to implement to mitigate the UIL to the best of your ability.

Understand the Business Goal

Before you start, you need to remember the goal: You are designing a business process to reduce the risk associated with the process. That risk includes UIL that arises from the process. This means that your focus is specifically on the process, and not on the user, except for the fact that users are a part of the process.

At this point, the primary focus is to consider how to make the process more secure. You need to understand what is the input of the business process, what is the output, and how to get from the input to the output in a way that reduces risk. As the user was an initial part of that system, it is likely that they will still be part of the system.

We describe that one of the problems with addressing UIL is the focus on making a more resilient user rather than a secure system. At this phase, it is likewise critical to focus on creating a system that solves a business problem versus specifically addressing the user problem.

Removing the User

In the ideal world, in Left of Boom you will completely remove the opportunity for UIL, because you take the user out of the process by the point of Boom. For example, with phishing messages, if you can completely filter out all phishing messages from a user's inbox, there is no potential loss for the user to initiate. Even though the user is still technically in the loop, they do not become involved. As we discussed earlier, when McDonald's implemented kiosks that allowed customers to place orders themselves in a store, there was no opportunity for cashiers to enter an order incorrectly, give the wrong change, and/or steal money.

In many cases, technology can remove the user from being in the position to create loss. This does not mean loss has been completely prevented, as the technology can create new types of loss. For example, if you assume that technology can remove all malicious phishing messages, and a malicious message slips through, there are no safeguards in place, and the loss can be catastrophic. In the case with McDonald's kiosks, some customers might not understand how to work the technology and might choose not to patronize the restaurant.

As you consider Left of Boom, you need to focus on the end goal of the process you are analyzing. If the goal of the process does not require a user to be involved, Left of Boom should involve determining how that can be accomplished.

Start Left of Boom

While we analyzed Left of Boom last, it is where to start first. You likely have better ideas of how the process that enables the loss can begin. You can begin to prevent the loss as early in the kill chain as possible. You may enact a process that dramatically changes the original process.

For this reason, you must consider that you might radically change the entire process. While there might be some similarities, you do not have to keep the process the same.

In the ideal world, you are involved in business processes as they are being defined. You can therefore design the processes fresh. However, even if there is a process in place initially, you should consider designing the process to mitigate the loss as early as possible.

This means that Boom and Right of Boom could be very different than initially studied. Your analysis therefore has to consider the change in the kill chain. While you may have identified countermeasures for Boom and Right of Boom, they might not be relevant.

Consider Technology

Remember that technology can be used to enhance the process in ways that might otherwise not be possible. McDonald's again is a simple and prime example of reducing UIL through the implementation of technology. The kiosks reduce UIL resulting from cashier accidents and malfeasance. They implemented cooking equipment and timers to ensure that food is properly cooked. The systems are tied to ordering systems that provide for just-in-time delivery of food so that there is no food wastage from accidents in ordering too much or too little food.

In the case of McDonald's, they are automating UIL away as a collateral benefit to the overall decreasing of operational costs, and providing for greater efficiencies. You likewise need to consider that proactively reducing UIL will likely result in operational efficiencies and therefore unintended returns on investments. Technology is one of those ways to do so.

Beyond the operational efficiencies, technology provides capabilities to mitigate UIL, before it can be initiated. For example, secure email gateways and other anti-phishing technologies can filter out attacks before they get to the users. Even if the technologies are not perfect, they still filter out well in excess of 99% of malicious emails. When you go to banks, casinos, and other facilities that deal with large volumes of cash, you find that there are machines used to count large stacks of cash, virtually eliminating counting errors.

Sometimes technology can provide capabilities that otherwise would not exist. More frequently, you will likely find that technology can restrict the potential damage of processes. Limiting access permissions on computer systems limits the amount of loss a user can implement. For example, if someone with access to a database can only see access to fields that they need to do their job, if their account is compromised, the scope of data compromise is likewise limited. Access cards that only provide access to needed facilities means that people can only compromise a portion of the facilities. Risk cannot be completely eliminated, but it can be reduced to necessary risk versus excessive risk.

You do not have to be a technology expert yourself, but you should be willing to do the appropriate research to find out what is the state of the art relevant to your own systems and processes. You should be very open to ask for help from the relevant departments throughout your organization, as they likely, or at least should, have people who track new technologies relevant to your environment.

After you have these technologies, they should be considered in relationship to how they impact the governance. Can user processes go away? Do procedures need to be created for configuring technology? Do guidelines have to be set for designing user interfaces? Again, you need to consider how, once technology is chosen, it should be implemented and embedded within the process.

Prioritize Potential Loss

As you go through your lists of UILs, it is clear that some losses are more costly and relevant than others. For example, if some losses, even if totally realized, are at best a nuisance, it is unlikely that you would or should spend limited resources to mitigate a nuisance. On the other hand, ransomware has and can cripple an organization, so you should ensure that you would invest more than adequate resources to mitigate that UIL.

As you start to consider countermeasures, you need to prioritize which losses you want to mitigate. You have limited resources, and you also have limited time. You also might want to start off small and pursue only one or two UILs to mitigate to get comfortable with the process.

As you do start, while you clearly want to mitigate your largest UILs, you also need to gain confidence and probably credibility with your organization. As we discuss in Chapter 20 on organizational issues, there are a variety concerns that you have to deal with beyond the technical and operational issues. As the proverbial eating of the elephant goes, you have to start with one bite. You are likely not going to be able to lead a complete rearchitecture of your organization and its business and technical processes without some form of proof.

Therefore, you need to choose your first efforts by considering both the scope of potential loss of a given UIL and the feasibility of implementing changes related to that UIL. This might involve level of effort, time to completion, impact to the organization, costs to implement, etc.

As we previously implied, the countermeasure you implement might very well mitigate other UILs that you didn't intend to address, by default. The likelihood of collateral mitigation might also impact which UILs you choose to address. For example, if you choose to mitigate loss resulting from lost mobile devices, you will likely find that this involves improving the security of all computers throughout the organization and thereby reduce loss from a wide variety of user actions.

While we would fully endorse addressing all potential UILs in a perfect world, we are not in a perfect world. You need to consider three criteria and then determine which UILs you want to focus on to begin. Those criteria are:

- Value of potential loss
- Ease and time in implementing mitigation
- Collateral impact

When you have the resulting priorities, you can potentially start to focus your efforts and get to work on mitigating the UILs.

Define Governance Thoroughly

We discuss governance in two sections; as in Left of Boom, there is a soft consideration of governance that might impact Boom and beyond. It is important to consider that governance will drive technology and awareness; or more specifically, at least it should.

We refer you to Chapter 13 on governance for details. To start, we are not necessarily concerned with standards at this point. Standards define high-level principles that address strategic concerns. In the ideal world, nothing you do regarding UIL should necessarily impact standards. That is, of course, assuming that standards exist. The reason we state this is because standards should not be changed based upon how a process is performed. The standards should be agnostic to implementation. This being said, we do recommend that after you finish defining the procedures and guidelines, you go back and review your standards to ensure that they are complete and provide for the appropriate authority that you need to implement the guidelines and procedures.

When you defined Left of Boom in Chapter 18 for each UIL, you likely defined a variety of paths from Boom back to the origin of the attacks. Those paths represent the multiple ways that can put a user in the position of initiating a loss. You have to consider each path for loss initiation. You can potentially combine paths when they are similar enough and can be addressed by the same governance, awareness, and technology. For example, if you determine that poor maintenance can initiate a loss, you possibly considered each piece of equipment. In most cases, you can create procedures that in some form specify to record and schedule preventative maintenance.

Similarly, you might determine that different types of UIL can be mitigated in the same way. For example, you might determine that employee health records, human resources information, financial records, and other forms of PII can all be governed under one overarching set of governance.

From this point, you step through the path and must determine at each step how that step can be performed in a way that will proactively mitigate the loss to the best extent possible. We use the word *best* as it might not be practical to mitigate a loss completely. Once you determine this, you need to create a procedure or guideline that defines the mitigation strategy. This can include defining the type of technology that you need or expect to implement the governance. You might want to note whether the technology is required or there can be alternatives, if not ideal.

Understand that sometimes you might not want to or need to define guidelines and procedures at each and every step. You may be able to combine steps as it makes sense when one seamlessly flows into another. You just need to ensure that there is a definition of the process and the associated concerns.

If there are decisions to be made, you need to identify the decision-making criteria. Sometimes that criteria could be to refer the decision to another party, such as a manager. You might contend that there is too wide of a variety of criteria to define in governance. That is possible, but you still need to define the criteria as well as possible. Author Ira Winkler was tasked with helping a major online gaming provider create antisocial engineering procedures to prevent people from calling into the service and tricking call center employees into giving the attackers control of someone else's account. This required creating a complicated decision tree based upon available information and whether or not the caller was able to answer the questions. There was the initial method of authentication and based on the caller's response, either they were given access to the account or they were presented with other questions. It was critical that the call center operator did not give hints, and the operator had no options except to follow the scripts as presented. There was also a verification process created to proactively contact the account holder after a certain level of effort was expended.

Your governance that you create for Left of Boom drives the governance at Boom. Boom then drives the required governance for Right of Boom. You need to ensure that you follow all potential paths (or at least as many paths as practical) and ensure that you define the process sufficiently so that it can be implemented with minimal discretion, while also driving the awareness and technology required to completely mitigate the problem.

No matter what the current process is, it is possible to drastically change it, if the findings warrant it. Again, the ideal situation is to potentially remove the UIL at Left of Boom.

The reality is that you will likely not make drastic changes to the process, but make it more streamlined and defined. For example, even with the best secure email gateway products, phishing messages will make their way past them. While that is not ideal, it is manageable if you prepare for the inevitable. For this reason, you should define the guidelines and procedures for each step or logical grouping of steps.

Matrix Technical Countermeasures

As you have the procedures identified for the UILs you intend to mitigate, you can begin to identify the technology required. This is a relatively straightforward process. There are many ways to do this, but we recommend a simple matrix for a variety of reasons.

As you go through the processes you identified, you need to record the technical countermeasures, their costs, and the scope of the benefits that they bring. Ideally, you will also record the potential benefit to other forms of UIL that you don't intend to explicitly mitigate.

For example, if you intend to mitigate the theft of PII with data leak prevention (DLP) software that can filter out personnel information from email messages, it can likewise be configured to filter out customer information, proprietary information, legal information, financial data, etc. There should be a great deal of unintended benefit in many of your identified countermeasures, and you should keep track of this to assist in your final determination of how you choose to invest your limited funding.

Creating the Matrix

The rows will represent the potential countermeasures. The first column will be the name of the technical countermeasure. The second column will be the approximate cost. The third columns and beyond represent the types of UIL you intend to mitigate. We also recommend adding a row at the top so that you can put in the likely value of a potential loss. This allows for making a true risk-based decision.

As you begin to address UIL, mark the cell representing that the countermeasure assists in mitigating the UIL. Also indicate in some form the relative importance and value of the countermeasure to mitigating that form of UIL.

You will add as many rows as required to record countermeasures, and as many columns as required to represent UIL. As you add new countermeasures and new classes of UIL, you go back and indicate in the boxes the potential effectiveness of the particular countermeasure in mitigating that UIL. Again, the goal is to identify all of the potential benefits of a countermeasure, as there should be benefits across multiple losses.

Figure 19.1 demonstrates one method to create a table. In this example, we use grayscale shading to indicate the value/importance of a countermeasure to mitigate the potential loss, along with the potential loss.

As you look at the graph, you might notice that the technical countermeasures to mitigate UIL 3 are more expensive than the potential loss. You might, therefore, choose not to mitigate that loss. However, you can see that Countermeasures 1 and 2 mitigate a significant amount of other loss. So while it might not be your specific intent to mitigate UIL 3, it will be mitigated by default in the mitigation of UIL 1 and UIL 4.

	Cost	UIL 1	UIL 2	UIL 3	UIL 4
Potential Loss		$1M	$200K	$200K	$50M
Countermeasure 1	$55K				
Countermeasure 2	$150K				
Countermeasure 3	$75K				
Countermeasure 4	$250K				

Figure 19.1: Sample countermeasure matrix

Similarly, you may find that in some cases, the cost to mitigate a UIL is not practical at all through the use of technology, and you might choose just to implement process change to mitigate as much of the loss as possible.

The goal is to identify the technical countermeasures that have true return on investment, prioritizing the countermeasures compared to the available resources. If you do not have sufficient resources to acquire the required technical countermeasures to mitigate reasonable UIL, you at least have a tool that quickly depicts the need. You can then ideally take that tool to your management to provide a business case for the additional resources.

Define Awareness

Awareness is intentionally last on the list, as you need to know specifically what to make people aware of. We constantly reiterate that awareness should be based on process. As technology is likely embedded within the process, awareness needs to include proper use of technology.

You need to ensure that people are specifically aware of how to perform their functions in a safe way, as well as how to properly use any technology that is part of those functions. The awareness program then needs to be implemented around those principles.

Using the principles in Chapter 15, you need to create an awareness program. The key is to keep the focus on how to implement process versus how not to do things wrong.

It's Just a Start

While we would love if everyone would follow this guidance for all processes within their organization, we realize that you must implement this strategy within a variety of constraints. As we reiterate throughout this chapter, you need to start where it is simple and the most valuable.

This is desirable for a variety of reasons. It allows you to determine where the process needs to be modified for your own circumstances. It also allows you to deal with potential shortcomings in a controlled circumstance. It also allows you to build up momentum, and gain confidence in your abilities and the process as a whole. Once you have success, you can then tackle additional UILs, while expanding into other business processes.

20 Implementation Considerations

We've recognized our users; determined administrative, technological, and operational approaches; defined the desired security-minded culture; created metrics for effectiveness and improvement; and identified methodologies to follow. Now you are almost ready to implement the loss mitigation strategy you've created to mitigate against user-initiated loss (UIL). Most organizations have ambitious goals for change, but far too often we see there is a tenacious gap between ambition and performance or strategy formulation and execution. These tend to be the most common areas for failure despite best efforts. Therefore, it is crucial to consider where you may encounter problems while holistically implementing our recommendations.

Studies and interviews find multiple organizational issues contributing to failed strategy execution. We can learn from failed implementations of other organizations just as we have backward-engineered countermeasures for UIL. Countless issues will arise during any strategic change. Identifying the potential hurdles in advance can provide a playbook for successfully overcoming common challenges encountered during similar efforts.

We find UIL and similar issues during mergers and acquisitions, strategic implementation, applying safety controls, and organization-wide changes. Three Mile Island, Honda, Chernobyl, Honeywell, U.S. Airways, American Airlines, Sprint, Time-Warner, and AOL are all examples of organizations that experienced failures in quality, safety, change management, and execution. Each of the examples is truly complex with multiple implementation challenges; however, the list of issues can be simplified for our purposes of mitigating UIL and implementing a loss prevention strategy.

Thinking of possible outcomes and planning accordingly, in advance, is something we often do individually. For example, when planning for a trip abroad, you will take measures to minimize loss of money, personal belongings, location, or life. You may take traveler's checks, a theft proof traveler's bag, virus-protective facemask, luggage identifiers, or a compass. You went through a process of figuring out what you wanted to protect, didn't want to lose, and identified countermeasures for mitigating against loss. Do you feel completely protected against potential loss while actively on your trip? Likely not. Challenges or situations you didn't think of may occur. Knowing that challenges can arise is important to ensuring your ability to be flexible, think critically, and tackle issues effectively. If you do lose your luggage, what do you do? You set your theft-proof bag down to take a better picture of something amazing and it was stolen at your feet. Now what?

The same concept applies to our organizations. Having an organizational strategy is part of successful implementation; however, effective execution is inclusive of identifying where issues may arise and planning accordingly.

You've Got Issues

As you execute the strategy, there are aspects of implementation you must know and prepare for. The considerations we discuss are not a comprehensive list; rather, they are some of the more common issues. As you go through them, consider whether they are likely to impact your efforts. If they might, you should at least begin to plan how to address them.

Weak Strategy

A tactical approach or list of things to do is often mislabeled as strategic objectives. It is easy to make that mistake. For example, all too often we rely on security awareness to educate our users as the sole effort to mitigate user error. Then, the security awareness plan is considered the strategy. As we have thoroughly covered, security awareness is simply a tactic of our overall strategy with the objective of educating users to minimize UIL.

It becomes too easy to confuse tactics with strategies when you are not provided with the proper perspective. A strategy is an overarching plan or set of goals. Tactics are steps to achieve the strategy. With the example of awareness, the goal is to reduce UIL. You need an overall strategy to figure out the life cycle of a loss and to mitigate it the way we recommend. Again, though, people confuse the tactic of awareness as a strategy. They might even confuse the tactic of endpoint security as a strategy. Both tactics fit within the strategy of mitigating UIL. If your sole responsibility is to implement awareness, then you might develop a strategy to specifically implement the awareness program. However, you must know where your efforts fit within the overall strategy.

As you consider a potential strategy, besides whether or not it is just an independent set of tactics, you need to consider whether the strategy is comprehensive and complete. It is typically easy to tell how strong a strategy is by seeing its completeness. You should have a team that provides the required expertise. There should be sufficient resources available to implement the strategy. The strategy should help you proactively understand what problems you may encounter.

Resources, Culture, and Implementation

Budget is often an elusive vision in the realms of security and risk management. Information is required from sources across the organization to forecast budgetary projections and must include objective, quantifiable metrics for cost savings. For example, if an organization wants to implement a cloud-based technology, you can state the implementation will cost $250,000 to replace on-site infrastructure with a cost savings of $2.5 million over three years, due to decreased operational and maintenance expenses. Additionally, the new solution may lower UIL by 50% based on the cost from UIL in previous years. If leadership does not approve the budget, there will be an increase in associated risk, and the leadership team would need to agree to sign off on risk acceptance in exchange.

The number of, availability, and capability of people resources are often overestimated. You must consider how large the organization is and how many people make up the workforce. Are people disbursed locally, regionally, or globally? Understanding where your people are located will provide insight to environmental, cultural, and operational aspects that require attention. You must consider the job types and descriptions of the people who will ultimately execute your strategy to account for their capability. Additionally, is resource capacity practiced within the organization? For example, if 70% of your workforce time is spent on operations, 20% on administrative duties, and 10% on new projects, do they have the capacity to take on additional efforts? The best strategy in the world will likely fail if the people responsible for implementation are functioning at more than 100% capacity.

The size, location, and type of organization (corporation, SME, micro, etc.) can pose challenges to strategic implementation. Author Tracy Celaya Brown worked with a health and wellness technology startup client experiencing a downturn in profits. The organization was small, ran a lean crew, and was in an exponential growth phase. The leadership team wanted to remain a lean group to maintain flexibility and profitability. As the company continued to grow, the initial employee base consistently pivoted products and processes without documentation to immediately satisfy the desires of potential clients.

While the tactic helped the company expand into different markets and increase revenues, the new employee base hired to handle new customers and incoming orders was left without documented processes and a legacy leadership team without time to devote to training. This resulted in an increase in erroneous orders, poor product quality, disgruntled customers, tainted brand image, and loss of revenue. The client worked with Tracy and successfully established a consistent product line with holistic processes for customer onboarding, order fulfillment, and customer maintenance. A focused product line allowed sales engineers to provide consistent offerings for clients that improved the productivity of employees because their efforts were no longer applied to customizing products on the whim and the quality of the product. Establishing holistic, security-minded processes provided thorough procedures for onboarding, maintaining, and off-boarding customers while mitigating potential UIL from missed steps or unclear expectations during verification, authentication, and communication for clients. While the organization was extremely agile, implementing a strategy in a fast-paced environment without an established structure or processes was near impossible.

In some cases, a startup culture is highly desired while the structure of larger organizations is considered stifling. However, providing structure and process can improve efficiency, security, and minimize UIL, even in startup cultures. For larger organizations, the proverbial red-tape or layered bureaucratic culture may feel like turning a battleship.

The culture of the organization is a serious consideration in ability and effectiveness and may affect the type and number of resources utilized. Fast and furious versus slow and steady will have unique challenges where UIL must be addressed, costs of UIL, and how to effectively mitigate against it.

Lack of Ownership and Accountability

In Chapter 12, we revisited TQM and the foundational principles of ownership and accountability. Business leaders must be fully committed to supporting and implementing the strategy. They must fully understand how the plan can improve the business along with the risks and costs associated with not implementing. Additionally, middle management and staff must be committed to accountability and follow through with delivering the strategy.

Organizations will achieve leadership engagement in different ways. In some cases, a top-down or bottom-up approach is used. Remember that our goal is to optimize UIL, and users are at every level within an organization. As we discussed early in the book, when users initiate loss, an organization's leadership, IT, security, and other groups like to label them as "stupid." This, however, begs the question: Does the term "stupid user" apply to leadership, if they don't care? Similarly, does "stupid user" apply to our security team or other business units? Personal jeopardy for leaders is increasing as they are being held accountable for UIL more and more. This accountability must be an effort distributed among everyone within the organization to create an environment where movement toward a common goal is conducted on one accord.

Despite the top-down or bottom-up approach, it is just as fundamentally important to have middle management and executive leadership support as it is to have frontline staff and individual contributor support. Consider tying strategy execution to performance management and let people identify their own goals aligned to strategic initiatives and maintain ongoing visibility and proof of progress throughout a specified period of time. Leadership is not limited to any one person with a specific title or position within an organization; rather, it is dependent upon the ability to effectively influence others. Organizations need leaders embedded within and capable of positively bringing others into unrealized futures.

One Effort at a Time

We discuss governance throughout the book, and it applies to strategic initiatives as well. Far too often, organizations have many strategic initiatives running simultaneously with nebulous objectives. Too many. There must be a thoughtful process for identifying, reviewing, measuring, and prioritizing strategic initiatives. Organizations are easily distracted and must maintain focus for the successful implementation of any strategy and to minimize UIL.

Similarly, it is possible that strategic initiatives might conflict with each other. If you, for example, are implementing new equipment that does require a major strategy and want to mitigate UIL related to poor equipment maintenance, you likely need to implement training. If, at the same time, you want to mitigate security-related UIL, you likely want to enhance awareness training. In certain environments, there are union contracts that limit the amount of training you can mandate to workers, which may be a contributing factor in determining prioritization of the effort.

Without a structured process for managing active initiatives and resulting benefits, there can be poor follow-through, chaotic implementation, inefficient use of resources, a lack of measurable effectiveness or performance factors, and failed implementation. Ensure there is a manageable number of goals, objectives, and programs in flight with clear expectations with the collection and analysis of metrics to support proof of satisfying the expectations.

Change Management

Changes within a business mean change management of the process for ensuring changes are smoothly implemented and successfully adopted. People want to know what is going on and why. You can help minimize pushback or resistance with communication. Yet, a lack of communication is a common point of failure with many organizations executing strategy. A thorough communication plan is a critical part of any solid change management plan and should be structured, timely, relative, and purposeful.

Apple Inc. executes a strong communication plan when announcing changes to a popular product to inform users, gain engagement, and obtain support. Apple is mindful with the message being delivered, keenly aware of the audience, and intentional about audience interpretation. For example, Apple proactively announces product changes, along with preparations required for the updates, and creates a sense of excitement and anticipation with carefully timed and crafted communication. Apple demonstrates transparency, authenticity, and connectedness when using effective communication that is timely with message consistency across distribution channels.

Poor communication plans can include a lack of clarity or purpose, misinformation, timing, distribution channels, and an inadequate consideration for the audience. Many political administrations implemented poor communication plans during the COVID-19 global lockdown with unrelated material and poorly structured daily briefings. The dreadful briefings left audiences confused about the accuracy of the information and purpose behind communication efforts.

Communication is a constantly developing skill, which requires a level of emotional intelligence and maturity on the part of the communicator and an understanding of those with whom you are communicating. Effective communication plans will clearly identify the audience, will be purposeful with what is communicated and why, and will include a calendar for when something is distributed using specific digital or written platforms. Additionally, multiple platforms and professionals exist to assist in crafting communication to increase attention, interpretation, and effectiveness. Ensure you and your team strive to continuously improve communication and have a change management plan prepared to over-communicate. Essentially, when you think you are sick of listening to yourself speak is when the message may be heard by others in the organization. The goal is to ensure the intended message is received by the targeted audience. For our purposes of mitigating UIL, ongoing communication is recommended to ensure our workforce understands their role in minimizing risk, techniques for avoiding UIL, and where additional resources are available for further education or use. Behavior change is both important and complex. A detailed, effective communication plan can be a tool for this purpose.

Adopting Changes

A commitment to change and personal accountability across all levels of the organization can greatly affect the successful adoption of major change initiatives. Every person has a level of tolerance for change that directly impacts the speed at which behavior changes are accepted and demonstrated.

Two particularly effective tools that deal with adapting to change and adopting new behaviors are the Kubler-Ross Change Curve and the J-Curve of Adoption (based on the Diffusion of Innovation theory). The following sections explore these models along with an adaptation to the J-Curve with *Crossing the Chasm*.

Kubler-Ross Change Curve

The Kubler-Ross Change Curve is a model effectively used by business leaders around the world to assist their workforce in successfully adapting to change. (See Figure 20.1.) The Kubler-Ross Change Curve initially identified the stages of grief and was later modified as the seven stages of change.

- Shock
- Denial
- Frustration
- Depression
- Experiment
- Decision
- Integration

During shock, one may feel surprise or shock at the event occurring. Denial is disbelief and a search for evidence that the change is not true. Frustration is one recognizing that the current situation is different and can sometimes include anger. Depression may set in with low mood or a lack of energy. Experiment is a phase of initial engagement with the new situation. Decision is learning how to work in the new situation and feeling more positive. Finally, integration is when changes are accepted and integrated with renewal.

Consider these stages when implementing change initiatives. For example, when implementing efforts to review and adjust existing processes with the intention of modifying to preemptively mitigate against UIL, the result will likely be new steps in an existing process or the elimination of old ways and expectation of behavior change to the new way. While the culture of an organization may be to embrace change, each organization consists of subcultures and individuals with their own tolerance for change. This means you must plan for change and how the individuals will move through a change curve personally and as a whole with the organization.

If an accountant has processed work a specific way for 10 years but the process is changed, the behavior must change. Let's say the accountant is not as flexible as the organization expects. Your team member may experience the phases of the change curve for varying lengths of time within each phase. The accountant may be in shock for a week, in denial for a week, frustrated for two months, depressed for a couple of days, and a little more willing for a week before ready to move on with the new way of working. In this case, one person could take a few months before behavior change is integrated. With a workforce of thousands of local and globally positioned team members, the layers of complexity compound. Understanding these phases can help when planning for change and determining an approach for implementing, communicating, and measuring the effectiveness and success of the change initiative.

The stages may not be experienced in a linear fashion, and some people may not experience all stages; however, the model may be helpful in addressing challenges to alleviate issues during implementation.

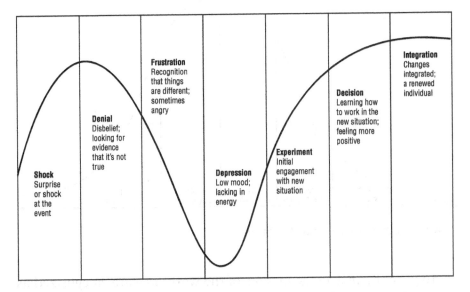

Figure 20.1: The Kubler-Ross Change Curve

J-Curve of Adoption or Diffusion of Innovation

Another model is the J-Curve of Adoption or Diffusion of Innovation. The Diffusion of Innovation is a theory developed by E. M. Rogers in 1962, explaining how and why innovative efforts or behaviors are adopted and diffused and communicated throughout a social system or population.

A common point of strategy implementation failure is when there is an unwillingness or inability to change. The J-Curve of Adoption identifies how the population of an organization may be categorized and provide an opportunity to customize change efforts based on the projected adoption rates across the organization. As you can see in Figure 20.2, the population breaks down into the following groups:

- Innovators = 2.5%
- Early Adopters = 13.5%
- Early Majority = 34%
- Late Majority = 34%
- Laggards = 16%

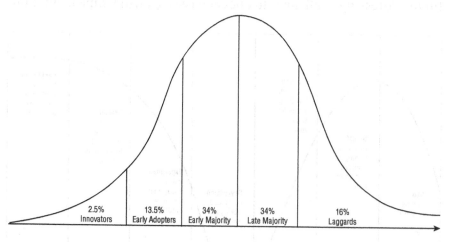

Figure 20.2: The J-Curve of Adoption

In general, an average of 2.5% of the workforce are categorized as innovators and welcome change; 13.5% are next to adopt change and labeled early adopters. The next 34% are considered the early majority, while the subsequent 34% are the late majority. The last 16% are labeled laggards. Willingness to change ensures the organization is nimble with an ability to adapt to change. Employees and leaders may become enthusiastic and more accountable, or willing, as change is successfully conducted. Performance management and individual goals are an accompanying approach for supporting change.

Geoffrey A. Moore created an adaption to the J-Curve introducing the chasm and the concept of a transition period between early adopters and the early majority. The adaptation is focused on marketing technologies to the mainstream market. As such, Moore refers to the early market adopters as enthusiasts and visionaries, while the mainstream market consumers are pragmatists, conservatives, and skeptics, respectively. However, he notes a chasm between the visionaries and pragmatists, which, if not addressed, can result in failure of adoption from the mainstream market. While there may be cracks between each segment, the chasm between the early market and mainstream is the most difficult to cross. However, once successfully crossed, momentum builds, which can move the masses toward adoption or positive change. Moore offers ideas for crossing the chasm with focused efforts, compelling factors for change, establishing credibility, adjusting the target audience as necessary, and guiding people through any fear of change to adopt the respective new idea, technology, or thing.

We see Moore's adaption to Rogers' J-Curve with the chasm that aligns with the period of disruption in Figure 20.3. Moore's reference is for disruptive technologies. For your purposes, you may consider the level of disruption expected from the introduced change or the maturity level of the organization to determine whether a chasm may exist and use the respective model in planning and executing change.

Looking at performance over time through disruptive change, we understand there must be alignment between leadership's expectations for achieving a desired state and the realization of the workforce's objectives. Likely long-standing processes are changing or new processes developed as you are implementing strategy with the goal to mitigate UIL. They will change how they work, and thus there will be a period of disruption and impact on performance. However, over time behavior changes are adopted and performance gradually improves. The key is to align desired outcomes to realistic expectations. See Figure 20.4.

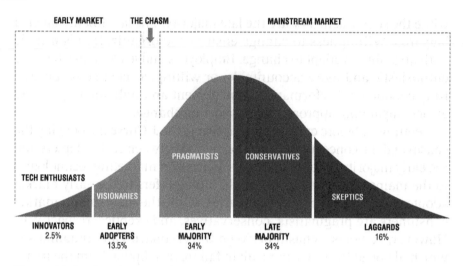

Figure 20.3: The chasm in the J-Curve

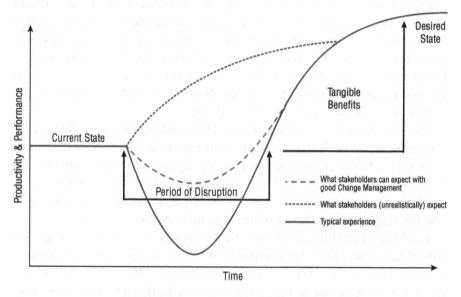

Figure 20.4: How good change management influences productivity and performance over time

Governance, Again

As the saying goes, "It takes a village," and everyone is responsible for mitigating risk and loss. Governance ensures your security strategy and efforts to minimize loss are intentional and well-supported, and we touch on these concepts in Chapters 8 and 9. It is the ongoing activity of identifying a desired outcome, what gaps are currently in place, determining what must be addressed, and prioritizing with the goal of mitigating UIL. It is through the governance process where continuous review, alignment to standards, and prioritization are reviewed on a steady cadence. You may consider this a feedback loop of sorts to track progress, revisit, and revise with metrics to support decisions.

Finally, consider enlisting the assistance of an empowered project management office (PMO) with professionals responsible for leading and driving change. A PMO will typically be aligned with an executive leadership committee and have visibility to enterprise-wide initiatives as part of effective portfolio management.

Business Case for a Human Security Officer

We have acknowledged that users are a choice attack vector, because the environment around the user is often weak. As a result, upwards of 90% of data breaches are a result of user failures. Remember that successful attacks against users result from a systematic failure of the entire security infrastructure and typically technology, governance, and awareness address these issues in silos without coordination. Security needs more significant change within organizational culture through reinforced strategy. Some would contend it is the CISO's job to do this; however, the CISO (or CIO) has an extensive field of responsibility and will have a team of people to delegate responsibilities. Similar to how organizations assign team members to oversee technology infrastructure security and another to oversee application security, we posit the creation of the human security officer (HSO).

The HSO is responsible for identifying vulnerabilities that could result in UIL and implementing a mitigation plan, which includes technology and sound governance. In security, our customers are the other business units, so this position would be more aligned with risk and business process with experience in security. This person is a security advocate who can speak the languages of business and IT and translate that into the language of risk. Given security awareness is aimed at educating users to keep from making poor security decisions or erroneous behaviors, the team would report to the HSO. Additionally, the HSO would recruit security champions to support security efforts across business units by extending a collaborative arm to assist leaders.

Some of the skills required for the position include consultative abilities, expert communication skills (verbal and written), pattern recognition, business acumen, relationship-building, and some security technical prowess. The HSO position requires a deeper level of responsibility and authority, but it is also collaborative, communicative, and consultative. The HSO reviews potential harmful user actions in various areas of the organization and holistically determines countermeasures to implement as preventative processes for user actions that can result in loss.

While an HSO might not be considered mandatory, the question is otherwise, "Who will be responsible for overseeing the comprehensive mitigation of UIL?" Again, all studies show that UIL initiates more than 90% of significant losses. We contend that this should be approached as a strategy, and there should be an individual whose sole responsibility is overseeing the reduction of these losses. What we have now are a set of uncoordinated tactics that produced the current, unacceptable results.

It Won't Be Easy

Many organizations often forgo risk management for the sake of convenience, which increases the potential for catastrophic UIL through failed strategy. We've reviewed multiple potential issues that may arise when implementing your larger security strategy. You must understand how your organization functions, know which contributing factors require consideration, and potentially use adoption models as a methodology for building out a comprehensive implementation plan. We understand change requires ongoing user support and reviewed how performance management can reinforce strategy and compliance to secure processes. Finally, we posited the human security officer (HSO) as a security advocate and business enabler. We also recommend that organizations create the position of HSO that serves as focal point for integrating the different disciplines involved. There are chief network architects, chief data architects, and chief security architects; why not an HSO to collaborate with the business and assist with holistically securing users? Successful strategy implementation is no easy task and is critical for an organization to maintain a competitive advantage despite an ever-growing threat landscape and evolving global markets.

21 If You Have Stupid Users, You Have a Stupid System

User error is a window into your system. User error, or more encompassing, user-initiated loss (UIL), which includes error and intentional acts, is not a specific problem with the user, but a problem of the entire system. Why was the user in a position to initiate loss? Why did the user initiate the loss? Why didn't the system stop the user? Why did the system allow the user's action to create such a loss?

The users can only act in a way that you allow them to act. They can only do what you put them in the position to do. Their actions should theoretically be limited to what is necessary, or should at least be expected. Does this mean that users are not "stupid" in that they lack intelligence or common sense? Not at all. At the end of the day, some of your users can be complete imbeciles.

Whether or not a given user is an imbecile, you need to design a system around the fact that any given user might be an imbecile. Likewise, you need to design a system around the fact that 3% to 5% of users will intentionally do harm if given the opportunity. Even if you hire only the most intelligent and honest people to work with your systems, they will inevitably initiate some form of loss due to carelessness, accidents, their compliance budget, and similar reasons. There will never be a system where all users act appropriately at all times. Even if all users always act appropriately, it is possible that the system will not function perfectly and will fail you.

A User Should Never Surprise You

People sometimes argue that they cannot be responsible for every action by every user, but the fact is that they are responsible for users' actions and dealing with their consequences. Even while you cannot foresee every possible UIL, you are still responsible for mitigating the losses. That does not mean that a user has to be prevented from initiating all possible losses. It is virtually impossible to ensure that a loss will never occur.

Although losses will occur, the one thing that should never happen is that you are caught by surprise. You should at least attempt to examine what types of losses can occur, what actions a user can take that can lead to loss, what the scope of the loss might be, what it would take to stop the loss, and, finally, whether it is worth stopping the loss. If you have thought through the process, you are better prepared when a user makes an action that initiates a loss.

Perform Some More Research

Throughout the book we discuss process improvement disciplines such as Six Sigma, safety science, counterterrorism, and others, and you should explore them further. Clearly, if one of the disciplines especially triggered your interest, you can start with it.

If your organization already implements one or more of these disciplines, you definitely want to research them further. For example, if you are in a manufacturing environment where there is a strong safety program, you likely want to talk to the people who run that program and find out how they implement it. Do they have books or standards that they use to design their program?

It does not hurt to be able to speak their language. More important, if you are going to implement a quality improvement process, you are more likely to get both approval and support by using a methodology they are already familiar with.

You may find that you have a variety of people available to support you. For example, if your organization already applies Six Sigma, you may find someone certified to assist you and take your effort well beyond what you could otherwise accomplish yourself.

We have no delusions that this book will make our readers complete experts in applying a systematic process to proactively mitigate loss. We do provide a good roadmap to allow you to step through the process and develop your expertise. However, by finding allies and team members with expertise, you can accelerate your efforts.

Start Somewhere

Unfortunately, the primary principle we present, specifically that a problem created by the user indicates a problem with the whole system, is not a commonly embraced concept throughout the business world. While safety science, TQM, accounting, and some other disciplines have adopted the concept in general, it appears that most technical, operational, and security programs have not.

Therefore, implementing the strategy becomes an uphill battle, and we see firsthand the criticism of our work from some security awareness professionals, who believe the answer to human error is simply making users more aware. Our touting of awareness as being important, but the least effective aspect of loss mitigation initially causes security awareness professionals concern. We want awareness professionals to become broader in their practice to include governance and determination of the appropriate technologies.

Despite possible initial lack of acceptance, you need to start somewhere. If you want to mitigate UIL, you have to acknowledge it as a systems problem. You need to address the organizational issues and begin making changes. We assume that readers of this book are involved with some aspect of loss mitigation. You might have to expand your responsibility into areas where you have no authority.

While Part IV provides an overall process that we want people to follow, we understand it may not be practical. So, for that reason, if you cannot implement the process as defined, pick the most obvious and pressing loss to address.

Throughout the book, we refer to phishing as an example. It is common. The losses are obvious. No matter how much awareness you provide, people will still eventually click a malicious link in an email. If your organization has not addressed phishing through a comprehensive approach of Left of Boom, Boom, and Right of Boom, it could be an easy place to start and get a quick win.

If you have other responsibilities and areas of authority, you might have trouble deciding where to start. One thing you can try is to ask yourself, "What is my greatest aggravation with my users initiating loss?" It can be that simple. Then start to implement the defined process to mitigate those losses. If it is a process where you have control, you should be able to enhance, if not rearchitect, the process. Minimally, you should strive to make your life easier.

Take Day Zero Metrics

Perhaps the biggest mistakes that we see people make when implementing loss reduction programs is a failure to take metrics before they start their efforts. From a personal benefits perspective, taking Day Zero metrics and then showing improvement can demonstrate your value to the organization. From a practical perspective, it allows you to measure and track improvements, allowing you to know whether you are actually improving the situation and whether to continue or modify your efforts.

As we discussed in Chapter 10, metrics that can highlight a financial return are best; however, any metrics that can demonstrate a potential benefit are helpful. You can begin by measuring whichever efforts you think are optimal for demonstrating the reduction of at least one category of UIL.

UIL Mitigation Is a Living Process

Once you choose a UIL to mitigate, you might be able to step through the process completely. You might want to just test it out less formally. Again, though, you need to start somewhere. You can use what you learned about the Boom cycle and countermeasures to develop and implement a process, ideally with the support of team members.

You will never implement a perfect program on your first time through. That is both expected and acceptable. It is practically impossible to implement a perfect program. Loss mitigation is about risk management, not perfection. Ideally, you at least do not leave the loss worse than when you started. If you collect metrics and study your successes and failures, you should be able to refine your process improvements. This is the most critical aspect.

Even if you have a firm grasp of your operational environment, you might not realize the full operational impact of changes that you want to make to processes. There might be some obscure purpose for a technology that is too expensive to replace. In one case, we implemented a system that involved installing an old software package on an outdated PC. The reason that we had to use the PC is that there was a special-purpose computer board inside of the computer. It served its basic purpose of receiving military communications, well. Replacing the PC would mean writing new software that would have to be tested and certified to military specifications, which is an excessively costly endeavor.

During the COVID-19 pandemic, many U.S. state unemployment insurance offices were hampered, because the software that processed unemployment claims was run on COBOL, which is a 60-year-old programming language. The underlying problem is that there were relatively few people with COBOL experience available to make the required enhancements to account for the increased processing load due to the massive increase in unemployment insurance claims.

While you ideally don't have to enhance relatively old systems in the middle of a pandemic, you still need to expect that there will be internal issues that you have to work around. This can be accomplished only when you are constantly monitoring your progress efficiently, especially your failures.

Grow from Success

If you proceed methodically, you should succeed or at least have an indication of how to make improvements in mitigating UIL. Quality improvement efforts, which are essentially what you are pursuing, involve a constant state of experimentation on how errors can be reduced.

Regardless of whether your initial efforts are completely or only partially successful, you should build upon those successes. Whether you continue to work on the same problem or you move on to a new problem, your early successes should help you gain both experience and support.

The support can come in many forms. Assuming you gathered metrics that demonstrate that you reduced risk and saved the organization money, you should have developed some credibility. This credibility could translate to a larger budget and more access to decision-makers and stakeholders. These people can give you support in pursuing other areas of UIL mitigation.

More important, the experience you will gain is priceless. You can first off grow from walking through a systematic process. No matter how long you have been pursuing your profession, every time you pursue a new discipline, there will be a learning curve that is accomplished only through hands-on experience. You learn what types of problems to expect, in which areas successes might come more quickly, red flags that might signal when to not pursue an endeavor, and so on.

For example, one of the greatest red flags we have identified as critical is when we are delegated to work with awareness professionals to reduce UIL. These people are well-meaning and might even be open to looking at UIL as a systemic problem, but many awareness professionals still want to put the focus on empowering users with information. Awareness has its place, but it is problematic if it is the primary focus of your efforts.

Similarly, sometimes we work with technologists who believe users are stupid and are the root of the problem. Occasionally, they even sabotage efforts, as they do not want to consider that they are potential causes and enablers of "stupidity." While you should avoid your own bias, it does not mean that you cannot develop your own profile of whom you should ask to work with in your efforts.

Experience can also allow you to see subtleties, so you know when your efforts are being productive or failing. The sooner you can pick up on trends, the sooner you can either take advantage of them or attempt to mitigate the potential setbacks.

If your first experiences are noticeably successful, that is awesome. However, do not be discouraged if there are mixed results. Few efforts ever go as planned, which is not so ironically the essence of risk management.

The Users Are Your Canary in the Mine

While we hope our readers will be able to apply the materials, we realize that most readers will primarily read this book to expand their general knowledge in business, risk, security, and other related topics. That still makes us happy.

If you get nothing else out of this book, we hope that we get the message across that your users are only part of the overall system. If a user "initiates a loss," the system as a whole has failed, not the user.

Throughout the technology world, and in most industries for that matter, practitioners bemoan the users for causing them trouble. While dealing with the problematic users is likely part of their responsibilities, and in some cases the actual reason for their job existing, the users can only create problems if they are put in the position to do so. Users can only cause damage if you both provide them with the ability to do so, and you fail to account for those damages.

The users may have their own responsibilities, but your system must account for all parts of the system to fail at some point individually. This includes the users. To not do so is not only a problem in part with the user, who may have failed to perform their responsibilities as specified, but also a problem with the system designers and maintainers, who failed to account for such a failure. As we reiterate many times, failure is expected and should be proactively accounted for, unless the risk for the resulting losses is deemed acceptable.

Your users are the analogous canaries in the coal mine. They reveal the problems you have. We also talk about the fallacy that if a user fails in most environments, traditional security and technology professionals state the figurative position that the canaries just need to be healthier and have gas masks. Clearly, this thought process is absurd.

That being said, you would not want an unhealthy canary that dies from random heart failure. That would clearly cause unnecessary panic in the coal mine. Likewise, you want your users to be made properly aware and receive the appropriate training. While the users do not have ultimate responsibility, they are a critical part of the system, and as such, they should be enabled to function at their best.

In the end, you cannot stop a user from theoretically demonstrating "stupidity." However, you can take steps to prevent that stupidity from resulting in a user-initiated loss. It's your job to do so. In your role, you are ultimately one more user, and your first responsibility is to recognize that so that you can begin by preventing loss that comes from your own errors. You *can* stop stupid. It all begins with you.

Index